ETHICS

Other Books in the Current Controversies Series:

ETHICS

David L. Bender, *Publisher*
Bruno Leone, *Executive Editor*

Katie de Koster, *Managing Editor*
Scott Barbour, *Senior Editor*

Carol Wekesser, *Book Editor*

CURRENT CONTROVERSIES

Cover photo: © Misha Derwitt/Magnum Photos

Library of Congress Cataloging-in-Publication Data

Ethics / Carol Wekesser, book editor.
    p. cm. — (Current controversies)
    Includes bibliographical references and index.
    ISBN 1-56510-231-2 (lib. bdg.) — ISBN 1-56510-230-4 (pbk.)
    1. Business ethics—United States. [1. Business ethics.]   I. Wekesser,
Carol, 1963-   . II. Series.
  HF5387.E823   1995
  174'.4—dc20   94-28195
                                                                        CIP
                                                                         AC

© 1995 by Greenhaven Press, Inc., PO Box 289009, San Diego, CA 92198-9009
Printed in the U.S.A.

Every effort has been made to trace the owners of copyrighted material.

Contents

together to create a world ethic in which all people and nations take responsibility for the local and global impacts of their actions.

Chapter 2: Is There a Lack of Professional Ethics in America?

Chapter 3: Is American Business Ethical?

Chapter 4: Do Ethical Business Practices Benefit Society?

No: Many Modern Biomedical Practices Are Unethical

Yes: Most Modern Biomedical Practices Are Ethical

women to become pregnant and bear children. This practice has been criticized by those who fear for the health of the mothers and the well-being of the children. Although some of these criticisms are well founded, the practice should be considered ethical and thought of as simply another reproductive right.

Chapter 6: What Measures Would Promote Ethical Behavior?

Foreword

By definition, controversies are "discussions of questions in which opposing opinions clash" (Webster's Twentieth Century Dictionary Unabridged). Few would deny that controversies are a pervasive part of the human condition and exist on virtually every level of human enterprise. Controversies transpire between individuals and among groups, within nations and between nations. Controversies supply the grist necessary for progress by providing challenges and challengers to the status quo. They also create atmospheres where strife and warfare can flourish. A world without controversies would be a peaceful world; but it also would be, by and large, static and prosaic.

The Series' Purpose

The purpose of the Current Controversies series is to explore many of the social, political, and economic controversies dominating the national and international scenes today. Titles selected for inclusion in the series are highly focused and specific. For example, from the larger category of criminal justice, Current Controversies deals with specific topics such as police brutality, gun control, white collar crime, and others. The debates in Current Controversies also are presented in a useful, timeless fashion. Articles and book excerpts included in each title are selected if they contribute valuable, long-range ideas to the overall debate. And wherever possible, current information is enhanced with historical documents and other relevant materials. Thus, while individual titles are current in focus, every effort is made to ensure that they will not become quickly outdated. Books in the Current Controversies series will remain important resources for librarians, teachers, and students for many years.

In addition to keeping the titles focused and specific, great care is taken in the editorial format of each book in the series. Book introductions and chapter prefaces are offered to provide background material for readers. Chapters are organized around several key questions that are answered with diverse opinions representing all points on the political spectrum. Materials in each chapter include opinions in which authors clearly disagree as well as alternative opinions in which authors may agree on a broader issue but disagree on the possible solutions. In this way, the content of each volume in Current Controversies mirrors the mosaic of opinions encountered in society. Readers will quickly realize that there are many viable answers to these complex issues. By questioning each author's conclusions, students and casual readers can begin to develop the critical thinking skills so important to evaluating opinionated material.

Current Controversies is also ideal for controlled research. Each anthology in the series is composed of primary sources taken from a wide gamut of informational categories including periodicals, newspapers, books, United States and foreign government documents, and the publications of private and public organizations. Readers will find factual support for reports, debates, and research papers covering all areas of important issues. In addition, an annotated table of contents, an index, a book and periodical bibliography, and a list of organizations to contact are included in each book to expedite further research.

Perhaps more than ever before in history, people are confronted with diverse and contradictory information. During the Persian Gulf War, for example, the public was not only treated to minute-to-minute coverage of the war, it was also inundated with critiques of the coverage and countless analyses of the factors motivating U.S. involvement. Being able to sort through the plethora of opinions accompanying today's major issues, and to draw one's own conclusions, can be a complicated and frustrating struggle. It is the editors' hope that Current Controversies will help readers with this struggle.

> *"Like most people, Americans are sometimes generous and compassionate, sometimes dishonest and untrustworthy."*

Introduction

Many statistics indicate that Americans are less ethical today than in previous decades. In the book *The Day America Told the Truth*, 64 percent of the 5,000 Americans interviewed agreed with the statement "I will lie when it suits me—as long as it doesn't cause any real damage." Seventy-four percent agreed that "I will steal from those who won't really miss it."

These statistics are alarming. But while Americans may not be very ethical (according to their own accounts), are they in fact *less* ethical than in previous decades? Gary Edwards of the Ethics Resource Center, a think tank that promotes and researches ethics, believes that they are. He writes:

> In some inchoate way we sense that things really *are* different now, that the balance [between good and evil] is lost and may not be restored. Our institutions decay and the moral memory of wisdom wanes, leaving us with the growing anxiety that if things are not worse now than they have been, they soon shall be.

There is a particular concern about the lack of ethics in young people, many of whom seem nonchalant about cheating, stealing, and other unethical behaviors. In a 1989 Girl Scouts of America study of students in grades 4 to 12, 65 percent of high school students reported they would cheat on an important exam, and 36 percent said they would lie to protect a friend. Almost half said they rely on "their own personal experience" as the basis for deciding what is true. The majority said they had no external moral code, either religious or secular, to guide them.

A CBS News report reveals much about how the ethical dilemmas of America's youth have changed in forty years. In the 1940s, according to the report, the top seven transgressions of schoolchildren were talking out of turn, chewing gum, making noise, running in halls, cutting in line, disobeying the dress code, and littering. By the 1980s the list had changed to include drug abuse, alcohol abuse, pregnancy, suicide, rape, robbery, and assault.

Why such a dramatic change? Edwards believes it is the decline of the institutions that once taught ethical values:

> In the 1940s and for generations before, we relied on family, religion, and

schools together to impart essential civic and moral values across generations. [Since then] we have witnessed the gradual erosion of the family, the secularization of our society, and the evacuation of values from public school instruction. The moral development of our children has suffered greatly.

Ethicist Michael Josephson agrees that families, schools, and other institutions are failing to teach children about ethics and about the negative consequences of unethical behavior. But after completing a two-year study on the ethics of high school and college students, Josephson concluded that a cynical and selfish attitude that pervades society also contributes to a lack of ethics among young people. As Josephson writes:

> The lax ethics, self-indulgence, and rationalizations expressed by today's youth reflect and magnify similar characteristics in society. . . . "Look-out-for-#1" rhetoric and an unremitting parade of bad examples engender cynicism and foster selfish attitudes that drive dishonest and irresponsible conduct. . . . Youth of today rarely hear invocations to morality and service. Instead, they hear "Greed is good," and other slogans that degrade traditional ethical values such as altruism, honor, and duty beyond self.

Josephson believes this cynicism and selfishness drive young people to think that unethical conduct is necessary to succeed in life. In his study, 75 percent said they think that "most people will cheat or lie when it is necessary to get what they want." A significant percentage agreed that "it is not unethical to do whatever you have to do to succeed if you don't seriously hurt other people."

Josephson's findings and those of other ethicists are cause for concern. But concern about the behavior and ethics of the young and of all of society is not new. Throughout human history social critics have lamented the lack of ethics in society. A prophet in the eighth century B.C. wrote that "the times are evil." Hundreds of years later Jesus Christ labeled his society "a wicked generation." As Edwards states, "Meanness, deceit, and avarice have been with us forever."

But if vices have always existed, so have virtues such as courage, love, and compassion. Josephson himself found that, in addition to his study's negative findings, many young people show "a high degree of caring and a willingness to help others." Of the respondents, nearly 90 percent said "being kind and caring" was very important. In a speech on America's ethical values, Jeffrey H. Coors, president of ACX Technologies, points to the generosity of Americans as evidence of their ethical nature:

> We are the most giving nation on earth. There is no tradition of benevolence that can compare in Asia, Latin America, Africa, or even Europe. Nowhere in the world is there a United Way or a Cancer Society like ours. No other nation supports missionaries to the same extent, and none can compare with America in support for private, independent education. . . . Americans donate about $100 billion to charity each year, mostly in the form of individual contributions. Remarkably, poor Americans give a higher percentage of their incomes than do their more affluent neighbors.

Introduction

Ethics: Current Controversies explores the ethics and lack of ethics in American society in the following chapters: What Motivates People to Behave Ethically? Is There a Lack of Professional Ethics in America? Is American Business Ethical? Do Ethical Business Practices Benefit Society? Are Modern Biomedical Practices Ethical? What Measures Would Promote Ethical Behavior? The contributors debate whether Americans are less ethical than in previous decades and discuss the role ethics plays in the many aspects of people's lives.

Chapter 1

What Motivates People to Behave Ethically?

CURRENT CONTROVERSIES

Chapter Preface

Definitions of "ethical behavior" vary from age to age and culture to culture. But in general "ethical behavior" includes the following qualities, among others: honesty, integrity, fairness, loyalty, kindness, courage, generosity, compassion, altruism, and unselfishness. When people display these qualities, they can be said to be behaving ethically.

The three institutions that have traditionally influenced people to behave ethically are the family, religion, and government. The family is the first social organization that children belong to, and the one from which they receive their first, and perhaps most important, lessons about ethics. "Train a child in the way he should go, and when he is old he will not turn from it," states one proverb. This belief—that children must be taught how to behave ethically, and that the family is the primary teacher—is commonly accepted by most societies.

Religion is the second force that motivates ethical behavior. All religions embody moral and ethical beliefs and codes that are conveyed in their traditions, symbols, myths, and tenets. For example, the Bible's Ten Commandments express the ethical principles central to Christianity.

The third influence on ethical behavior is government and its laws. Alexander Hamilton wrote in one of *The Federalist* papers that "government has been instituted . . . because the passions of men will not conform to the dictates of reason and justice, without constraint." Hamilton understood that many people need the "constraint" of laws to behave legally and ethically. Others obey laws out of a respect for their nation and government. Philosopher Jean-Jacques Rousseau is one who believed that people owe their nation "the most precious thing possessed by man, the morality of his actions and the love of virtue."

Family, religion, and government have traditionally been powerful motivating forces for ethical behavior. But statistics show that most Americans today do not credit these institutions for their ethical behavior. In a poll reported in the book *The Day America Told the Truth*, 93 percent of respondents said they themselves—not their church, government, or family—determine what is moral and what is not. Harvard professors Amar Bhide and Howard H. Stevenson believe that "most of us choose virtue because we want to believe in ourselves and have others respect and believe in us."

Both why people behave ethically and how to motivate ethical behavior have been debated for thousands of years by philosophers and theologians. In more recent years sociologists, ethicists, criminologists, psychiatrists, and others have joined the debate in the belief that understanding people's motivations for behaving ethically might enable society to improve the behavior of criminals and others who behave unethically. In the following chapter, the contributors discuss and debate these issues.

Belief in God Motivates People to Behave Ethically

by Benedict de Spinoza

About the author: *Benedict de Spinoza (1632-1677) was a Dutch philosopher. Born a Sephardic Jew, as a young man he was excommunicated from the Jewish community for his thoughts and practices. Spinoza proposed that people are guided by their own natures, and that virtuous people understand their own natures and ultimately seek to understand the nature of God. Spinoza wrote the books* A Treatise on Religious and Political Philosophy, Political Treatise, *and* Ethics, *from which this viewpoint is excerpted.*

I should like to say a few words about perfection and imperfection, and about good and evil. If a man has proposed to do a thing and has accomplished it, he calls it perfect, and not only he, but every one else who has really known or has believed that he has known the mind and intention of the author of that work will call it perfect too. For example, having seen some work (which I suppose to be as yet not finished), if we know that the intention of the author of that work is to build a house, we shall call the house imperfect; while, on the other hand, we shall call it perfect as soon as we see the work has been brought to the end which the author had determined for it. But if we see any work such as we have never seen before, and if we do not know the mind of the workman, we shall then not be able to say whether the work is perfect or imperfect. This seems to have been the first signification of these words; but afterwards men began to form universal ideas, to think out for themselves types of houses, buildings, castles, and to prefer some types of things to others; and so it happened that each person called a thing perfect which seemed to agree with the universal idea which he had formed of that thing, and, on the other hand, he called a thing imperfect which seemed to agree less with his typical conception, although, according to the intention of the workman, it had been entirely com-

Benedict de Spinoza, from *The Ethics of Spinoza*, translated by W.H. White and revised by A.H. Stirling. Reprinted by permission of Oxford University Press.

pleted. This appears to be the only reason why the words *perfect* and *imperfect* are commonly applied to natural objects which are not made with human hands; for men are in the habit of forming, both of natural as well as of artificial objects, universal ideas which they regard as types of things, and which they think nature has in view, setting them before herself as types too; it being the common opinion that she does nothing except for the sake of some end. When, therefore, men see something done by nature which does not altogether answer to that typal conception which they have of the thing, they think that nature herself has failed or committed an error, and that she has left the thing imperfect. Thus we see that the custom of applying the words *perfect* and *imperfect* to natural objects has arisen rather from prejudice than from true knowledge of them. For . . . nature does nothing for the sake of an end, for that eternal and infinite Being whom we call God or Nature acts by the same necessity by which He exists; . . . He acts by the same necessity of nature as that by which He exists. The reason or cause, therefore, why God or nature acts and the reason why He exists are one and the same. Since, therefore, He exists for no end, He acts for no end; and since He has no principle or end of existence, He has no principle or end of action. A final cause, as it is called, is nothing, therefore, but human desire, in so far as this is considered as the principle or primary cause of anything. For example, when we say that the having a house to live in was the final cause of this or that house, we merely mean that a man, because he imagined the advantages of a domestic life, desired to build a house. Therefore, having a house to live in, in so far as it is considered as a final cause, is merely this particular desire, which is really an efficient cause, and is considered as primary, because men are usually ignorant of the causes of their desires; for, as I have often said, we are conscious of our actions and desires, but ignorant of the causes by which we are determined to desire anything. . . .

> *"The highest virtue of the mind is to understand or know God."*

The Virtue of Knowing God

The highest good of the mind is the knowledge of God, and the highest virtue of the mind is to know God.

The highest thing which the mind can understand is God, that is to say, Being absolutely infinite, and without whom nothing can be nor can be conceived, and therefore that which is chiefly profitable to the mind, or which is the highest good of the mind, is the knowledge of God. Again, the mind acts only in so far as it understands, and only in so far can it be absolutely said to act in conformity with virtue. To understand, therefore, is the absolute virtue of the mind. But the highest thing which the mind can understand is God (as we have already demonstrated), and therefore the highest virtue of the mind is to understand or know God. Q.E.D. . . .

The good which every one who follows after virtue seeks for himself he will desire for other men; and his desire on their behalf will be greater in proportion as he has a greater knowledge of God.

Men are most profitable to man in so far as they live according to the guidance of reason, and therefore, according to the guidance of reason, we necessarily endeavour to cause men to live according to the guidance of reason. But the good which each person seeks who lives according to the dictates of reason, that is to say, who follows after virtue, is to understand, and therefore the good which each person seeks who follows after virtue he will also desire for other men. Again, desire, in so far as it is related to the mind, is the essence itself of the mind. But the essence of the mind consists in knowledge, which involves the knowledge of God, and without this knowledge the essence of the mind can neither be nor be conceived; and therefore the greater the knowledge of God which the essence of the mind involves, the greater will be the desire with which he who follows after virtue will desire for another the good which he seeks for himself.   Q.E.D.

The good which a man seeks for himself and which he loves he will love more unchangeably if he sees that others love it, and therefore he will endeavour to make others love it; and because this good is common to all and all can rejoice in it, he will endeavour (by the same reasoning) to cause all to rejoice in it, and he will do so the more, the more he rejoices in this good himself. Q.E.D.

> *"The good which each person seeks who follows after virtue he will also desire for other men."*

He who strives from an affect alone to make others love what he himself loves, and to make others live according to his way of thinking, acts from mere impulse, and is therefore hateful, especially to those who have other tastes and who therefore also desire, and by the same impulse strive to make others live according to their way of thinking.

Again, since the highest good which men seek from an affect is often such that only one person can possess it, it follows that persons who love are not consistent with themselves, and, whilst they delight to recount the praises of the beloved object, fear lest they should be believed. But he who endeavours to lead others by reason does not act from impulse, but with humanity and kindness, and is always consistent with himself.

The Guidance of Reason

Everything which we desire and do, of which we are the cause in so far as we possess an idea of God, or in so far as we know God, I refer to *Religion*. The desire of doing well which is born in us, because we live according to the guidance of reason, I call *Piety*. The desire to join others in friendship to himself, with which a man living according to the guidance of reason is possessed, I call

Chapter 1

Honour. I call that thing *Honourable* which men who live according to the guidance of reason praise; and that thing, on the contrary, I call *Base* which sets itself against the formation of friendship. . . .

It is by the highest right of nature that each person exists, and consequently it is by the highest right of nature that each person does those things which follow from the necessity of his nature; and therefore it is by the highest right of nature that each person judges what is good and what is evil, consults his own advantage as he thinks best, avenges himself, and endeavours to preserve what he loves and to destroy what he hates. If men lived according to the guidance of reason, every one would enjoy this right without injuring any one else. But because men are subject to affects, which far surpass human power or virtue, they are often drawn in different directions, and are contrary to one another, although they need one another's help.

In order, then, that men may be able to live in harmony and be a help to one another, it is necessary for them to cede their natural right, and beget confidence one in the other that they will do nothing by which one can injure the other.

Atheism Motivates People to Behave Ethically

by Friedrich Nietzsche

About the author: *Friedrich Nietzsche (1844-1900) was a German philosopher, author, and poet. He is renowned for his statement, "God is dead," by which he meant that religion had lost its meaningfulness and efficacy in modern society. He rejected Christianity, arguing that its values were based on fear and resentment, that it incorrectly accepted all people as equals, and that it denied this world in favor of an illusory other world. Nietzsche's concept of the "superman"—the passionate individual able to control and utilize passions creatively—expressed his view of the ideal manner of human existence. He wrote the books* Thus Spake Zarathustra *and* Beyond Good and Evil, *from which this viewpoint is excerpted.*

The human soul and its frontiers, the compass of human inner experience in general attained hitherto, the heights, depths and distances of this experience, the entire history of the soul *hitherto* and its still unexhausted possibilities: this is the predestined hunting-ground for a born psychologist and lover of the "big-game hunt." But how often must he say despairingly to himself: "one man! alas, but one man! and this great forest and jungle!" And thus he wishes he had a few hundred beaters and subtle well-instructed tracker dogs whom he could send into the history of the human soul and there round up *his* game. In vain: he discovers again and again, thoroughly and bitterly, how hard it is to find beaters and dogs for all the things which arouse his curiosity. The drawback in sending scholars out into new and dangerous hunting grounds where courage, prudence, subtlety in every sense are needed is that they cease to be of any use precisely where the "*big* hunt," but also the big danger, begins—precisely there they do lose their keenness of eye and keenness of nose. To divine and establish, for example, what sort of history the problem of *knowledge and conscience* has had in the soul of *homines religiosi* one would oneself perhaps have to be as profound, as wounded, as monstrous as Pascal's intellectual conscience was—and

Excerpted from Friedrich Nietzsche, *Beyond Good and Evil*, translated by R.J. Hollingdale. London: Penguin Classics, 1973. Translation ©1972 by R.J. Hollingdale. Reprinted by permission of Penguin Books Ltd.

then there would still be needed that broad heaven of bright, malicious spirituality capable of looking down on this turmoil of dangerous and painful experiences, surveying and ordering them and forcing them into formulas.—But who could do me this service! And who could have the time to wait for such servants!—They appear too rarely, they are at all times so very improbable! In the end one has to do everything *oneself* if one is to know a few things oneself: that is to say, one has *much* to do!—But a curiosity like mine is after all the most pleasurable of vices—I beg your pardon! I meant to say: the love of truth has its reward in Heaven, and already upon earth.—

Suicide of Reason

The faith such as primitive Christianity demanded and not infrequently obtained in the midst of a sceptical and southerly free-spirited world with a centuries-long struggle between philosophical schools behind it and in it, plus the education in tolerance provided by the *Imperium Romanum*—this faith is *not* that gruff, true-hearted liegeman's faith with which a Martin Luther, say, or an Oliver Cromwell, or some other northern barbarian of the spirit cleaved to his God and his Christianity; it is rather that faith of Pascal which resembles in a terrible fashion a protracted suicide of reason—of a tough, long-lived, wormlike reason which is not to be killed instantaneously with a single blow. The Christian faith is from the beginning sacrifice: sacrifice of all freedom, all pride, all self-confidence of the spirit, at the same time enslavement and self-mockery, self-mutilation. There is cruelty and religious Phoenicianism in this faith exacted of an over-ripe, manifold and much-indulged conscience: its presupposition is that the subjection of the spirit is indescribably *painful*, that the entire past and habitude of such a spirit resists the *absurdissimum* which "faith" appears to it to be. Modern men, with their obtuseness to all Christian nomenclature, no longer sense the gruesome superlative which lay for an antique taste in the paradoxical formula "god on the cross." Never and nowhere has there hitherto been a comparable boldness in inversion, anything so fearsome, questioning and questionable, as this formula: it promised a reevaluation of all antique values.—It is the orient, the *innermost* orient, it is the oriental slave who in this fashion took vengeance on Rome and its noble and frivolous tolerance on Roman "catholicism" of faith; and it has never been faith but always freedom from faith, that half-stoical and smiling unconcern with the seriousness of faith, that has enraged slaves in their masters and against their masters. "Enlightenment" enrages: for the slave who wants the unconditional, he understands in the domain of morality too only the tyrannical, he loves as he hates, without nuance, into the depths of him, to the point of pain, to the point of sickness—the great *hid-*

> *"The Christian faith is . . . sacrifice of all freedom, all pride, all self-confidence of the spirit."*

den suffering he feels is enraged at the noble taste which seems to *deny* suffering. Scepticism towards suffering, at bottom no more than a pose of aristocratic morality, was likewise not the least contributory cause of the last great slave revolt which began with the French Revolution.

The Dangers of Christianity

Wherever the religious neurosis has hitherto appeared on earth we find it tied to three dangerous dietary prescriptions: solitude, fasting and sexual abstinence—but without our being able to decide with certainty which is cause here and which effect, or *whether* any relation of cause and effect is involved here at all. The justification of the latter doubt is that one of the most frequent symptoms of the condition, in the case of savage and tame peoples, is the most sudden and most extravagant voluptuousness which is then, just as suddenly, reversed into a convulsion of penitence and a denial of world and will: both perhaps interpretable as masked epilepsy? But nowhere is it more necessary to renounce interpretations: around no other type has there grown up such an abundance of nonsense and superstition, none seems to have hitherto interested men, even philosophers, more—the time has come to cool down a little on this matter, to learn caution: better to look away, *to go away.* . . .

It seems that their Catholicism is much more an intrinsic part of the Latin races than the whole of Christianity in general is of us northerners; and that unbelief consequently signifies something altogether different in Catholic countries from what it does in Protestant—namely a kind of revolt against the spirit of the race, while with us it is rather a return to the spirit (or lack of spirit—) of the race. We northerners are undoubtedly descended from barbarian races also in respect of our talent for religion: we have *little* talent for it. We may except the Celts, who therefore supplied the best soil for the reception of the Christian infection in the north—the Christian ideal came to blossom, so far as the pale northern sun permitted it, in France. How uncongenially pious are to our taste even these latest French sceptics when they have in them any Celtic blood! How Catholic, how un-German does August Comte's sociology smell to us with its Roman logic of the instincts! How Jesuitical that clever and charming cicerone of Port-Royal, Charles-Augustin Sainte-Beuve, despite all his hostility towards the Jesuits! And even more so Ernest Renan: how inaccessible to us notherners is the language of a Renan, in whom every other minute some nothingness of religious tension topples a soul which is in a refined sense voluptuous and relaxed! . . .

What astonishes one about the religiosity of the ancient Greeks is the tremendous amount of gratitude that emanates from it—the kind of man who stands

> *"Why atheism today?—'The father' in God is thoroughly refuted. . . . He does not hear—and if he heard he would still not know how to help."*

thus before nature and before life is a very noble one!—Later, when the rabble came to predominate in Greece, *fear* also overran religion; and Christianity was preparing itself.—

The passion for God: there is the peasant, true-hearted and importunate kind, like Luther's—the whole of Protestantism lacks southern *delicatezza*. There is an oriental ecstatic kind, like that of a slave who has been undeservedly pardoned and elevated, as for example in the case of Augustine, who lacks in an offensive manner all nobility of bearing and desire.

> *"The concepts 'God' and 'sin' will one day seem to us of no more importance than a child's toy and a child's troubles seem to an old man."*

There is the womanly tender and longing kind which presses bashfully and ignorantly for a *unio mystica et physica:* as in the case of Madame de Guyon. In many cases it appears strangely enough as a disguise for the puberty of a girl or a youth; now and then even as the hysteria of an old maid, also as her final ambition—the church has more than once canonized the woman in question.

Hitherto the mightiest men have still bowed down reverently before the saint as the enigma of self-constraint and voluntary final renunciation: why did they bow? They sensed in him—as it were behind the question-mark presented by his fragile and miserable appearance—the superior force that sought to prove itself through such a constraint, the strength of will in which they recognized and knew how to honour their own strength and joy in ruling: they honoured something in themselves when they honoured the saint. In addition to this, the sight of the saint aroused a suspicion in them: such an enormity of denial, of anti-nature, will not have been desired for nothing, they said to themselves. Is there perhaps a reason for it, a very great danger about which the ascetic, thanks to his secret visitors and informants, might possess closer knowledge? Enough, the mighty world learned in face of him a new fear, they sensed a new power, a strange enemy as yet unsubdued—it was the "will to power" which constrained them to halt before the saint. They had to question him—.

In the Jewish "Old Testament," the book of divine justice, there are men, things and speeches of so grand a style that Greek and Indian literature have nothing to set beside it. One stands in reverence and trembling before these remnants of what man once was and has sorrowful thoughts about old Asia and its little jutting-out promontory Europe, which would like to signify as against Asia the "progress of man." To be sure: he who is only a measly tame domestic animal and knows only the needs of a domestic animal (like our cultured people of today, the Christians of "cultured" Christianity included—) has no reason to wonder, let alone to sorrow, among those ruins—the taste for the Old Testament is a touchstone in regard to "great" and "small"—: perhaps he will find the New Testament, the book of mercy, more after his own heart (there is in it a great deal of the genuine delicate, musty odour of devotee and petty soul). To have glued this New Testament, a species of rococo taste in every respect, on to the Old Testament to form a *single* book, as "bible," as "the book of books": that is perhaps the greatest piece of temerity and "sin against the spirit" that literary Europe has on its conscience.

Why Atheism?

Why atheism today?—"The father" in God is thoroughly refuted; likewise "the judge," "the rewarder." Likewise his "free will": he does not hear—and if he heard he would still not know how to help. The worst thing is: he seems incapable of making himself clearly understood: is he himself vague about what he means?—These are what, in course of many conversations, asking and listening, I found to be the causes of the decline of European theism; it seems to me that the religious instinct is indeed in vigorous growth—but that it rejects the theistic answer with profound mistrust. . . .

There is a great ladder of religious cruelty with many rungs; but three of them are the most important. At one time one sacrificed human beings to one's god, perhaps precisely those human beings one loved best—the sacrifice of the first-born present in all prehistoric religions belongs here, as does the sacrifice of the Emperor Tiberius in the Mithras grotto on the isle of Capri, that most horrible of all Roman anachronisms. Then, in the moral epoch of mankind, one sacrificed to one's god the strongest instincts one possessed, one's "nature"; the joy of *this* festival glitters in the cruel glance of the ascetic, the inspired "anti-naturist." Finally: what was left to be sacrificed? Did one not finally have to sacrifice everything comforting, holy, healing, all hope, all faith in a concealed harmony, in a future bliss and justice? Did one not have to sacrifice God himself and out of cruelty against oneself worship stone, stupidity, gravity, fate, nothingness? To sacrifice God for nothingness—this paradoxical mystery of the ultimate act of cruelty was reserved for the generation which is even now arising: we all know something of it already.—

He who, prompted by some enigmatic desire, has, like me, long endeavoured to think pessimism through to the bottom and to redeem it from the half-Christian, half-German simplicity and narrowness with which it finally presented itself to this century, namely in the form of the Schopenhaueran philosophy; he who has really gazed with an Asiatic and more than Asiatic eye down into the most world-denying of all possible modes of thought—beyond good and evil and no longer, like Buddha and Arthur Schopenhauer, under the spell and illusion of morality—perhaps by that very act, and without really intending to, may have had his eyes opened to the opposite ideal: to the ideal of the most exuberant, most living and most world-affirming man, who has not only learned to get on and treat with all that was and is but who wants to have it again *as it was and is* to all

> *"What wisdom there is in the fact that men are superficial."*

eternity, insatiably calling out *da capo* not only to himself, but to the whole piece and play, and not only to a play but fundamentally to him who needs precisely this play—and who makes it necessary: because he needs himself again and again—and makes himself necessary—What? And would this not be—

> *circulus vitiosus deus?*

> *"Piety . . . [is] the subtlest and ultimate product of the* **fear** *of truth."*

With the strength of his spiritual sight and insight the distance, and as it were the space, around man continually expands: his world grows deeper, ever new stars, ever new images and enigmas come into view. Perhaps everything on which the spirit's eye has exercised its profundity and acuteness has been really but an opportunity for its exercise, a game, something for children and the childish. Perhaps the most solemn concepts which have occasioned the most strife and suffering, the concepts "God" and "sin," will one day seem to us of no more importance than a child's toy and a child's troubles seem to an old man—and perhaps "old man" will then have need of another toy and other troubles—still enough of a child, an eternal child!

Indifference to Religion

Has it been observed to what extent a genuine religious life (both for its favourite labour of microscopic self-examination and that gentle composure which calls itself "prayer" and which is a constant readiness for the "coming of God"—) requires external leisure or semi-leisure, I mean leisure with a good conscience, inherited, by blood, which is not altogether unfamiliar with the aristocratic idea that work *degrades*—that is to say, makes soul and body common? And that consequently modern, noisy, time-consuming, proud and stupidly proud industriousness educates and prepares precisely for "unbelief" more than anything else does? Among those in Germany for example who nowadays live without religion, I find people whose "free-thinking" is of differing kinds and origins but above all a majority for those in whom industriousness from generation to generation has extinguished the religious instincts: so that they no longer have any idea what religions are supposed to be for and as it were merely register their existence in the world with a kind of dumb amazement. They feel they are already fully occupied, these worthy people, whether with their businesses or with their pleasures, not to speak of the "fatherland" and the newspapers and "family duties": it seems that they have no time at all left for religion, especially as it is not clear to them whether it involves another business or another pleasure—for they tell themselves it is not possible that one goes to church simply to make oneself miserable. They are not opposed to religious usages; if participation in such usages is demanded in certain cases, by the state for instance, they do what is demanded of them as one does so many things—with patient and modest seriousness and without much curiosity and discomfort—it is only that they live too much aside and outside even to feel the need for any for or against in such things. The great majority of German middle-class Protestants can today be numbered among these indifferent people, especially in the great industrious centres of trade and commerce; likewise the great majority of industrious scholars and the entire university equipage (excepting the theologians, whose possibility and presence there provides the psychologist with ever more and ever subtler enigmas to solve). Pious or even merely church-going people seldom realize *how much* good will, one might even say willfulness, it requires nowadays for a German scholar to take the problem of religion seriously; his whole trade (and as said above, the tradesmanlike industriousness to which his modern conscience obliges him) disposes him to a superior, almost good-natured merriment in regard to religion, sometimes mixed with a mild contempt directed at the "uncleanliness" of spirit which he presupposes wherever one still belongs to the church. It is only with the aid of history (thus *not* from his personal experience) that the scholar succeeds in summoning up a reverent seriousness and a certain shy respect towards religion; but if he intensifies his feelings towards it even to the point of feeling grateful to it, he has still in his own person not got so much as a single step closer to that which still exists as church or piety: perhaps the reverse. The practical indifference to religious things in which he was born and raised is as a rule sublimated in him into a caution and cleanliness which avoids contact with religious people and things; and it can be precisely

> *"Christianity has been the most fatal kind of self-presumption ever."*

the depth of his tolerance and humanity that bids him evade the subtle distress which tolerance itself brings with it.—Every age has its own divine kind of naïvety for the invention of which other ages may envy it—and how much naïvety, venerable, childlike and boundlessly stupid naïvety there is in the scholar's belief in his superiority, in the good conscience of his tolerance, in the simple unsuspecting certainty with which his instinct treats the religious man as an inferior and lower type which he himself has grown beyond and *above*—he, the little presumptuous dwarf and man of the mob, the brisk and busy head- and handyman of "ideas," of "modern ideas"!

Fear Leads People to Religion

He who has seen deeply into the world knows what wisdom there is in the fact that men are superficial. It is their instinct for preservation which teaches them to be fickle, light and false. Here and there, among philosophers as well as artists, one finds a passionate and exaggerated worship of "pure forms": let no one doubt that he who *needs* the cult of surfaces to that extent has at some time or other made a calamitous attempt to get *beneath* them. Perhaps there might even exist an order of rank in regard to these burnt children, these born artists who can find pleasure in life only in the intention of falsifying its image (as it were in a long-drawn-out revenge on life—): one could determine the degree to which life has been spoiled for them by the extent to which they want to see its image falsified, attenuated and made otherworldly and divine—one could include the *homines religiosi* among the artists as their *highest* rank. It is the profound suspicious fear of an incurable pessimism which compels whole millennia to cling with their teeth to a religious interpretation of existence: the fear born of that instinct which senses that one might get hold of the truth *too soon*, before mankind was sufficiently strong, sufficiently hard, sufficient of an artist. . . . Piety, the "life in God," would, viewed in this light, appear as the subtlest and ultimate product of the *fear* of truth, as the artist's worship of an intoxication before the most consistent of all falsifications, as the will to inversion of truth, to untruth at any price. Perhaps there has up till now been no finer way of making man himself more beautiful than piety: through piety man can become to so great a degree art, surface, play of colours, goodness, that one no longer suffers at the sight of him.—

> *"A shrunken, almost ludicrous species, a herd animal, something full of good will, sickly and mediocre has been bred, the European of today."*

To love men *for the sake of God*—that has been the noblest and most remote feeling attained to among men up till now. That love of man without some sanctifying ulterior objective is one piece of stupidity and animality *more*, that the inclination to this love of man has first to receive its measure, its refinement, its grain of salt and drop of amber from a higher inclination—whatever man it was who first felt and "experienced" this, however much his tongue may have faltered as it sought to express such a delicate thought, let him be holy and venerated to us for all time as the man who has soared the highest and gone the most beautifully astray! . . .

The Danger of Saving the Weak

Among men, as among every other species, there is a surplus of failures, of the sick, the degenerate, the fragile, of those who are bound to suffer. . . . Now what is the attitude of [Christianity and Buddhism] towards this *surplus* of unsuccessful cases? They seek to preserve, to retain in life, whatever can in any way be preserved, indeed they side with it as a matter of principle as religions *for sufferers*, they maintain that all those who suffer from life as from an illness are in the right, and would like every other feeling of life to be counted false and become impossible. However highly one may rate this kindly preservative solicitude, inasmuch as, together with all the other types of man, it has been and is applied to the highest type, which has hitherto almost always been the type that has suffered most: in the total accounting the hitherto *sovereign* religions are among the main reasons the type "man" has been kept on a lower level—they have preserved too much of that *which ought to perish*. We have inestimable benefits to thank them for; and who is sufficiently rich in gratitude not to be impoverished in face of all that the "spiritual men" of Christianity, for example, have hitherto done for Europe! And yet, when they gave comfort to the suffering, courage to the oppressed and despairing, a staff and stay to the irresolute, and lured those who were inwardly shattered and had become savage away from society into monasteries and houses of correction for the soul: what did they have to do in addition so as thus, with a good conscience, as a matter of principle, to work at the preservation of everything sick and suffering, which means in fact and truth at the *corruption of the European race?* Stand all evaluations *on their head—that* is what they had to do! And smash the strong, contaminate great hopes, cast suspicion on joy in beauty, break down everything autocratic, manly, conquering, tyrannical, all the instincts proper to the highest and most successful of the type "man," into uncertainty, remorse of conscience, self-destruction, indeed reverse the whole love of the earthly and of dominion over the earth into hatred of the earth and the earthly—*that* is the task the church set itself and had to set itself, until in its evaluation "unworldliness," "unsensuality," and "higherman" were finally fused together into *one* feeling. Supposing one were able to view the strangely painful and at the same time coarse and subtle comedy of European Christianity with the mocking and unconcerned eye of an Epicurean god, I believe there would be no end to one's laughter and amazement: for does it not seem that *one* will has dominated Europe for eighteen centuries, the will to make of man a *sublime abortion?* But he who, with an opposite desire, no longer Epicurean but with some divine hammer in his hand, approached this almost deliberate degeneration and stunting of man such as constitutes the European Christian (Pascal for instance), would he not have to cry out in rage, in pity, in horror: "O you fools, you presumptuous, pitying fools, what have you done! Was this a work for your hands! How you have bungled and botched my beautiful stone! What a thing for *you* to take upon yourselves!"—What I am saying is: Christianity has been the most fatal kind of self-presumption ever. Men not high or hard enough for the artistic refashioning of *mankind*; men not strong or farsighted enough for the sublime self-constraint needed to *allow* the foreground law of thousandfold failure and perishing to prevail; men not noble enough to see the abysmal disparity in order of rank and abysm of rank between man and man—it is *such* men who, with their "equal before God," have hitherto ruled over the destiny of Europe, until at last a shrunken, almost ludicrous species, a herd animal, something full of good will, sickly and mediocre has been bred, the European of today.

A Moral Character and Good Fortune Help People Behave Ethically

by Mortimer J. Adler

About the author: *Mortimer J. Adler is a noted philosopher, educator, and author of numerous books, including* Desires, Right and Wrong: The Ethics of Enough, *from which this viewpoint is excerpted. Adler is the editor in chief of the series* Great Books of the Western World.

Right thinking is less than enough for habitual right desire. It may be necessary for the acknowledgment of moral problems, and even for some understanding of how they can be solved; but it is insufficient for their solution. It does not produce moral virtue, or the habit of right desire, which is an indispensable means to living well.

In turn, moral virtue is necessary, but it is also by itself insufficient for the successful pursuit of happiness, ethically conceived. Having the habit of right desire, which is moral virtue, must be present as a necessary condition for human beings to act righteously for the most part, but it is insufficient to guarantee that result.

Why are all these things true? As to the first, because a person can know and understand the truths of moral philosophy without possessing the habit of right desire that constitutes a virtuous character. That reason, by the way, is the reason why Aristotle said it was futile to give lectures on ethics to the young, the immature.

Two Kinds of Desires

The reason why persons of good moral character may infrequently commit wrong acts is that we have two kinds of desire—sensitive or sensual desires, and rational desires that are acts of the intellectual appetite, which is the will. These two kinds of desire often operate simultaneously in particular cases, but they seldom act cooperatively, but rather in conflict.

When this occurs and virtuous individuals succumb to the sensual desires, which motivate them to act contrary to their rational desires, Aristotle calls the wrong actions that then result acts of incontinence. Incontinence is the reason why having a habit of right desire does not guarantee that persons of good character always act as they should. Moral virtue is necessary but insufficient.

> *"Moral virtue is necessary but insufficient."*

A more important reason why moral virtue is necessary but insufficient is that it is not the only factor required for the pursuit of happiness as the ultimate goal of right desire. The other factor required is good luck, or what Aristotle calls "the blessings of good fortune." Like moral virtue it is necessary, but also insufficient.

Let us now examine these three factors, which are insufficient or less than enough that is needed for solving moral problems and leading a good life.

Virtue Cannot Be Taught

We are indebted to Plato for the insight that moral virtue is not teachable. His dialogue the *Meno* opens with the question "whether [moral] virtue is acquired by teaching or by practice; or if neither by teaching nor practice, then whether it comes to man by nature, or in what other way."

The dialogue contains a good example of teaching, in which Socrates teaches a slave boy how to learn the solution of a problem in geometry. Clearly, moral virtue cannot be acquired in the way in which such knowledge is learned, certainly not by the asking and answering of questions, nor by lecturing.

The full reason why this is so does not become clear in Plato's dialogue. It is Aristotle's definition of moral virtue as a habit of choice that helps us to understand why it is not acquired by teaching. The fact that moral virtue is a habit eliminates one of the alternatives mentioned by Plato. Habits are acquired; therefore, moral virtue is not by nature. We are not born virtuous.

The other alternative mentioned by Plato—by practice—comes nearer to the answer. We all know that habits are formed by the repetition of the same action time and time again. Anyone who has practiced playing the piano or another musical instrument is kept at it by the maxim "Practice makes perfect." A well-executed performance results from the habit formed by conscientious and diligent practice.

Choosing to Be Taught

But are there not music teachers who teach students how to play instruments well? The kind of teaching they do is usually called coaching. They supervise the practice by telling the student, step by step, what to do and what not to do, and as the practicing proceeds, they stop it every time the learner makes a mistake and they require him to do it correctly, over and over again, until the student does it in a satisfactory manner.

On the assumption that the person who is the student wishes to learn, the individual willingly complies with such instruction. At no point does he consider whether he should or should not do what the coach prescribes. He does not exercise any choice about whether he will or will not submit to the advice of the coach and follow the rules laid down.

In that word "choice" lies the answer, especially if the choice is understood to be free choice. Moral virtues are habits of choice, said Aristotle. Habits of choice can be formed only by acts of choice. Those acts of choice are made by individuals when they are confronted with alternatives that solicit their response: this versus that apparent good, this apparent good versus this real good; this versus that real good here and now. . . .

Is Knowledge Necessary?

Returning to the point that initiated this discussion, one part of the answer is now clear. A person who has learned the truths of moral philosophy has acquired knowledge that by itself is insufficient for that individual's acquirement of a good moral character. Knowing the truths of moral philosophy, a person may still turn out to be a knave or a villain.

Knowledge and understanding are intellectual virtues. No one disputes the fact that a person can have intellectual virtues to a high degree without being a person of admirable moral character. A college student of philosophy can pass a course in ethics with a high grade and at the same time exhibit disgraceful habits of desire and action.

> *"We are not born virtuous."*

Learning the truths of moral philosophy may be insufficient for the acquirement of moral virtue, but is it necessary even though insufficient? The fact that persons entirely innocent of moral philosophy are often persons of good moral character shows that it cannot be necessary. While not necessary, it may be still recommended not merely because the pursuit of truth is always commendable, but also because understanding the truths of moral philosophy reinforces right desire when it is challenged by the temptations of seductive apparent goods that should be shunned.

A Conflict of Desires

Is there anyone who has not experienced remorse for having made a wrong choice or committed a wrong deed? How is it that we can know what is right and not choose it, or know what is wrong and still do it?

The words used in the confession of sins are clear on this point. "We have done the things we ought not to have done, and we have failed to do what we ought to have done." When Socrates said that knowledge is virtue, he asserted the opposite. Our knowing what is right necessitates our doing what is right.

Therein lies the error made by Socrates.

As I intimated earlier, Aristotle's analysis of incontinence in Book VII of his *Ethics* supplies us with the answer. We have two kinds of desire, not one: sensual desires and rational desires, desires of the intellectual appetite or will. They frequently come into conflict with one another, as most of us know from personal experience or from the vicarious experience of reading novels or seeing dramas in which the conflict between reason and the passions is central to the narrative or action.

Important Choices

We make important choices many times in the course of our lives. They are always made at a particular time and place and under particular circumstances. The alternatives with which we are confronted simultaneously may be objects of sensual desire, on the one hand, and objects of rational desire, on the other hand.

Intellectually knowing what is really good for us to choose, our intellectual appetite or will tends toward the objects of rational desire. Attributing apparent goodness to sensually attractive objects, our sensitive desires tend toward those objects.

When the objects of rational desire are remote real goods—goods that cannot be obtained at the moment of choice—and the objects of sensitive desire are sensually present apparent goods, obtainable here and now, it is easy to give in to the temptations of immediately obtainable goods and hard to postpone the gratification of desire by choosing goods that are obtainable only in the long run.

When persons make choices they later regret, or suffer remorse for choices they failed to make, what Aristotle called their incontinence consists in their refusal to defer gratification. He also tells us that the urge toward immediate gratification of desire is a typically childish indulgence in pleasures, meaning thereby not only the pleasures of the flesh, but also the pleasures that consist in being pleased when we get the things we want at the moment we want them.

Acquiring moral virtue, forming the habit of right desire, is thus seen to be a process of conquering one's childish tendencies toward indulgence in immediate gratifications.

> *"Our knowing what is right necessitates our doing what is right."*

This is not a complete account of all conflicts between reason and the passions. Objects of desire are not always pleasures of the flesh, or even objects that are immediately obtainable and pleasing in the sense that they satisfy our desires. Money, fame, and power are not objects of this sort. Nevertheless, they arouse passions which drive us to make wrong choices.

The fourth book of Spinoza's *Ethics* is entitled "Of the passions or of human bondage." The freedom we have lost when we are in bondage to the passions is the freedom of being able to will as we ought. That freedom is enjoyed only by persons of moral virtue. They have acquired that freedom by acquiring the habit of right choice, the habit of willing as one ought.

In a treatise on happiness or the good life, Augustine declared that happy is the person who, in the course of a complete life, has satisfied all desires, *provided that the individual desired nothing amiss.* If desiring nothing amiss is having the habit of right desire, then Augustine's declaration is another statement of a mistake we have already discussed—the error of thinking that moral virtue is not only necessary but also sufficient for happiness or leading a good life.

> *"Acquiring moral virtue . . . is . . . a process of conquering one's childish tendencies toward indulgence in immediate gratifications."*

Aristotle would correct Augustine's error by adding another proviso. He would say that happiness consists in a complete life in which all one's desires are satisfied provided (a) the individual desires nothing amiss and also provided (b) that goods which are not wholly within the power of individuals to obtain for themselves are obtained partly as the result of good luck or the blessings of good fortune.

The second proviso is expressed in the definition of happiness that Aristotle formulates in Chapter 10 of Book I of his *Ethics*. There he says that happiness is attained only in a complete life; that it involves activity in accordance with moral virtue; and that it also must be accompanied by a moderate possession of wealth. Since wealth is an external good, a possession rather than a personal perfection, such as the virtues, moral and intellectual, we can correctly expand the mention of wealth to include other external goods.

External goods are goods that are never wholly within our power to obtain for ourselves. Good luck or the blessings of good fortune may bestow them upon us or help us to obtain them. The benefactions of just government secure for us or help us to obtain the real goods to which we have a natural and unalienable human right.

Being a Citizen

Being the citizen of a society the government of which is distributively just is certainly a blessing of good fortune. It is a blessing that does not befall a large part of the human race.

It is not only external goods, such as wealth, that are not wholly within the power of individuals to obtain for themselves, and so depend for their attainment either upon good luck or upon the benefactions of a just government. What is true of wealth is also true of health, of liberty, of knowledge, even of friendships; in fact, of all real goods except moral virtue, and of many innocuous apparent goods as well. Except for moral virtue, which is wholly within our power to acquire by free choice, all other goods partly depend on external circumstances—on the condition of the physical environment in which one happens to live and on the institutions and enactments of the government under which one happens to live.

The truth we have just considered can be briefly summarized by saying that there are two indispensable conditions requisite for happiness, ethically conceived. One is moral virtue. The other is good luck, or the blessings of good fortune. Both are necessary conditions, but neither by itself is a sufficient condition.

The lives of persons having moral virtue can be blemished and, even in extreme cases, ruined by the adversities of outrageous fortune. Persons having all the blessings of good fortune can ruin their own lives or seriously blemish them by the vices to which they are addicted.

Aristotle is the only moral philosopher in the Western tradition who makes good luck as well as moral virtue a necessary condition of a life that is morally good as well as one that is enriched by the attainment of all real goods and many apparent goods that are innocuous. That is why I think his *Ethics* is the only sound and pragmatic moral philosophy that has made its appearance in the last twenty-five centuries.

If this unique feature of Aristotle's *Ethics* were not true, all the social, political, and economic reforms that have occurred in the last twenty-five centuries would be shorn of meaning and purpose. They were all instituted and enacted in order to bestow upon human beings the external conditions they need for a good human life. If moral virtue were sufficient for the successful pursuit of happiness, human beings could lead good human lives under the deprivations imposed upon them by the deplorable conditions under which a great many still live.

> *"The lives of persons having moral virtue can be . . . ruined by the adversities of outrageous fortune."*

The goal at which a just government should aim would not be the happiness of all its citizens. That would be entirely within their own power to pursue by acquiring moral virtue.

Morally virtuous chattel slaves and morally virtuous disfranchised females could lead good human lives; so, too, could those living in dire poverty or suffering from serious illness without adequate medical care.

In the lives of most of us, there is an imperfection that only the most fortunate completely escape. Most of us suffer personal tragedies in which we are confronted with having to choose between alternatives, neither of which is desirable or good. We are thus compelled to take unto ourselves, by free choice, an evil that we would otherwise strive to avoid.

A Philosophy of Caring Motivates People to Behave Ethically

by Nel Noddings

About the author: *Nel Noddings is an associate professor of education at Stanford University in California and is the author of* Caring: A Feminine Approach to Ethics and Moral Education, *from which this viewpoint is excerpted.*

Ethics, the philosophical study of morality, has concentrated for the most part on moral reasoning. Much current work, for example, focuses on the status of moral predicates and, in education, the dominant model presents a hierarchical picture of moral reasoning. This emphasis gives ethics a contemporary, mathematical appearance, but it also moves discussion beyond the sphere of actual human activity and the feeling that pervades such activity. Even though careful philosophers have recognized the difference between "pure" or logical reason and "practical" or moral reason, ethical argumentation has frequently proceeded as if it were governed by the logical necessity characteristic of geometry. It has concentrated on the establishment of principles and that which can be logically derived from them. One might say that ethics has been discussed largely in the language of the father: in principles and propositions, in terms such as justification, fairness, justice. The mother's voice has been silent. Human caring and the memory of caring and being cared for, which I shall argue form the foundation of ethical response, have not received attention except as outcomes of ethical behavior. One is tempted to say that ethics has so far been guided by Logos, the masculine spirit, whereas the more natural and, perhaps, stronger approach would be through Eros, the feminine spirit. I hesitate to give way to this temptation, in part because the terms carry with them a Jungian baggage that I am unwilling to claim in its totality. In one sense, "Eros" does capture the flavor and spirit of what I am attempting here; the notion of psychic relatedness lies at the heart of the ethic I shall propose. In another sense, however, even "Eros" is masculine in its roots and fails to capture the receptive rationality of caring that is characteristic of the feminine approach.

Moral Attitude, Not Moral Reasoning

When we look clear-eyed at the world today, we see it wracked with fighting, killing, vandalism, and psychic pain of all sorts. One of the saddest features of this picture of violence is that the deeds are so often done in the name of principle. When we establish a principle forbidding killing, we also establish principles describing the exceptions to the first principle. Supposing, then, that we are moral (we are principled, are we not?), we may tear into others whose beliefs or behaviors differ from ours with the promise of ultimate vindication.

This approach through law and principle is not, I suggest, the approach of the mother. It is the approach of the detached one, of the father. The view to be expressed here is a feminine view. This does not imply that all women will accept it or that men will reject it; indeed, there is no reason why men should not embrace it. It is feminine in the deep classical sense—rooted in receptivity, relatedness, and responsiveness. It does not imply either that logic is to be discarded or that logic is alien to women. It represents an alternative to present views, one that begins with the moral attitude or longing for goodness and not with moral reasoning. . . .

Ethics and Caring

It is generally agreed that ethics is the philosophical study of morality, but we also speak of "professional ethics" and "a personal ethic." When we speak in the second way, we refer to something explicable—a set of rules, an ideal, a constellation of expressions—that guides and justifies our conduct. One can, obviously, behave ethically without engaging in ethics as a philosophical enterprise, and one can even put together an ethic of sorts—that is, a description of what it means to be moral—without seriously questioning what it means to be moral. Such an ethic, it seems to me, may or may not be a guide to moral behavior. It depends, in a fundamental way, on an assessment of the answer to the question: What does it mean to be moral? This question will be central to our investigation. I shall use "ethical" rather than "moral" in most of our discussions but, in doing so, I am assuming that to behave ethically is to behave under the guidance of an acceptable and justifiable account of what it means to be moral. To behave ethically is not to behave in conformity with just any description of morality,

> *"Human caring and the memory of caring and being cared for . . . have not received attention."*

and I shall claim that ethical systems are not equivalent simply because they include rules concerning the same matters or categories. . . .

I want to build an ethic on caring, and I shall claim that there is a form of caring natural and accessible to all human beings. Certain feelings, attitudes, and memories will be claimed as universal. But the ethic itself will not embody a set of universalizable moral judgments. Indeed, moral judgment will not be its central concern. It is very common among philosophers to move from the question: What is morality? to the seemingly more manageable question: What is a moral judgment? Fred Feldman, for example, makes this move early on. He suggests:

> Perhaps we can shed some light on the meaning of the noun "morality" by considering the adjective "moral." Proceeding in this way will enable us to deal with a less abstract concept, and we may thereby be more successful. So instead of asking "What is morality?" let us pick one of the most interesting of these uses of the adjective "moral" and ask instead, "What is a moral judgment?"

Now, I am not arguing that this move is completely mistaken or that nothing can be gained through a consideration of moral judgments, but such a move is not the only possibility. We might choose another interesting use of the adjective and ask, instead, about the moral impulse or moral attitude. The choice is important. The long-standing emphasis on the study of moral judgments has led to a serious imbalance in moral discussion. In particular, it is well known that many women—perhaps most women—do not approach moral problems as problems of principle, reasoning, and judgment. . . . If a substantial segment of humankind approaches moral problems through a consideration of the concrete elements of situations and a regard for themselves as caring, then perhaps an attempt should be made to enlighten the study of morality in this alternative mode. Further, such a study has

> *"Many women . . . do not approach moral problems as problems of principle, reasoning, and judgment."*

significant implications, beyond ethics, for education. If moral education, in a double sense, is guided only by the study of moral principles and judgments, not only are women made to feel inferior to men in the moral realm but also education itself may suffer from impoverished and one-sided moral guidance.

So building an ethic on caring seems both reasonable and important. One may well ask, at this point, whether an ethic so constructed will be a form of "situation ethics." It is not, certainly, that form of act-utilitarianism commonly labeled "situation ethics." Its emphasis is not on the consequences of our acts, although these are not, of course, irrelevant. But an ethic of caring locates morality primarily in the pre-act consciousness of the one-caring. Yet it is not a form of agapism. There is no command to love nor, indeed, any God to make the commandment. Further, I shall reject the notion of universal love, finding it unattainable in any but the most abstract sense and thus a source of distraction. While much of what will be developed in the ethic of caring may be found, also, in Christian ethics, there will be major and irreconcilable differences. Human love, human caring, will be quite enough on which to found an ethic.

We must look even more closely at that love and caring. . . .

How are we to make judgments of right and wrong under this ethic? First, it is important to understand that we are not primarily interested in judging but, rather, in heightening moral perception and sensitivity. But "right" and "wrong" can be useful.

Suppose a mother observes her young child pulling the kitten's tail or picking it up by the ears. She may exclaim, "Oh, no, it is not nice to hurt the kitty," or, "You must not hurt the kitty." Or she may simply say, "Stop. See—you are hurting the kitty," and she may then take the kitten in her

> *"Building an ethic on caring seems both reasonable and important."*

own hands and show the child how to handle it. She holds the kitten gently, stroking it, and saying, "See? Ah, ah, kitty, nice kitty. . . ." What the mother is supposing in this interaction is that the realization that his act is hurting the kitten, supplemented by the knowledge of how to avoid inflicting hurt, will suffice to change the child's behavior. If she believes this, she has no need for the statement, "It is wrong to hurt the kitty." She is not threatening sanctions but drawing dual attention to a matter of fact (the hurting) and her own commitment (I will not hurt). Beyond this, she is supposing that her child, well-cared-for himself, does not want to inflict pain.

Now, I am not claiming through use of this illustration that moral statements are mere expressions of approval or disapproval, although they do serve an expressive function. A. J. Ayer, who did make a claim of this sort before modifying his position somewhat, uses an illustration very like the one just given to support an emotivist position. But even if it were possible to take a purely analytic stance with respect to moral theory, as Ayer suggests he has done, that is certainly not what I intend to do. One who labels moral statements as expressions of approval or disapproval, and takes the matter to be finished with that, misses the very heart of morality. He misses the commitment to behave in a fashion compatible with caring. Thus he misses both feeling and content. I may, after all, express my approval or disapproval on matters that are not moral. Thus it is clear that when I make a moral judgment I am doing more than simply expressing approval or disapproval. I am both expressing my own commitment to behave in a way compatible with caring and appealing to the hearer to consider what he is doing. I may say first to a child, "Oh! Don't hurt the kitty!" And I may then add, "It is wrong to hurt the kitty." The word is not necessary, strictly speaking, but I may find it useful.

What do I mean by this? I certainly mean to express my own commitment, and I show this best by daily example. But I may mean to say more than this. I may explain to the child that not only do I feel this way but that our family does, that our community does, that our culture does. Here I must be very careful. Our community may say one thing and do quite another. Such contradiction is even more likely at the level of "our culture." But I express myself doubly in words and in acts, and I may search out examples in the larger culture to convince the child that significant others do feel this way. The one-caring is careful to distinguish between acts that violate caring, acts that she herself holds wrong, and those acts that "some people" hold to be wrong. She need not be condescending in this instruction. She is herself so reluctant to universalize beyond the demands of caring that she cannot say, "It is wrong," to everything that is illegal, church-forbidden, or contrary to a prevailing etiquette. But she can raise the question, attempt to justify the alien view, express her own objections, and support the child in his own exploration.

The Importance of Feeling

Emotivists are partly right, I think, when they suggest that we might effectively substitute a statement describing the fact or event that triggers our feeling or attitude for statements such as "It is wrong to do *X*." When I say to my child, "It is wrong to hurt the kitty," I mean (if I am not threatening sanctions) to inform him that he is hurting the kitten and, further, that I believe that if he perceives he is doing so, he will stop. I am counting on his gradually developing ability to feel pain in the other to induce a decision to stop. To say, "It is wrong to cause pain needlessly," contributes nothing by way of knowledge and can hardly be thought likely to change the attitude or behavior of one who might ask, "Why is it wrong?" If I say to someone, "You are hurting the cat," and he replies, "I know it—so what? I like hurting cats," I feel "zero at the bone." Saying to him, "It is wrong to hurt cats," adds little unless I intend to threaten sanctions. If I mean to equate "It is wrong to hurt cats" with "There will be a sure and specific punishment for hurting cats," then it would be more honest to say this. One either feels a sort of pain in response to the pain of others, or one does not feel it. If he does feel it, he does not need to be told that causing pain is wrong. If he does not feel it in a particular case, he may remember the feeling— as one remembers the sweetness of love on hearing a certain piece of music— and allow himself to be moved by this remembrance of feeling. For one who feels nothing, directly or by remembrance, we must prescribe reeducation or exile. Thus, at the foundation of moral behavior—as we have already pointed out—is feeling or sentiment. But, further, there is commitment to remain open to that feeling, to remember it, and to put one's thinking in its service. It is the particular commitment underlying genuine expressions of moral judgment—as well as the special content—that the emotivist misses.

> *"The caring attitude that lies at the heart of all ethical behavior is universal."*

The one-caring, clearly, applies "right" and "wrong" most confidently to her own decisions. This does not, as we have insisted before, make her a relativist. The caring attitude that lies at the heart of all ethical behavior is universal. . . . In general the one-caring evaluates her own acts with respect to how faithfully they conform to what is known and felt through the receptivity of caring. But she also uses "right" and "wrong" instructively and respectfully to refer to the judgments of significant others. If she agrees because the matter at hand can be assessed in light of caring, she adds her personal commitment and example; if she has doubts—because the rule appealed to seems irrelevant or ambiguous in the light of caring—she still acknowledges the judgment but adds her own dissent or demurrer. Her eye is on the ethical development of the cared-for and, as she herself withholds judgment until she has heard the "whole story," she wants the cared-for to encounter others, receive them, and reflect on what he has received. Principles and rules are among the beliefs he will receive, and she wants him to consider these in the light of caring.

But is this all we can say about right and wrong? Is there not a firm foundation in morality for our legal judgments? Surely, we must be allowed to say, for example, that stealing is wrong and is, therefore, properly forbidden by law. Because it is so often wrong—and so easily demonstrated to be wrong—under an ethic of caring, we may accede that such a law has its roots *partly* in morality. We may legally punish one who has stolen, but we may not pass moral judgment on him until we know why he stole. An ethic of caring is likely to be stricter in its judgment, but more supportive and corrective in following up its judgment, than ethics otherwise grounded. . . .

> *"Far from being romantic, an ethic of caring is practical, made for this earth."*

The lessons in "right" and "wrong" are hard lessons—not swiftly accomplished by setting up as an objective the learning of some principle. We do not say: It is wrong to steal. Rather, we consider why it was wrong or may be wrong in this case to steal. We do not say: It is wrong to kill. By setting up such a principle, we also imply its exceptions, and then we may too easily act on authorized exceptions. The one-caring wants to consider, and wants her child to consider, the act itself in full context. She will send him into the world skeptical, vulnerable, courageous, disobedient, and tenderly receptive. The "world" may not depend upon him to obey its rules or fulfill its wishes, but you, the individual he encounters, may depend upon him to meet you as one-caring. . . .

The Toughness of Caring

An ethic built on caring is thought by some to be tenderminded. It does involve construction of an ideal from the fact and memory of tenderness. The ethical sentiment itself requires a prior natural sentiment of caring and a willingness to sustain tenderness. But there is no assumption of innate human goodness. . . .

We have memories of caring, of tenderness, and these lead us to a vision of what is good—a state that is good-in-itself and a commitment to sustain and enhance that good (the desire and commitment to be moral). But we have other memories as well, and we have other desires. An ethic of caring takes into account these other tendencies and desires; it is precisely because the tendency to treat each other well is so fragile that we must strive so consistently to care.

Far from being romantic, an ethic of caring is practical, made for this earth. Its toughness is disclosed in a variety of features, the most important of which I shall try to describe briefly here.

First, since caring is a relation, an ethic built on it is naturally other-regard-ing. Since I am defined in relation, I do not sacrifice myself when I move toward the other as one-caring. Car-ing is, thus, both self-serving and other-serving. Willard Gaylin de-scribes it as necessary to the survival of the species: "If one's frame of refer-ence focuses on the individual, caring seems self-sacrificing. But if the focus is on the group, on the species, it is the ultimate self-serving device—the sine qua non of survival."

> *"An ethic of caring is a tough ethic."*

Clearly, this is so. But while I am drawn to the other, while I am instinctively called to nurture and protect, I am also the initiator and chooser of my acts. I may act in accordance with that which is good in my deepest nature, or I may seek to avoid it—either by forsaking relation or by trying to transform that which is feeling and action into that which is all propositional talk and princi-ple. If I suppose, for example, that I am somehow alone and totally responsible for either the apprehension or creation of moral principles, I may find myself in some difficulty when it comes to caring for myself. If moral principles govern my conduct with respect to others, if I must always regard the other in order to be moral, how can I properly meet my own needs and desires? How can I, morally, care for myself?

Caring for Self

An ethic of caring is a tough ethic. It does not separate self and other in car-ing, although, of course, it identifies the special contribution of the one-caring and the cared-for in caring. In contrast to some forms of agapism, for example, it has no problem in advocating a deep and steady caring for self. In a discus-sion of other-regarding forms of agapism, Gene Outka considers the case of a woman tied to a demanding parent. He explores the possibility of her finding justification for leaving in an assessment of the greatest good for all concerned, and he properly recommends that her own interests be included. In discussing the insistence of some agapists on entirely other-regarding justification, he ex-plores the possibility of her breaking away "to become a medical doctor," thereby satisfying the need for multilateral other-interests. The one-caring throws up her hands at such casting about for reasons. She needs no special jus-tification to care for herself for, if she is not supported and cared-for, she may be entirely lost as one-caring. If caring is to be maintained, clearly, the one-caring must be maintained. She must be strong, courageous, and capable of joy. . . .

The ethical responsibility of the one-caring is to look clear-eyed on what is happening to her ideal and how well she is meeting it. She sees herself, perhaps, as caring lovingly for her parent. But perhaps he is cantankerous, ungrateful, rude, and even dirty. She sees herself becoming impatient, grouchy, tired, and filled with self-pity. She can stay and live by an honestly diminished ideal—"I am a tired, grouchy, pitiful caretaker of my old father"—or she can free herself to whatever degree she must to remain minimally but actually caring. The ethical self does not live partitioned off from the rest of the person. Thinking guided by caring does not seek to justify a way out by means of a litany of predicted "goods," but it seeks a way to remain one-caring and, if at all possible, to enhance the ethical ideal. In such a quest, there is no way to disregard the self, or to remain impartial, or to adopt the stance of a disinterested observer. Pursuit of the ethical ideal demands impassioned and realistic commitment.

We see still another reason for accepting constraints on our ethical ideals. When we accept honestly our loves, our innate ferocity, our capacity for hate, we may use all this as information in building the safeguards and alarms that must be part of the ideal. We know better what we must work toward, what we must prevent, and the conditions under which we are lost as ones-caring. Instead of hiding from our natural impulses and pretending that we can achieve goodness through lofty abstractions, we accept what is there—all of it—and use what we have already assessed as good to control that which is not-good.

The Ethical Ideal

Caring preserves both the group and the individual and, as we have already seen, it limits our obligation so that it may realistically be met. It will not allow us to be distracted by visions of universal love, perfect justice, or a world unified under principle. It does not say, "Thou shalt not kill," and then seek other principles under which killing is, after all, justified. If the other is a clear and immediate danger to me or to my cared-fors, I must stop him, and I might need to kill him. But I cannot kill in the name of principle or justice. I must meet this other—even this evil other—as one-caring so long as caring itself is not endangered by my doing so. I must, for example, oppose capital punishment. I do not begin by saying, "Capital punishment is wrong." Thus I do not fall into the trap of having to supply reasons for its wrongness that will be endlessly disputed at a logical level. I do not say, "Life is sacred," for I cannot name a source of sacredness. I may point to the irrevocability of the decision, but

> *"Pursuit of the ethical ideal demands impassioned and realistic commitment."*

this is not in itself decisive, even for me, because in many cases the decision would be just and I could not regret the demise of the condemned. (I have, after all, confessed my own ferocity; in the heat of emotion, I might have torn him to shreds if I had caught him molesting my child.)

My concern is for the ethical ideal, for my own ethical ideal and for whatever part of it others in my community may share. Ideally, another human being should be able to request, with expectation of positive response, my help and comfort. If I am not blinded by fear, or rage, or hatred, I should reach out as one-caring to the proximate stranger who entreats my help. This is the ideal one-caring creates. I should be able to respond to the condemned man's entreaty, "Help me." We must ask, then, after the effects of capital punishment on jurors, on judges, on jailers, on wardens, on newspersons "covering" the execution, on ministers visiting the condemned, on citizens affirming the sentence, on doctors certifying first that the condemned is well enough to be executed and second that he is dead. What effects have capital punishment on the ethical ideals of the participants? For me, if I had to participate, the ethical ideal would be diminished. Diminished. The ideal itself would be diminished. My act would either be wrong or barely right—right in a depleted sense. I might, indeed, participate ethically—rightly—in an execution but only at the cost of revising my ethical ideal downward. If I do not revise it and still participate, then my act is wrong, and I am a hypocrite and unethical. It is the difference between "I don't believe in killing, but . . ." and "I did not believe in killing cold-bloodedly, but now I see that I must and for these reasons." In the latter case, I may retain my ethicality, but at considerable cost. My ideal must forever carry with it not only what I would be but what I am and have been. There is no unbridgeable chasm between what I am and what I will be. I build the bridge to my future self, and this is why I oppose capital punishment. I do not want to kill if other options are open to me,

> *"Our own ethicality is not entirely 'up to us.'. . . We depend upon each other even for our own goodness."*

and I do not want to ask others in the community to do what may diminish their own ethical ideals. . . .

No Nation Can Be Ethical

The duty to enhance the ethical ideal, the commitment to caring, invokes a duty to promote skepticism and noninstitutional affiliation. In a deep sense, no institution or nation can be ethical. It cannot meet the other as one-caring or as one trying to care. It can only capture in general terms what particular ones-caring would like to have done in well-described situations. Laws, manifestos, and proclamations are not, on this account, either empty or useless; but they are limited, and they may support immoral as well as moral actions. Only the individual can be truly called to ethical behavior, and the individual can never give way to encapsulated moral guides, although she may safely accept them in ordinary, untroubled times.

Everything depends, then, upon the will to be good, to remain in caring relation to the other.

A Sense of Global Responsibility Would Motivate People to Behave Ethically

by Hans Küng

About the author: *Hans Küng is a Swiss Roman Catholic theologian, and a professor at Tübingen University in Germany. A critic of papal authority, in 1979 he was stripped of his right to teach as an official Roman Catholic theologian. Küng is the author of* Infallible? An Inquiry *and* Global Responsibility: In Search of a New World Ethic, *from which this viewpoint is excerpted.*

The catastrophic economic, social, political and ecological developments of both the first and the second halves of the century necessitate a world ethic if humankind is to survive on this earth. Diagnoses of disaster have been of little help to us here. Nor might a pragmatic social technology without foundations for values, of a Western or Eastern tendency, be enough. But without morality, without universally binding ethical norms, indeed without 'global standards', the nations are in danger of manoeuvring themselves into a crisis which can ultimately lead to national collapse, i.e. to economic ruin, social disintegration and political catastrophe.

An Ethical System Is Necessary

In other words, we need reflection on ethics, on the basic moral attitude of human beings; we need an ethical system, a philosophical or theological theory of values and norms, to direct our decisions and actions. The crisis must be seen as an opportunity, and a 'response' must be found to the 'challenge'. But an answer in negative terms can hardly be enough if ethics is not to degenerate into a technique for repairing defects and weaknesses. So we must take the

Excerpted from *Global Responsibility*, translated from the German *Projekt Weltethos*, published by R. Piper GmbH & Co. KG, Munich, 1990. Copyright ©1990 by Hans Küng. English translation copyright ©1991 by John Bowden. Reprinted by permission of The CROSSROAD Publishing Company, New York.

trouble to give a positive answer to the question of a world ethic. We begin with the basic question of any ethics. Why ethics at all? Why be moral?

Beyond Good and Evil?

(a) Why not do evil?

Why should people do good and not evil? Why are not human beings 'beyond good and evil' (F. Nietzsche) and only obligated to their 'will to power' (success, riches and contentment)? Elementary questions are often the most difficult of all—and such questions no longer arise just for the 'permissive' West. Much—morals, laws and customs—that was taken for granted down the centuries because it was supported by religious authority is no longer taken for granted nowadays all over the world. Questions like these occur to every individual:

–Why should human beings not lie to, deceive, rob their fellows if this is to their advantage and in any particular instance one does not have to fear discovery and punishment?

–Why should the politician resist corruption if he can be sure of the discretion of the one who offers the bribe?

–Why should a businessman (or a bank) set a limit to the profit motive, if greed, if the slogan 'get rich', is preached publicly without any moral constraints?

> *"Without morality . . . the nations are in danger of manoeuvring themselves into a crisis."*

–Why should someone engaged in embryo research (or a research institute) not develop a commercial technique for implantation which guarantees the production of flawless embryos and throws the surplus on the rubbish heap?

–Why should unwanted (say, female) offspring whose sex has been determined before birth not be liquidated right away?

But the questions are also addressed to the great collectives. Why may a people, a race, a religion, not hate, harass and, if that is its concern, even exile or liquidate a minority of another kind, another faith, or even one that is 'foreign'?

But enough of negatives!

(b) Why do good?

Here, too, questions arise first for the individual:

–Why should people be friendly, compassionate and even ready to help instead of being heedless and brutal; why should a young person renounce the use of force and in principle opt for non-violence?

–Why should a businessman (or a bank) behave with absolute correctness even when there are no controls? Why should a trade union official fight not only for an organization but also for the common good, even if it damages his or her own career?

–Why should human beings never be the object of commercialization and industrialization (the embryo as a marketable article and an object of trade) for scientists, doctors involved in implantation and their institutes, but always be legal subjects and goals of the process?

But here too questions are addressed to the great collectives:

–Why should one people show tolerance, respect and even appreciation to another?

–Why should one race show these to another?

–Why should one religion show these to another?

–Why should those in authority in the nations and religions in all circumstances commit themselves to peace and never to war?

So to put the basic question once again: why should human beings—understood as individuals, groups, nations or religions—act in a human, truly human way? And why should they do this unconditionally—that is, in every case? And why should they all do this, and no class, clique or group be excepted? That is the basic question for every ethics.

No Democracy Without Basic Consensus

(a) The dilemma of democracy

It may be evident that here we have a basic problem of Western democracy about which we are not to moralize in a self-righteous way but on which we are to reflect self-critically. For on the basis of its self-understanding the free democratic state—in contrast to the mediaeval clerical ('black') state or the modern totalitarian ('brown' or 'red') state—must be neutral in its world-view. That means that it must tolerate different religions and confessions, philosophies and ideologies. And beyond question this represents tremendous progress in the history of humankind, with the result that nowadays, all over the world, there is tremendous longing for freedom and human rights which no Western intellectual who constantly enjoys Western freedom should disavow as 'typically Western'. Given its constitution, the democratic state must observe, protect and further freedom of conscience and religion, freedom of the press and of assembly, and everything that is counted among modern human rights. Nevertheless, in all this the state may not decree any interpretation of life or lifestyle; it may not prescribe any supreme values and ultimate norms by law, if it is not to violate the neutrality of its world-view.

Here, obviously, is the basis of the dilemma of any modern democratic state (whether in Europe, America, India or Japan): it has to take into account precisely that which it may not

> *"Without a minimal basic consensus on certain values, norms and attitudes, no human society worth living in is possible."*

prescribe by law. If the different world-views within it are to live together, the pluralistic society in particular needs a basic consensus to which these world-views contribute, to bring about the formation of a consensus which is not 'strict' or total, but 'overlapping' (John Rawls). How far this 'overlapping' basic ethical consensus must go in particular instances depends on the historical situation. Thus for a long time people did not have to worry, say, about the preservation and protection of non-human nature, which nowadays is important for survival. So the consensus must constantly be found afresh in a dynamic process.

(b) A minimum of common values, norms and attitudes

Nowadays there is largely agreement here. Without a minimal basic consensus on certain values, norms and attitudes, no human society worth living in

> *"The key concept for our strategy for the future must be: human responsibility for this planet."*

is possible in either a smaller or a larger community. Even a modern democracy cannot function without such a basic consensus, which constantly has to be rediscovered in dialogue; indeed it collapses into chaos or a dictatorship—as was shown, say, by the Weimar republic between 1919 and 1933.

What does a minimal basic consensus mean? I shall clarify this on a few points:

- What is the presupposition of internal peace in a smaller or larger community? An agreement that social conflicts will be solved without violence.
- What is the presupposition of economic and legal order? An agreement that a particular order and laws will be obeyed.
- What is the presupposition for institutions which support this order and yet are subject to constant historical change? The will at least to go on giving them tacit assent.

But it is a fact that conversely, in the ideological controversies of a technological world which has become abstract and impossible to survey, in some places the reaction is always one of terror that there will be even more acceptance of Machiavellianism in politics, sharkish methods in the stock market and libertinism in private life. Once again, what we need here is not moralizing, but reflection.

(c) Freely chosen ties

If modern society is to function, the question of the aims and the 'ligatures' (to use Ralf Dahrendorf's phrase), the freely chosen bonds of the individual, may not be neglected. These ties may not become fetters and chains for men and women, but must be help and support. And fundamental to human life is a commitment to a direction in life, to values, to norms, to attitudes, to a meaning in life: one which—unless everything is deceptive—is transnational and transcultural.

People are normally conscious of the ineradicable longing to hold on to something, to rely on something, to have a standpoint in the bewilderingly complex technological world and in the errors and confusions of their private life, to follow some guideline, to have some standards, to have a goal. In short, people feel the longing to possess something like a basic ethical orientation. And though communication open on all sides, which is stressed so much by social psychology, is doubtless important in a modern society made uncertain by excessive information and disinformation; although the model of an 'alternative dispute resolution' which has been proposed for legal practice is doubtless also important legally, without any ties to meaning, values and norms people will not be able to act in a truly human way in matters large or small.

But what could be the maxims for the future in this context? What would be the ethical goal for the third millennium? What would be the slogan for a strategy of the future?

The key concept for our strategy for the future must be: human responsibility for this planet, a planetary responsibility.

The Slogan of the Future: Planetary Responsibility

(a) An ethic of responsibility in place of an ethic of success or disposition
Calling for global responsibility is first and foremost the opposite of calling for what is a mere ethic of success: it is the opposite of an action for which the end sanctifies the means and for which whatever functions, brings profit, power or enjoyment, is good. This in particular can lead to crass libertinism and Machiavellianism. Such an ethic can have no future.

Nor, however, can a mere dispositional ethics have a future either. Orientated on an idea of value seen more or less in isolation (justice, love, truth), it is concerned only with the purely inner motivation of the agent, without bothering about the consequences of a decision or an action, with the concrete situation, its demands and effects. Such an 'absolute' ethic is unhistorical in a dangerous way (it ignores the complexity of the historical situation as it has developed); it is unpolitical (it ignores the complexity of the given social structures and power-relationships); but precisely in this respect, if need be it can justify even terrorism on grounds of disposition.

By contrast, an ethics of responsibility, of the kind that the great sociologist Max Weber proposed in the revolutionary winter of 1918/19, might have some future. Even according to Weber, such an ethic is not 'without a disposition'; however, it always asks realistically about the foreseeable 'consequences' of our action and takes responsibility for them: 'to this degree a dispositional ethics and an ethics of responsibility are not absolute opposites, but supplement each other; it takes both of them to make the authentic person who can have the "call to politics".' Without a dispositional ethics, the ethics of responsibility would decline into an ethics of success regardless of disposition, for which the end justifies any means. Without an ethics of responsibility, dispositional ethics would decline into the fostering of self-righteous inwardness.

> *"An ethics of responsibility . . . might have some future."*

Since the First World War, however, human knowledge and power have grown immeasurably—with extremely dangerous long-term consequences for the generations to come. This is demonstrated to us particularly in the spheres of nuclear energy and gene technology. At the end of the 1970s the German-American philosopher Hans Jonas therefore thought through 'the principle of responsibility' in a completely changed world situation in a new and comprehensive way for our technological civilization: in the light of the danger to the ongoing existence of the human species. This involves action in global responsibility for the whole of the biosphere, lithosphere, hydrosphere and atmosphere of our planet. And this includes a self-imposed limitation by human beings on their freedom in the present for the sake of their survival in the future—one need think only of the energy crisis, the exhaustion of natural resources and population growth. So a new kind of ethic is called for out of concern for the future (which makes people wise) and reverence for nature.

(b) Responsibility for our neighbours, the environment and the world after us
So in concrete terms, the slogan for the third millennium should run: world society is responsible for its own future! This is responsibility for our society and environment and also for the world after us. Those responsible in the various regions, religions and ideologies of the world are called on to learn to think and act in a global context. Here there are certainly particular demands on three regions of the world which are economic leaders: the European community, North America and the Pacific area. They also have a responsibility which they cannot get rid of, for the development of other regions of the world: Eastern Europe, Latin America, Southern Asia and Africa—where now, after the encouraging developments in Eastern Europe [the collapse of communism], one also longs for positive changes.

> *"The slogan for the third millennium should run: world society is responsible for its own future!"*

So on the threshold of the third millennium the cardinal ethical question is raised all the more urgently. On what basic conditions can we survive, survive as human beings, on a habitable earth, and give human form to our individual and social life? On what presuppositions can human civilization be rescued for the third millennium? What basic principles should be followed by the leading forces in politics, economics, science and the religions? And on what basis can the individual, too, achieve a happy and fulfilled existence?

Humans Must Remain the Subject

(c) Human beings: the goal and criterion
The answer is that human beings must become more than they are; they must become more human! What is good for human beings is what preserves and furthers their humanity and makes it succeed—and does so in quite a different way from before. Human beings must exhaust their human potential in an unprecedented way to produce the most humane society possible and an intact en-

vironment. For the possibilities of humanity that they can activate are greater than the *status quo*. To this extent the realistic principle of responsibility and the 'utopian' principle of hope (Ernst Bloch) belong together.

So there is nothing against the present-day 'self-tendencies' (self-determination, experience of self, self-discovery, self-realization, self-fulfillment)—as long as they are not detached from responsibility for oneself and the world, from responsibility for our fellow human beings, for society and nature; as long as they do not deteriorate into narcissistic reflection on and autistic relationship to the self. Self-assertion and unselfishness need not be mutually exclusive. Identity and solidarity are both required for the formation of a better world.

> *"Human beings must become more than they are; they must become more human!"*

But whatever projects one plans for a better human future, the basic ethical principle must be that human beings may never be made mere means. They must remain an ultimate end, and always be a goal and criterion—since Kant that has been a way of formulating the categorical imperative. Money and capital are means, as work is a means. Science, technology and industry are also means. They too are in no way 'value-free', 'neutral', but in each individual case have to be assessed and used in terms of the degree to which they serve human development. For example, manipulation of genes in human gametes is therefore legitimate only to the degree that it serves the protection, preservation and humanization of human life; research which uses up the embryo is a human experiment which is to be strictly repudiated as being inhumane.

Business Ethics

And as for business: I once heard the American management guru Professor Peter Drucker, who has announced the replacement of the 'business society' by the 'knowledge society', in which education and training would have a key position, remark that 'Profit is not a goal but a result'. But we already know now that computers and machines too, cybernetics and management, organization and system are there for human beings and not vice versa. In other words: human beings must always remain the subject and never become the object. What holds for politics on a large scale also applies in the everyday handling of business (as economic psychologists and business specialists are also telling us): 'The "human factor" is the central driving force or restraining element in business and in global events' (Roland Müller). Or as Knut Bleicher puts it in a comparison of management analysis in different cultures (USA—Europe—Japan): 'It is not machines which produce inventions and innovations, but people who are motivated to set their intellect to recognizing opportunities, avoiding risks and creating new economic, social and technological conditions through their activities. Instead of material capital which was decisive for the success of businesses in times of stable developments, it is now human capital that determines the future success of a business'. Humankind will not be saved by the computer but by human beings.

(d) Ethics as public concern

Hence we can recognize as a programmatic demand that ethics, which in modern times has increasingly been regarded as a private matter, must again become a public concern of prime importance in postmodernity—for human well-being and for the survival of humankind. Here it is not enough to employ ethical experts in the various social institutions in individual cases. In view of the tremendous complexity of the problems and the specialization of science and technology, ethics itself needs to be institutionalized. It has already progressed further in this direction in North America than in Europe and Japan: ethical commissions, chairs in ethics and codes of ethics have been created, especially in the spheres of biology, medicine, technology and economy (e.g. a code of business ethics which, for example, resolutely attacks increasing corruption).

Economic Thought and Action

It should not be forgotten that economic thought and action, too, are not value-free or value-neutral. For example the view that it is the exclusive concern of a business to make a profit and that the maximization of profit is the best and only contribution of a business to the prosperity of a society is increasingly being regarded as an outdated standpoint, even among economists and business specialists. Economists, too, are reflecting nowadays on the fact that the great European theoreticians on economics and society from Aristotle and Plato through Thomas Aquinas to the moral philosopher Adam Smith, the founder of modern economics, have seen economics and politics in an overall ethical context.

But those who act ethically do not therefore act in an unbusinesslike way; they take precautions against crises. Some major firms have had to suffer serious losses before learning that the most successful business economically is not the one which has no concern for the ecological, political or ethical implications of its products, but the one which takes these into account—possibly making short-term sacrifices—and so from the start avoids painful penalties and legal restrictions.

Just as the social and ecological responsibility of business cannot simply be foisted on to politicians, so moral and ethical responsibility cannot simply be foisted on to religion.

> *"Humankind will not be saved by the computer but by human beings."*

There are businessmen who are even asked at the dinner table by their critical sons and daughters whether such a split between economics and morality, between a purely profit-orientated business at work and ethical private life at home is still credible. No, ethical action should not be just a private addition to marketing plans, sales strategies, ecological bookkeeping and social balance-sheets, but should form the natural framework for human social action. For even the market economy, if it is to function socially and be regulated ecologically, needs people who are supported by very definite convictions and attitudes. Indeed, in general it may be said:

(e) No ordering of the world without a world ethic

For one thing is certain: human beings cannot be improved by more and more laws and regulations, nor can they be improved simply by psychology and sociology. In matters great and small people are confronted with the same situation: knowing about things is not the same as knowing about meanings; regulations are not in themselves orientations, nor are laws morals. Even the law needs a moral foundation! The ethical acceptance of the laws (which the state provides with sanctions and can impose by force) is the presupposition of any political culture. What is the use of more and more laws to individual states or organizations, whether these are the European Community, the United States of America or the United Nations, if a majority of people has no intention of keeping them and constantly finds enough ways and means of irresponsibly imposing their own or collective interests? In the early 1990s, for example, because of the new drug wave, the US National Council on Crime and Delinquency estimates that new cells must be built for 460,000 new prisoners and in all 35 billion dollars must be spent. On economic grounds alone, therefore, the demand for more supervision, police, prisons and stronger laws cannot be the only solution for coping with such difficult problems of our time. In addition to the question of the financing of a replacement for the cocaine plantations in South America there is obviously also a basic educational problem (in the family, in schools, in groups and in the public) in North America and in Europe. *Quid leges sine moribus* runs a Roman saying: What is the use of laws without morals?

Certainly all the states of the world have an economic and legal order, but this will not function in any state in the world without an ethical consensus, an ethic of its citizens on the basis of which democratic constitutions can function. Certainly the international community of states has also created trans-national, trans-cultural and trans-religious legal structures (without which international treaties would be sheer self-deception); but what is a world order without a binding and obligatory ethic for the whole of humankind—for all its time-conditioned nature—i.e. without a world ethic? Not least, the world market calls for a world ethic. The world economy can less than ever tolerate areas with utterly different ethics or even ethics which are contradictory on central points. What is the use of prohibitions with an ethical foundation in one country (one thinks of particular manipulations of finances or the stock market, or of aggressive research into gene technology) if they can be got round by going to other countries? If ethics is to function for the well-being of all, it must be indivisible. The undivided world increasingly needs an undivided ethic.

Chapter 2

Is There a Lack of Professional Ethics in America?

Chapter Preface

Polls in recent years show that Americans have less trust in government officials, doctors, journalists, and the clergy than ever before. But the professionals least trusted by many Americans are lawyers. In a poll by the *National Law Journal*, 60 percent of respondents said they had a "fair" or "poor" impression of lawyers. In an American Bar Association poll of the general public, only 22 percent described lawyers as "honest and ethical."

Attorney and former Maryland assemblyman Luiz R.S. Simmons believes many of the public's criticisms of lawyers are accurate. He argues that lawyers themselves are often unethical, and that "the modern lawyer refuses to accept professional responsibility for the unethical or immoral conduct of clients." Simmons maintains that the lawyers' code of professional responsibility is partly to blame. This code requires lawyers to work for the client's cause if that cause is not criminal. Unfortunately, not everything that is "not criminal" is ethical. Lawyers, adhering to the code, may focus only on winning a case, not on whether the client's cause is ethical.

Defenders of the law profession point out that lawyers exist only because Americans seek out their services. As Wes Hanson, editor of the quarterly *Ethics: Easier Said Than Done*, states, "There is hypocrisy from some of us who are keen to exercise our rights (and then some) but quick to criticize the 'litigiousness' of society and the tactics it takes an advocate or defender to win in our adversarial system." Some defenders believe that much of the public's criticism is simply "sour grapes"—that is, envy of professionals who are well paid and high in status. Finally, defenders maintain that unethical lawyers are a small minority of the profession, and that the actions of this minority should not be used to label the entire profession untrustworthy.

The trustworthiness of lawyers and other professionals is the subject of the following chapter. The contributors discuss why Americans are distrustful of professionals and to what extent this distrust is based on fact.

Lawyers Are Unethical

by **Warren E. Burger**

About the author: *Warren E. Burger was chief justice of the U.S. Supreme Court from 1969 to 1986.*

The reputation of the legal profession is at its lowest ebb since I first started practicing law more than 60 years ago. With ever increasing frequency, the public is questioning the competence, integrity and honesty of lawyers. Indeed, over just the past few years, a number of judges and all too many lawyers have been guilty of self-dealing and other forms of professional misconduct in and out of the courtroom. These transgressions not only diminish the public's confidence in the profession, but they also subtly undermine the public's respect for the rule of law.

Many are concerned by the bar's seeming indifference toward the preservation of a fair and well-functioning legal system. With damaging results for the impartiality of juries and the judicial process, too many lawyers are "trying their cases" on the courthouse steps to newspaper and television reporters. The proliferation of huckster advertising also exploits our legal system by generating counterproductive or frivolous litigation. And all too often, lawyers fail to recognize how ridiculous litigation threatens access to our courts for those with legitimate claims. As officers of the court, lawyers should seek to eliminate, not exacerbate, those trends.

A Lawyer's "Calling"

The law historically has been viewed as a learned profession rather than a trade. As such, a lawyer's "calling" goes beyond his or her immediate financial interest. Lawyers have viewed themselves as statesmen and have served as problem-solvers, harmonizers, and peacemakers—the healers of conflict, not its promoters or "gunslingers." The legal profession, in short, abided by standards that were above the minimum commands of the law. All of the profession's current problems—the eroding public respect for lawyers, the lack of professional dignity and civility on the part of many lawyers, and lawyers' insensitivity to the litigation explosion—are clear indications that the professionalism of the bar has been in sharp decline.

What is the antidote for this decline? I believe it lies in a recommitment of lawyers, and particularly the organized bar, to the higher meaning of professionalism. The annual meeting of the American Bar Association . . . is a good occasion to restate these timeless principles.

With 400,000 or so members, the ABA is one of the world's most powerful professional associations. As such, the association has heavy public responsibilities. Its obligations include maintaining standards for education and admission to the bar, ensuring professional competence, prescribing and enforcing ethical standards, preserving the quality, integrity and independence of judges, and promoting improvement in the functioning of courts.

> *"The public is questioning the competence, integrity and honesty of lawyers."*

Harvard Law School Dean Roscoe Pound, one of history's most distinguished commentators on the role of the legal profession, summed up this mission when he observed: "By a bar association, then, we mean an organization of lawyers to promote and maintain the practice of law as a profession, that is, as a learned art pursued in the spirit of a public service—in the spirit of a service of furthering the administration of justice through and according to law." Dean Pound firmly believed that bar associations were the first line of defense in upholding the honor of the legal profession.

Has the ABA satisfied these public responsibilities? A book from the Federalist Society—"The ABA in Law and Social Policy: What Role?"—reveals that too much of the ABA's power and resources are directed at controversial political issues rather than at matters relating principally to the practice of law and the functioning of the legal system.

In recent years, the ABA has adopted formal policy positions on abortion, affirmative action, AIDS, funding for the arts, gun control, homelessness, nuclear proliferation, parental leave, sexual orientation, health care and a wide variety of other social issues. At the same time, the ABA has done little or nothing to attack the root causes of the public's loss of confidence in the legal profession and the judicial system.

What, for example, has the ABA done about the problem of lawyer advertising? It has compromised professional integrity by drafting the Model Rules of Professional Conduct so as to prohibit only advertising that makes "false or misleading" statements. Because making such statements could also subject a lawyer to civil or criminal liability, this alleged "standard" makes no distinction between what is legal and what is professional.

Advertising Gimmicks

At no time has the ABA made the obvious point that just because the First Amendment permits certain conduct, that conduct is not necessarily ethically appropriate. Moreover, the ABA has done little to address advertising gimmicks—such as "first consultation free" and the like—that are frequently employed to entice law-abiding citizens to exploit the legal system for personal profit.

Nor has the ABA done much to address the fact that our society is drowning in litigation. One has only to look at the overworked system of justice, the delays in trials, the clogs businessmen face in commerce, and a medical profession rendered overcautious for fear of malpractice suits to realize that civil justice reform should be a high priority. Yet the ABA prefers to resist or ignore proposals such as contingency fee caps, widespread adoption of no-fault automobile insurance, and aspects of product liability or tort reform.

Instead of confronting such problems, the ABA has become involved in contentious and partisan battles regarding public policy and political issues. Passage of resolutions regarding divisive social questions naturally involves much lobbying and debate, which leave delegates much less time to address subjects related to the practice of law.

The issue of abortion, for example, dominated at least three recent ABA annual meetings. . . . In addition to wasting time, staking out positions on hotly contested social and political issues can have serious long-term costs. As my colleague Justice Lewis Powell noted while serving as president of the ABA: "The association's responsibilities relate primarily to the legal profession, and these could not be discharged if our membership were lost, fractionated or embittered by involvement in political controversy."

> *"Just because the First Amendment permits certain conduct, that conduct is not necessarily ethically appropriate."*

The ABA was formed during the Jacksonian era to counter the deterioration of the bar's reputation for competence and integrity. It is imperative for it to embrace this noble and important mission once again. The ABA must devote more of its influence to a serious examination of the profession of lawyering and less to special interest politics and social engineering.

The Media Are Unethical

by Stephen Hess

About the author: Stephen Hess is a senior fellow at the Brookings Institution in Washington, D.C. He has been an advisor to four presidents and has taught courses about the relationship between government and the press at Harvard University in Cambridge, Massachusetts, and Johns Hopkins University in Baltimore, Maryland.

Betwen 1992 and 1994, NBC settled out of court with General Motors over the network's faking of two GM truck crashes, and psychoanalyst Jeffrey Masson won a libel suit against freelance writer Janet Malcolm for her *New Yorker* story profiling him. These two events have focused public attention on where journalism ends and fiction begins.

Dateline Dishonesty

On 17 November 1992 *Dateline NBC* aired a 15-minute segment about the safety of GM pickup trucks manufactured between 1973 and 1987 with the gasoline tanks mounted outside the trucks' underframe. Critics contend that this model explodes in side-impact accidents. The NBC program staged two crashes, which culminated in a 56-second scene, a driver's view of the last moments before impact, and a fire that an on-camera safety consultant described as a "holocaust." The segment's reporter said that the crash had punctured a hole in the gas tank.

A subsequent investigation by GM proved that the story was fraudulent on five counts. First, NBC had attached remote-controlled model rocket igniters to the trucks. Second, while one truck failed to catch fire, the fire on the other truck lasted for only 15 seconds, and the filming of the fire had been enhanced by multiple camera angles. Third, there was no puncture in the gas tank. Fourth, a previous owner of the truck had lost the gas cap and the gas leakage resulted from an ill-fitting replacement. Fifth, the truck was being driven at faster speeds than were reported on the program.

In an on-air apology on 9 February 1993, Jane Pauley told viewers that the incendiary devices were "a bad idea from start to finish." And co-host Stone

Stephen Hess, "Where Journalism Ends and Fiction Begins," *The Responsive Community*, Spring 1994. Reprinted by permission of *The Responsive Community*, 2020 Pennsylvania Ave. NW, Suite 282, Washington, DC 20006.

Phillips added, "We have also concluded that unscientific demonstrations should have no place in hard news stories at NBC." GM then dropped its lawsuit and NBC agreed to pay the expenses of GM's investigation, estimated at $2 million. Media reporter Howard Kurtz called it "one of the most embarrassing episodes in modern television history."

NBC later hired outside lawyers to conduct an investigation of what had gone wrong. The report concluded, "Taping a crash fire was at least as important a goal as proving that the GM trucks were defective." The president of NBC, Robert C. Wright, issued his statement: "These journalistic and administrative failures are indefensible."

New York, New York

A more complicated but equally embarrassing incident was the conclusion of a lawsuit by Jeffrey Masson against Janet Malcolm. Malcolm's two-part profile of Masson in the *New Yorker* had appeared in 1983 after Masson had been dismissed from his curatorial position at the Freud Archives in London. Masson contended that five quotations had been fabricated. In the profile, for instance, he was supposed to have said that he would have turned the Freud Archives into "a place of sex, women, fun."

After a monthlong trial (May–June 1993), a San Francisco jury found that all the quotations were fabrications and that two of them (including "sex, women, fun") met the three criteria for libel as defined by the Supreme Court: that the quotations were made up or substantially altered, that the plaintiff suffered damages, and that the writer acted deliberately and with "reckless disregard." The jury could not agree on a monetary award.

The trial also delved into Malcolm's writing techniques, notably what she called "compression," or combining quotations from conversations held at different times. A 1986 deposition from William Shawn, then the editor of the *New Yorker*, said, "This is done frequently for literary reasons. It must never be done to distort anything or deceive anybody or done to the disadvantage of anybody." But more journalists would agree with *New York Times* columnist Anna Quindlen: "Grinding up a number of encounters and molding them into one entity, a kind of journalistic paté, is beyond the pale."

> *"These journalistic and administrative failures are indefensible."*

Much of the contested material in the Masson profile appeared in a very long monologue placed at the restaurant Chez Panisse in Berkeley. Malcolm testified that many of these words had been spoken over the telephone or in her New York kitchen. In her first draft the scene of the monologue was the Berkeley Pier and it was shifted indoors by her editor (and husband), Gardner Botsford, to simplify the story's narrative.

Malcolm's work is part of a continuum of controversial compositions that goes back to the publication in the *New Yorker* of Truman Capote's "In Cold Blood." That mid-1960s real-life story of the murder of a Kansas family employed all the techniques of fiction while claiming to be "immaculately factual." But how factual can quotations be when the reporter did not hear them? The same question was raised about *The Final Days*, a 1976 book about President Nixon by Bob Woodward and Carl Bernstein, and in 1984, *New Yorker* writer Alastair Reid, obviating such a question, admitted that his reporting was a distilled melange of things he had seen and heard in different places. Reid, and perhaps the others, were imposing their wills on events and other people's words in order "to make [in Reid's judgment] the larger truth."

Facts Kneaded and Rolled

Which brings us back to NBC's setting fire to a GM truck. Is this incident merely an aberration, a dishonest moment on a news medium that otherwise conforms to the standards of mainstream print journalism? Is it proof that TV news is intellectually dishonest, a massing of sound bites and pictures in support of predetermined conclusions? Is it proof that the image-based journalism of television is in the process of creating a different standard of truth? It is all three.

> *"Surreptitious eavesdropping [and] assuming a false identity . . . are standard techniques on the CBS program* **60 Minutes** *and similar shows."*

The TV newsmagazine format is now so popular and so profitable that it is even beginning to dominate prime-time programming. At the same time, the newsmags have become the motor force of the networks' news divisions, affecting personnel and resources decisions. Their influence on dinnertime news programs—still watched nightly by 30 million people in the U.S.—is also evident from the increased use of features with names like *American Agenda* and *Eye on America*, which borrow newsmag techniques.

The TV newsmag was born on 24 September 1968 when the news division of CBS first aired a topical prime-time variety show called *60 Minutes*. By 1979 *60 Minutes* was the most widely viewed program in the nation. According to its executive producer, Don Hewitt, it is "the biggest moneymaker in the history of broadcasting," having earned $1 billion for CBS—clearly worth imitating. In 1993 the networks (ABC, CBS, NBC) were producing seven newsmags and had at least three more in the pipeline. In 1987 Rupert Murdoch's Fox stations introduced *A Current Affair*, a highly sensationalist newsmag that was also imitated by other syndicated programs.

The mid-1980s was a period of flux in the television industry. Murdoch was laying plans to create a fourth network, and the three major networks were changing hands: ABC was acquired by Capitol Cities; Loews bought 25 percent of CBS and made investor Lawrence Tisch its president; General Electric replaced RCA as the parent company of NBC. The networks had always viewed their news operations as loss leaders, good public relations for a government-regulated industry. But times were tough in the news business, and the new corporate owners were offended by waste and redundancy. Soon, Dan Rather was publicly scolding his new bosses on the op-ed page of the *New York Times:* "Do the owners and officers of the new CBS see news as a trust . . . or only as a business venture?" As anchor, however, he was only entitled to the next-to-last word. The new owners wanted—and got—scaled-down news operations, and they substituted newsmags, which were cheap and network owned, for dramas and sitcoms, which were expensive and owned by others.

> *"Balance is clearly not the objective."*

Don Hewitt's newsmag formulation moved the journalist to stage center, transforming the reporter from an objective observer into a Dick Tracy–like protagonist. Reporter-detective outlines the case, searches for clues, stalks the transgressor (often a corporation or a government agency), and, if possible, brings the perpetrator to justice. Reporter-detective, especially if played by Mike Wallace, even wears a trench coat, and, according to media scholar Richard Campbell, "may appear in as many as 40 or 50 shots in a 120-shot, 14-minute segment."

Questionable Techniques

Just as Capote drew on the conventions of fiction in his "nonfiction novel," Hewitt and his disciples adopted the techniques of Hollywood screen imaging. Villains are always shown in extreme close-up (extreme villains, such as the Shah of Iran, have both forehead and chin cut from the frame, while middling villains usually just lose the tops of their heads). The reporter-detective, on the other hand, is seen from a distance.

Hidden camera investigations, often with reporters operating in disguise, have become another staple, especially on ABC's *PrimeTime Live*, whose executive producer has said he would like to do a hidden-camera story every week. "Journalistic practices that would get you fired from the *Chicago Tribune* or the *New York Times*—surreptitious eavesdropping or assuming a false identity—are standard techniques on the CBS program *60 Minutes* and similar shows," lamented Richard Harwood, a former ombudsman of the *Washington Post*.

Other techniques that are used at various times, in hard news shows as well as newsmags, include simulation of events by actors, music to heighten mood, changes in sequencing, fast-cutting that reduces sound bites to a sentence, "generic images" for illustrative purposes, weighted expert opinions, and ambush interviews. There are countless examples:

- ABC's *World News Tonight* used an employee to play an American diplomat handing a briefcase to a Soviet agent.

- The *CBS Evening News* used a rap-music video of President Bush repeating "read my lips" to synthesizer accompaniment.
- Ted Koppel's *Nightline*, during an interview with a Rodney King trial juror, used music that TV critic John Carmody described as an "almost ominous chord—faintly reminiscent of the note sounded when Rick sees Ilsa for the first time since Paris."
- The *NBC Nightly News* used images of dead fish to illustrate a 1993 story about alleged overcutting in Idaho's Clearwater National Forest. The fish turned out to be neither dead nor from Clearwater, and Tom Brokaw apologized on a later broadcast.
- An animal rights segment on *60 Minutes* had a 5:1 ratio of expert opinion in favor of one side, according to the count of one media critic.

Balance is clearly not the objective. The producer of CNN's *Network Earth* series said, "Indeed, [balance] can be debilitating. Can we really afford to wait for our audiences to come to its [*sic*] own conclusions? I think not." The objective is usually sting—which is why ambush interviews are so effective for newsmags. Interviews in which a trapped suspect refuses to answer the reporter-detective's questions serve simultaneously to underline the target's guilt (Why else wouldn't he talk?) and create an illusion of fairness and balance (He was given the chance, after all).

Television Is Different

Is the fire on *Dateline NBC* an indicator of dishonesty in TV news? Clearly, when that program's producers arranged to insure that a GM truck would explode, they violated the network's written policy: "If it isn't happening, you cannot make it happen. Make no effort to change or dramatize what is happening." Still, when the *New York Times*, *New York Daily News*, *Washington Post*, *USA Today*, and *New Yorker* had similar problems with fabrications, the journalism community regarded them as having harbored a sloppy editor or a bent reporter, not of being innately dishonest. The NBC incident, at one level, should be viewed as a similar aberration.

On another level the breach of standards at NBC is more than a blip on journalism's ethical echocardiogram. Increasing institutional pressures in the news business—particularly in television—to cut ethical corners make hoaxes like NBC's much more likely. TV pictures are increasingly coming from freelancers, syndicates, ama-

> *"Increasing institutional pressures in the news business . . . to cut ethical corners make hoaxes . . . much more likely."*

teurs who happen upon a scene, and groups trying to interest TV programs in their points of view—in short, from people whose credibility and news judgments are questionable. In 1986 ABC's *World News Tonight* purchased and aired a videotape that purported to show the nuclear meltdown at Chernobyl but turned out to be of a cement factory in Trieste, Italy.

Even if NBC's GM truck segment was an aberration, it still illustrates that TV news is intellectually dishonest. The newsmag report was designed to *show* that the trucks were defective, not to *test* whether the trucks were defective. All journalists start with a hunch. The purpose of reporting should be to test these hunches. When reporters simply marshal facts, quotations, or pictures to support their hypotheses, they sell out their mission.

As the TV news industry has trimmed operations, smaller staffs increasingly need each assigned story to be usable. Moreover, fewer interviews and less time per story both limit the testing of a hypothesis. Redundancy is now viewed as a problem rather than as rigor; reporters seek to gather no more information than a story can use. TV news now has no interest in the complexities of a story if it doesn't mesh with the producers' preconceived notion of what that story will be. Inevitably then, the story's hypotheses are self-fulfilling.

TV news began as an illustration of events, not unlike a courtroom sketch. The fictions of presentation were modest—such as the reverse-question technique, where interview questions and answers are filmed separately. TV journalists generally stuck to the standards of print reporting.

Times have changed. Indeed, as the newsmags increasingly place journalists in prime time, their success will be measured by showbiz standards. An irate professor at the Columbia School of Journalism wrote in the *Wall Street Journal* after the NBC-GM controversy that "TV 'news' is today increasingly peopled with 'journalists' who are often little more than actors playing the role of journalist." While the comment slights some very competent people, it is likely that their most valuable on-camera skills have nothing to do with news gathering. As Everette Dennis points out, poll data show that "many respondents could not tell the difference between serious evening news programs, talk shows, and programs that use a news format but which are designed to titillate and entertain."

TV's image-based journalism is a conveyor of information through moving pictures, and as such, its truth must be filmed. That is why it was so important to the *Dateline NBC* producers to set the truck on fire. This different standard will become more pronounced as the older generation of TV journalists (who learned their craft on newspapers or wire services) leaves the scene. TV's "New News," as it is already called by advocates, suggests a brave new future for the world of television reporting. Stretched by the potential of filmmaking, it seeks to adjust truth to incorporate and accept changing frame space, rearranging sequences, fast-cutting, adding music, even reenacting events: the larger truth, it will be claimed, truth in spirit if not in detail. And perhaps then, as Richard Reeves writes, "Situations such as the pickup truck scandal are going to happen again and again, and each time it will seem less important, as fact and filmmaking merge into a new, nonlinear information form." Is it too late to relearn a lesson from novelist and journalist John Hersey? In the autumn of 1980 he bluntly stated the case: "The writer of fiction must invent. The journalist must not invent."

A Lack of Ethics in Science Threatens Society

by Michael Crichton

About the author: *Michael Crichton is the author of numerous books, including the best-sellers* The Andromeda Strain, Rising Sun, The Terminal Man, The Great Train Robbery, *and* Jurassic Park, *from which the following viewpoint is excerpted.*

The late twentieth century has witnessed a scientific gold rush of astonishing proportions: the headlong and furious haste to commercialize genetic engineering. This enterprise has proceeded so rapidly—with so little outside commentary—that its dimensions and implications are hardly understood at all.

The Greatest Revolution

Biotechnology promises the greatest revolution in human history. By the end of this decade, it will have outdistanced atomic power and computers in its effect on our everyday lives. In the words of one observer, "Biotechnology is going to transform every aspect of human life: our medical care, our food, our health, our entertainment, our very bodies. Nothing will ever be the same again. It's literally going to change the face of the planet."

But the biotechnology revolution differs in three important respects from past scientific transformations. First, it is broad-based. America entered the atomic age through the work of a single research institution, at Los Alamos. It entered the computer age through the efforts of about a dozen companies. But biotechnology research is now carried out in more than 2,000 laboratories in America alone. Five hundred corporations spend five billion dollars a year on this technology.

Second, much of the research is thoughtless or frivolous. Efforts to engineer paler trout for better visibility in the stream, square trees for easier lumbering, and injectable scent cells so you will always smell of your favorite perfume may seem like a joke, but they are not. Indeed, the fact that biotechnology can be applied to the industries traditionally subject to the vagaries of fashion, such as cosmetics and leisure activities, heightens concern about the whimsical use of this powerful new technology.

Third, the work is uncontrolled. No one supervises it. No federal laws regulate it. There is no coherent government policy, in America or anywhere else in the world. And because the products of biotechnology range from drugs to farm crops to artificial snow, an intelligent policy is difficult.

But most disturbing is the fact that no watchdogs are found among scientists themselves. It is remarkable that nearly every scientist in genetics research is also engaged in the commerce of biotechnology. There are no detached observers. Everybody has a stake.

From Good Principles to Profits

The commercialization of molecular biology is the most stunning ethical event in the history of science, and it has happened with astonishing speed. For four hundred years since Galileo, science has always proceeded as a free and open inquiry into the workings of nature. Scientists have always ignored national boundaries, holding themselves above the transitory concerns of politics and even wars. Scientists have always rebelled against secrecy in research, and have even frowned on the idea of patenting their discoveries, seeing themselves as working to the benefit of all mankind. And for many generations, the discoveries of scientists did indeed have a peculiarly selfless quality.

When, in 1953, two young researchers in England, James Watson and Francis Crick, deciphered the structure of DNA, their work was hailed as a triumph of the human spirit, of the centuries-old quest to understand the universe in a scientific way. It was confidently expected that their discovery would be selflessly extended to the greater benefit of mankind.

> *"The commercialization of molecular biology is the most stunning ethical event in the history of science."*

Yet that did not happen. Thirty years later, nearly all of Watson and Crick's scientific colleagues were engaged in another sort of enterprise entirely. Research in molecular genetics had become a vast, multibillion-dollar commercial undertaking, and its origins can be traced not to 1953 but to April 1976.

That was the date of a now famous meeting, in which Robert Swanson, a venture capitalist, approached Herbert Boyer, a biochemist at the University of California. The two men agreed to found a commercial company to exploit Boyer's gene-splicing techniques. Their new company, Genentech, quickly became the largest and most successful of the genetic engineering start-ups.

Designer Genes

Suddenly it seemed as if everyone wanted to become rich. New companies were announced almost weekly, and scientists flocked to exploit genetic research. By 1986, at least 362 scientists, including 64 in the National Academy, sat on the advisory boards of biotech firms. The number of those who held equity positions or consultancies was several times greater.

It is necessary to emphasize how significant this shift in attitude actually was. In the past, pure scientists took a snobbish view of business. They saw the pursuit of money as intellectually uninteresting, suited only to shopkeepers. And to do research for industry, even at the prestigious Bell or IBM labs was only for those who couldn't get a university appointment. Thus the attitude of pure scientists was fundamentally critical toward the work of applied scientists, and to industry in general. Their long-standing antagonism kept university scientists free of contaminating industry ties, and whenever debate arose about technological matters, disinterested scientists were available to discuss the issues at the highest levels.

But that is no longer true. There are very few molecular biologists and very few research institutions without commercial affiliations. The old days are gone. Genetic research continues, at a more furious pace than ever. But it is done in secret, and in haste, and for profit.

Lawyers Are Becoming More Ethical

by Nancy Wride

About the author: *Nancy Wride is a staff writer for the* Los Angeles Times *newspaper.*

Let's say you're in law school. The first reaction you get is a slow, sly nod. Ahhhhh, gonna make the big bucks. Drive a nice car. Wear expensive suits with tasseled loafers. Overcharge people for coffee breaks with other lawyers. Say, nudge, nudge, what do you call 500 lawyers at the bottom of the ocean? An excellent start. Heh, heh.

Not exactly a profession with a noble reputation these days.

But that may be changing slowly with new programs such as the one in California at Orange County's only accredited law school, where new students will be required to do free legal work for the poor and needy in order to graduate.

Western State University College of Law in Fullerton is only the second California law school, and the largest in the country, to insist that aspiring barristers perform at least 20 hours of pro bono work. Already, about 200 students have volunteered.

It is an effort that appears to be growing nationally to instill a sense of ethics and social responsibility in budding lawyers, say program directors.

A Trend

"Two years ago [1991], there were only four law schools in the country that had pro bono requirements, and now there are 12 [including Loyola Law School in Los Angeles], so definitely there's a trend," says Paul Belden, spokesman for the National Association for Public Interest Law, a Washington, D.C.–based coalition of student groups aimed at getting more lawyers into pro bono work.

"These requirements are one way to get there if you want a whole generation of people committed to pro bono work. This is a crucial part of being a lawyer."

"The thing when you're a lawyer is, you have a lot of power and authority, and if you don't have a conscience you're in a position to do a lot of harm," says John C. Monks, president of the 2,500-student Western State University. "But relating it to the pro bono program, I think there is some clear benefit to making students aware of poor people's needs, the needs of the homeless, the abused.

"My main hope," he adds, "is that not only would they become sensitive to that, but they would continue to give their time to people who can't afford it."

The term *pro bono* is a shortened version of the Latin *pro bono publico*, which means, "for the public good." Tulane University in Louisiana was the country's first law school to require it. When the first class required to do pro bono work graduated in 1990, members were surveyed about the new program.

Of 253 students, 65% said their work with the needy had increased their willingness to do pro bono work, and 72% said their hands-on experience had increased their confidence in their own ability to handle cases for indigent clients. The class provided 6,500 hours of free legal work to the community.

The impact on students, and those results, were part of what clicked through Jeremy Miller's head when the Western State ethics professor first started considering requiring law students to do free legal work. "As an ethics professor, this is much easier and better than just telling your students, 'Help the poor.' They actually do it," Miller says.

"We wanted . . . to play down the stereotype that lawyers just want to make money."

He had attended Tulane and followed the progress of its pro bono program, and he polled a class about it. It was decidedly enthusiastic.

At the same time, the leadership of Delta Theta Phi, Western State's largest student organization on campus, had been stewing over the same idea.

"We were going to do it anyway, on a smaller and voluntary basis," says Judi Copenbarger, 29, of Anaheim Hills, vice dean of the organization. She hopes to go into estate planning law until her student loans are paid off, then pursue pediatrics.

Students and Pro Bono Work

Other campus organizations like the student bar association were polled for a reaction to the pro bono requirement.

Faculty and students on a committee studying pro bono initially anticipated some resistance to the added time burden. About 60% of Western State's students are part-timers who take four years to get through law school.

"The only concern was from a few students worried about time demands," Miller says. "Even among those who won't be required to do the work to graduate, there are 300 interested students willing to do it."

"Our people were very gung-ho," says Keith Youngblood, the 33-year-old vice president of the Black Law Student Association. He hopes to specialize in international law, particularly representing minority businesses. "We wanted exposure in L.A., not just Orange County, and to play down the stereotype that lawyers just want to make money."

The requirement started as a pilot program at the Fullerton campus (the others are in Irvine and San Diego). But officials are encouraging students at the other branches to voluntarily participate.

Students entering the university in the fall of 1993 were the first affected. Once they complete enough course work to become upper-class students, they will be required to perform 20 hours of pro bono work, and can choose from a list of law firms, community groups and public interest organizations. Or they can work with clients of Western State's legal clinic. The Orange County public defender's office has already asked for help, Miller said.

Because the students will not yet be licensed, their work must be closely monitored by practicing lawyers. The university is hoping that the pro bono program will provide an opportunity for lawyers not presently doing free legal work to start contributing through the students they oversee.

"I think it's wonderful," says Susan Allen-Perry, 37, of Lynwood, who was a major force in convincing the faculty that students would not resist the pro bono work requirement.

"As students we have to give back . . . and to realize there will always be people in need."

A second-year student, Allen-Perry and the others involved with getting the pro bono program launched are fairly typical at Western State. Judi Copenbarger and her husband, Larry, 28, the parents of a 3- and a 4-year-old, come from a family of lawyers but worked in another family business until switching to law. Youngblood had been an industrial engineer for McDonnell Douglas.

Allen-Perry has a 5-year-old daughter and works part time at Bullock's. She has a brother who is a sports agent and a husband who is an actor, so she hopes to practice entertainment and sports law, maybe representing theatrical performers.

"But a small aspect of what I want to do is work with men's rights in family law," she says. "I'm concerned in a small percentage of cases when men should get custody of their kids and don't. . . . You do one kind of work and get paid so that you can do good things [for free]. . . ."

> *"We have to give back . . . and to realize there will always be people in need."*

Youngblood, the father of a 3-week-old, works now for a Tustin lawyer but hopes to do pro bono work for his wife's Los Angeles church, where he sees a demand for free legal help, especially among older people.

"I'm hoping," Miller added, "that students will learn that law can be a very honorable profession."

Most Journalists Are Ethical

by Lou Prato

About the author: *Lou Prato is director of broadcasting of the Medill News Service in Washington, D.C., and associate professor of journalism at Northwestern University in Evanston, Illinois. He is also treasurer of the Washington-based Radio and Television News Directors Association.*

Whenever one criticizes the media on grounds of bias, misrepresentation, or any other ethical or journalistic lapse, care should be taken not to be too sweeping in scope. Blaming the generic "media" for the sins of a few is often more egregious than the specific transgression itself. . . .

The journalistic perversions at *Dateline NBC* and *60 Minutes* certainly tarnish all newspeople, even those anonymous hard-working folk far from the New York network headquarters in the cornfields of Iowa or the snowy vistas of Alaska.

But there are thousands of responsible, principled, and trustworthy journalists working in television, radio, newspapers, and magazines. They should be respected and appreciated for the traditional and objective journalism they practice every day as a matter of routine, and they should be acclaimed whenever their work is exemplary. The performance by the local broadcasting and print media during the 1992 Florida hurricane and the 1993 Midwest flooding is proof that responsible, honorable journalism still exists.

"Us-versus-Them" Atmosphere

It is counterproductive for anyone attempting to make journalists more accountable and more virtuous to tar the work of the entire profession. That can only intensify the "us-versus-them" atmosphere that pervades the media and deters many journalists from conceding their mistakes or indiscretions.

Similarly, one also must be judicious when continually complaining about the media's liberal bias. "The media" is not monolithic. Despite what some conservative critics may believe, there are plenty of journalists who do not subscribe

From Lou Prato, "The Sterility of Stereotyping the Media." This article appeared in the December 1993 issue and is reprinted with permission from *The World & I*, a publication of The Washington Times Corporation, copyright ©1993.

to a particular political doctrine, and there are many others with the integrity to subordinate their personal beliefs to their professional responsibilities. CNN's Reid Collins, ABC's Brit Hume, and NBC's Tim Russert are TV network types that come quickly to mind. There are thousands of others much less known.

Yes, a liberal bias exists throughout the media. . . . There is more widespread acceptance of that premise today among the media themselves than there was in 1964, when Goldwater Republicans made it a cause célèbre at the GOP convention in San Francisco, or than there was in 1969,

> *"There are thousands of responsible, principled, and trustworthy journalists."*

when Vice President Spiro Agnew created a nationwide uproar with his castigation of the "Eastern liberal media establishment."

Nowadays, the conservative viewpoint is heard and seen more often, too. William F. Buckley and the *Wall Street Journal* have been joined by such contemporary watchdogs as Rush Limbaugh and L. Brent Bozell's Media Research Center.

But in their zeal to expose the media's liberal bias, some conservative operatives have acted in as irresponsible a manner as their opponents. They utilize fallacious statistics or make ludicrous, deceptive claims to support their often narrow perspective.

Frequently, it is simply a matter of exaggeration. Reed Irvine's motives may be genuine, but at times what he and his Accuracy in Media organization say about allegedly biased news coverage is more hyperbole than fact.

Criticism Must Be Fair

Sometimes, the claim of liberal bias is specious. Statistics are often manipulated intentionally in an attempt to make a salient point. Many conservatives gloated when the ultraliberal Fairness and Accuracy in Reporting (FAIR) was exposed for misusing statistics about the abuse of women during the Super Bowl. But one must be constantly reminded that credibility works both ways. If the ultimate goals are to achieve fairness in reporting and the lessening of the liberal bias, then it is imperative that the criticism itself be fair, honest, and equitable.

Stereotyping is wrong and often odious, whether it involves a class of people or a profession. The "media" is not unscrupulous or biased, but individuals working in it are. Those are the ones who need to be exposed and chastised.

There also is a theme that runs through much of the criticism of deception and bias that tabs television news as the main culprit. Newspapers and magazines are often elevated to a more puritanical level. . . .

Within the entire journalistic profession, there is an inherent bias in favor of print. Most print journalists denigrate TV news as inadequate, inept, and worse. This is not the forum to debate the issue. But print bias is mentioned here because this writer believes it distorts the validity of criticism. Faulting TV news for most of journalism's serious ills ignores the all too frequent abuses in newspapers and magazines. It also is hypocritical. What better way to distract the public from one's own shortcomings than by focusing attention on those of a competitor?

Eliminating this print bias may be impossible, but to alleviate it one must start in the journalism and communications schools, because that's where it originates. It's also where much of the liberalism propagates.

A Lack of Introspection

Reform of journalism education may be critical for the "media" to overcome its blunders and its biases. But it is highly unlikely that the entrenched power structure of academia will ever allow the reform to happen.

No, it will be up to individual professors, many fighting the systematic biases of their colleagues, to continue stressing to their students the precepts and principles of traditional journalism. They must show how the distortions and deceptions by some professionals hurt the credibility of all. They must emphasize fairness and focus on ethics.

"Responsible, honorable journalism still exists."

But dedicated professors and responsive students are not enough. Professional journalists need to look inside themselves, too. Perhaps the poorest reaction to the accusations of misrepresentation and liberal bias is that many self-righteous journalists refuse to admit that they have a problem.

That, fundamentally, is what is really wrong with the "media."

The Threat Posed by Unethical Scientists Has Been Exaggerated

by Paul Kurtz

About the author: *Paul Kurtz is professor emeritus of philosophy at the State University of New York in Buffalo. He is also the founding chairman of the Committee for the Scientific Investigation of Claims of the Paranormal (CSICOP), which publishes the quarterly* Skeptical Inquirer.

It is paradoxical that today, when the sciences are advancing by leaps and bounds and when the earth is being transformed by scientific discoveries and technological applications, a strong antiscience counterculture has emerged. This contrasts markedly with attitudes toward science that existed in the nineteenth and the first half of the twentieth centuries. Albert Einstein perhaps best typified the high point of the public appreciation of scientists that prevailed at that time. Paul De Kruif (1926), in his book, *The Microbe Hunters*, described the dramatic results that scientists could now achieve in ameliorating pain and suffering and improving the human condition. John Dewey, perhaps the most influential American philosopher in the first half of this century, pointed out the great pragmatic benefits to humankind from the application of scientific methods of thinking to all aspects of human life. But today the mood has radically changed.

A 1993 essay in *Time* magazine by D. Overbye begins with the following ominous note:

> Scientists, it seems, are becoming the new villains of Western society. . . . We read about them in newspapers faking and stealing data, and we see them in front of congressional committees defending billion-dollar research budgets. We hear them in sound bites trampling our sensibilities by comparing the Big Bang or some subatomic particle to God.

An editorial in *Science* magazine, referring to the *Time* essay, comments:

> Does this reflect a growing antiscience attitude? If so, the new movie *Jurassic*

Paul Kurtz, "The Growth of Antiscience," *Skeptical Inquirer*, Spring 1994. Reprinted with permission.

Park is not going to help. According to both the writer and producer, the movie intentionally has antiscience undertones. Press accounts say that producer Steven Spielberg believes science is "intrusive" and "dangerous."

It is not only outsiders who are being critical. In recent speeches and publications, George Brown, chairman of the House Space, Science and Technology Committee, has seemed to question the very value of science. Brown has observed that despite our lead in science and technology, we still have many societal ills such as environmental degradation and unaffordable health care. Science, he says, has "promised more than it can deliver." Freeman Dyson seems to share some of this view. In a recent Princeton speech, he states, "I will not be surprised if attacks against science become more bitter and more widespread in the next few years, so long as the economic inequities in our society remain sharp and science continues to be predominantly engaged in building toys for the rich."

"Are these just isolated events, or is something more going on?" asks Richard S. Nicholson in the editorial quoted above.

A further sign that science has lost considerable prestige is the rejection of the superconducting supercollider project by the U.S. Congress. Although the chief reason given was the need to cut the national deficit, one cannot help but feel that this decision reflects the diminishing level of public confidence in scientific research.

Philosophical Attacks on Science

There have always been two cultures existing side by side, as Lord C. P. Snow has shown. There has been a historic debate between those who wish to advance scientific culture and those who claim that there are "two truths." According to the latter, there exists, along with cognitive scientific knowledge, a mystical and spiritual realm and/or aesthetic and subjective aspects of experience. The two cultures do not live side by side in peaceful coexistence any longer; in recent decades there have been overt radical attacks on science that threaten its position in society.

From within philosophy dissent has come from two influential areas. First, many philosophers of science, from Kuhn to Feyerabend, have argued that there is no such thing as scientific method, that scientific knowledge is relative to sociocultural institutions, that paradigm shifts occur for extra-rational causes, and that therefore the earlier confidence that there are objective methods for testing scientific claims is mistaken.

"Science has lost considerable prestige."

This critique is obviously greatly exaggerated. It is true that science functions in relation to the social and cultural conditions in which it emerges, and it is true that we cannot make absolute statements in science. Nonetheless, there are reliable standards for testing claims and some criteria of objectivity, and these transcend specific social and cultural contexts. How does one explain the vast body of scientific knowledge we possess? A specific claim in science cannot be said to be the same as a poetic metaphor or a religious tenet, for it is tested by its experimental consequences in the real world.

The second philosophical attack comes from the disciples of Heidegger, especially the French postmodernists, such as Derrida, Foucault, Lacan, and Lyotard. They argue that science is only one mythic system or narrative among many others. They maintain that by deconstructing scientific language, we discover that there are no real standards of objectivity. Heidegger complained that science and technology were dehumanizing. Foucault pointed out that science is often dominated by power structures, bureaucracy, and the state, and that the political and economic uses of science have undermined the pretensions of scientific neutrality. Some of these criticisms are no doubt valid, but they are overstated. If the alternative to objectivity is subjectivity, and if there are no warranted claims to truth, then the views of the postmodernists cannot be said to be true either. Surely we can maintain that the principles of mechanics are reliable, that Mars is a planet that orbits the sun, that cardiovascular diseases can be explained causally and preventive measures taken to lower the risk, that the structure of DNA is not simply a social artifact, nor insulin a cultural creation .

> *"In recent decades there have been overt radical attacks on science that threaten its position in society."*

The postmodern critics of "modernity" are objecting to the rationalist or foundationalist interpretations of science that emerged in the sixteenth and seventeenth centuries, and perhaps rightly so. For the continuous growth and revision of scientific theories demonstrates that any "quest for certainty" or "ultimate first principles" within science is mistaken. Nonetheless, they go too far in abandoning the entire modern scientific enterprise. The scientific approach to understanding nature and human life has been vindicated by its success; and its premises, I submit, are still valid. What are some of the characteristics of this modern scientific outlook as it has evolved today?

First, science presupposes that there *are* objective methods by which reliable knowledge can be tested. Second, this means that hypotheses and theories can be formulated and that they can be warranted (*a*) by reference to the evidence, (*b*) by criteria of rational coherence, and (*c*) by their predicted experimental consequences. Third, modern scientists find that mathematical quantification is a powerful tool in establishing theories. Fourth, they hold that there are causal regularities and relationships in our interactions with nature that can be discovered. Fifth, although knowledge may not be universal, it is general in the sense that it goes beyond mere subjective or cultural relativity and is rooted in an intersubjective and intercultural community of inquirers. Sixth, as the progressive and fallible character of science is understood, it is seen that it is difficult to reach absolute or final statements, that science is tentative and probabilistic, and that scientific inquiry needs to be open to alternative explanations. Previous theories are therefore amenable to challenge and revision, and selective and constructive skepticism is an essential element in the scientific outlook. Seventh is the appreciation of the fact that knowledge of the probable causes of phenomena as discovered by scientific research can be applied, that powerful technological inventions can be discovered, and that these can be of enormous benefit to human beings.

> *"The scientific approach to understanding nature and human life has been vindicated by its success."*

Fascination with the Paranormal

Yet the scientific approach, which has had such powerful effectiveness in extending the frontiers of knowledge, is now under heavy attack. Of special concern has been the dramatic growth of the occult, the paranormal, and pseudosciences, and particularly the promotion of the irrational and sensational in these areas by the mass media. We allegedly have been living in the New Age. Side by side with astronomy there has been a return to astrology, and concomitant with psychology there was the growth of psychical research and parapsychology. The paranormal imagination soars; science fiction has no bounds. This is the age of space travel, and it includes abductions by extraterrestrial beings and unidentified flying objects from other worlds. The emergence of a paranormal worldview competes with the scientific worldview. Instead of tested causal explanations, the pseudosciences provide alternative explanations that compete in the public mind with genuine science. The huge increase in paranormal beliefs is symptomatic of a profound antiscience attitude, which has not emerged in isolation but is part of a wider spectrum of attitudes and beliefs.

The readers of the *Skeptical Inquirer* are no doubt familiar with the singular role of CSICOP [Committee for the Scientific Investigation of Claims of the Paranormal] in evaluating claims made about the paranormal and by fringe sciences. Our basic aim is to contribute to the public appreciation for scientific inquiry, critical thinking, and science education. We need to be equally concerned, I submit, about the growth of antiscience in general.

The most vitriolic attacks on science in recent decades have questioned its benefits to society. To a significant extent these criticisms are based on ethical considerations, for they question the value of scientific research and the scientific outlook to humankind. Here are 10 categories of such objections. There are no doubt others.

1. After World War II great anxiety arose about a possible nuclear holocaust. This fear is not without foundation; for there is some danger of fallout from nuclear accidents and testing in the atmosphere, and there is the threat that politi-

cal or military leaders might embark, consciously or accidentally, upon a devastating nuclear war. Fortunately, for the moment the danger of a thermonuclear holocaust has abated, though it surely has not disappeared. However, such critiques generated the fear of scientific research, and even, in some quarters, the view that physicists were diabolical beings who, in tinkering with the secrets of nature, held within their grasp the power to destroy all forms of life on this planet. The fear of nuclear radiation also applies to nuclear power plants. The accident at Chernobyl magnified the apprehension of large sectors of the world's population that nuclear energy is dangerous and that nuclear power plants should be closed down. In countries like the United States, no nuclear power plants are being built, although France and many other countries continue to construct them. The nuclear age has thus provoked an antinuclear reaction, and the beneficent symbol of the scientist of the past, Albert Einstein, has to some been transmogrified into a Dr. Strangelove. Although some of the apprehensions about nuclear radiation are no doubt warranted, to abandon nuclear fuel entirely, while the burning of fossil fuels pollutes the atmosphere, leaves few alternatives for satisfying the energy needs of the world. This does not deny the need to find renewable resources, such as solar and wind power, but will these be sufficient?

Environmental Fears

2. The fear of science can also be traced to some excesses of the environmental movement. Although the environmentalists' emphasis on ecological preservation is a valid concern, it has led at times to the fear that human technology has irreparably destroyed the ozone layer and that the greenhouse effect will lead to the degradation of the entire planet. Such fears often lead to hysteria about all technologies.

3. In large sectors of the population, there is a phobia about any kind of chemical additive. From the 1930s to the 1950s, it was widely held that "better things and better living can be achieved through chemistry" and that chemicals would improve the human condition. Today there is, on the contrary, a widespread toxic terror—of PCBs and DDT, plastics and fertilizers, indeed of *any* kind of additive—and there is a worldwide movement calling for a return to nature, to organic foods and natural methods. No doubt we need to be cautious about untested chemical additives that may poison the ecosystem, but we should not forget that the skilled use of fertilizers led to the green revolution and a dramatic increase in food production that reduced famine and poverty worldwide.

> *"The nuclear age has . . . provoked an antinuclear reaction, and . . . Albert Einstein has to some been transmogrified into a Dr. Strangelove."*

4. Suspicion of biogenetic engineering is another dimension of the growth of

antiscience. From its very inception biogenetic research has met opposition. Many feared that scientists would unleash a new, virulent strain of *E. coli* bacteria into sewer pipes—and then throughout the ecosystem—that would kill large numbers of people. Jeremy Rifkin and others have demanded that all forms of biogenetic engineering research be banned because of its "dehumanizing" effect. A good illustration of this can be seen in the film *Jurassic Park*, produced by Steven Spielberg. Here not only does a Dr. Frankenstein seek to bring back the dead, but we are warned that a new diabolical scientist, in cloning dinosaurs, will unleash ominous forces across the planet. Although there may be some dangers in biogenetic engineering, it offers tremendous potential benefit for humankind—for the cure of genetic diseases as well as the creation of new products. Witness, for example, the production of synthetic insulin.

5. Another illustration of the growth of antiscience is the widespread attack on orthodox medicine. Some of these criticisms have some merit. With the advances of the scientific revolution and the growth of medical technology, we have been able to extend human life, yet many people are kept alive against their will and suffer excruciating pain; and the right to die has emerged as a basic ethical concern. Medical ethicists have correctly pointed out that the rights of patients have often been ignored by the medical and legal professions. In the past physicians were considered authoritarian figures, whose wisdom and skills were unquestioned. But to many vociferous critics today, doctors are demons rather than saviors. The widespread revolt against animal research is symptomatic of the attack on science. Granted that animals should not be abused or made to suffer unnecessary pain, but some animal rights advocates would ban all medical research on animals.

> *"Biogenetic engineering . . . offers tremendous potential benefit for humankind."*

6. Another illustration of antiscience is the growing opposition to psychiatry. Thomas Szasz has no doubt played a key role here. As a result of his works, large numbers of mental patients were deinstitutionalized. *One Flew Over the Cuckoo's Nest*, by Ken Kesey (1962), dramatizes the view that it is often the psychiatrist himself who is disturbed rather than the patient. Many, like Szasz, even deny that there are mental illnesses, though there seems to be considerable evidence that some patients do suffer behavioral disorders and exhibit symptoms that can be alleviated by anti-psychotic drugs.

7. Concomitant with the undermining of public confidence in the practice of medicine and psychiatry has been the phenomenal growth in "alternative health cures," from faith healing and Christian Science to the relaxation response, iridology, homeopathy, and herbal medicines. This is paradoxical, because medical science has made heroic progress in the conquering of disease and the development of antibiotics and the highly successful techniques of surgical inter-

vention. These have all been a boon to human health. But now the very viability of medical science itself has been questioned.

8. Another area of concern is the impact of Asian mysticism, particularly since World War II, whereby Yoga medita-
tion, Chinese Qigong, gurus, and spir-
itualists have come into the Western
world arguing that these ancient
forms of knowledge and therapy can
lead to spiritual growth and health in
a way that modern medicine does not. Unfortunately, there are very few reliable clinical tests of these so-called spiritual cures. What we have are largely anecdo-
tal accounts, but they hardly serve as objective tests of alternative therapies.

> *"The very viability of
> medical science itself
> has been questioned."*

The Threat Posed by Religious Fundamentalism

9. Another form of antiscience is the revival of fundamentalist religion even within advanced scientific and educational societies. Fundamentalists question the very foundation of scientific culture. Indeed, in the modern world, it is religion, not science, that seems to have emerged as the hope of humankind. Far more money is being poured into religion than into scientific research and edu-
cation. Especially symptomatic is the continued growth of "scientific creation-
ism" and widespread political opposition to the teaching of evolution in the schools, particularly in the United States.

10. A final area of antiscience is the growth of multicultural and feminist cri-
tiques of science education, particularly in the universities and colleges. The multiculturist view is that science is not universal or transcultural, but relative to the culture in which it emerges. There are, we are told, non-Western and primitive cultures that are as "true" and "valid" as the scientific culture of the Western world. This movement supports the complete relativization of scientific knowledge. The radical feminist indictment of "masculine bias" in science maintains that science has been the expression of "dead, white Anglo-Saxon males"—from Newton to Faraday, from Laplace to Heisenberg. What we must do, the extremists of these movements advise, is liberate humanity from cultural, racist, and sexist expressions of knowledge, and this means scientific ob-
jectivity as well. The positive contribution of these movements, of course, is that they seek to open science to more women and minorities. The negative dimension is that multiculturalist demands on education tend to weaken an under-
standing of the rigorous intellectual standards essential for effective scientific inquiry. Clearly we need to appreciate the scientific contribution of many cultures and the role of women in science throughout history; on the other hand, some multicultural critics undermine the very possibility of objective science.

What I have presented is a kaleidoscope illustration of many current trends that are undermining and threaten the future growth of science. They raise many questions. Why has this occurred? How shall those who believe in the value of scientific methods and the scientific outlook respond?

This is a complex problem, and I can only suggest some possible solutions. But unless the scientific community and those connected with it are willing to take the challenge to science seriously, then I fear that the tide of antiscience may continue to rise. Scientific research surely will not be rejected where there are obvious technological uses to be derived from it, at least insofar as economic, political, and military institutions find these profitable. But the decline in the appreciation of the methods of science and in the scientific outlook can only have deleterious effects upon the long-term role of science in civilization.

One reason for the growth of antiscience is a basic failure to educate the public about the nature of science itself. Of crucial significance is the need for public education in the aims of science. We need to develop an appreciation of the general methods of scientific inquiry, its relationship to skepticism and critical thinking, and its demand for evidence and reason in testing claims to truth. The most difficult task we face is to develop an awareness that the methods of science should not only be used in the narrow domains of the specialized sciences, but should also be generalized, as far as possible, to other fields of human interest.

We also need to develop an appreciation for the cosmic outlook of science. Using the techniques of scientific inquiry, scientists have developed theories and generalizations about the universe and the human species. These theories often conflict with theological viewpoints that for the most part go unchallenged. They also often run counter to mystical, romantic, and aesthetic attitudes. Thus it is time for more scientists and interpreters of science to come forward to explain what science tells us about the universe: for example, they should demonstrate the evidence for evolution and point out that creationism does not account for the fossil record; that the evidence points to a biological basis for the mind and that there is no evidence for reincarnation or immortality. Until the scientific community is willing to explicate openly and defend what science tells us about life and the universe, then I fear it will continue to be undermined by the vast ignorance of those who oppose it.

In this process of education, what is crucial is the development of scientific literacy in the schools and in the communications media. Recent polls have indicated that a very small percentage of the U.S. population has any understanding of scientific principles. The figures are similar for Britain, France, and Germany, where large sectors of the population are abysmally unaware of the nature of the scientific outlook. Thus we need to educate the public about how science works and what it tells us about the world, and we should make sure this understanding is applied to all fields of human knowledge.

> *"One reason for the growth of antiscience is a basic failure to educate the public about the nature of science itself."*

The growth of specialization has made this task enormously difficult. Specialization has enabled people to focus on one field, to pour their creative talents into solving specific problems, whether in biology or physics, mathematics or economics. But we need to develop generalists as well as specialists. Much of the fear and opposition to science is due to a failure to understand the nature of scientific inquiry. This understanding should include an appreciation for what we know and do *not* know. This means not only an appreciation of the body of reliable knowledge we now possess, but also an appreciation of the skeptical outlook and attitude. The interpreters of science must go beyond specialization to the general explication of what science tells us about the universe and our place in it. This is unsettling to many within society. In one sense, science is the most radical force in the modern world, because scientists need to be prepared to question everything and to demand verification or validation of any claims.

Scientists Must Have Courage

The broader public welcomes scientific innovation. Every new gadget or product and every new application in technology, where it is positive, is appreciated for its economic and social value. What is not appreciated is the nature of the scientific enterprise itself and the need to extend the critical methods of science further, especially to ethics, politics, and religion. Until those in the scientific community have sufficient courage to extend the methods of science and reason as far as they can to these other fields, then I feel that the growth of antiscience will continue.

Now it is not simply the task of scientists who work in the laboratory, who have a social responsibility to the greater society; it is also the task of philosophers, journalists, and those within the corporate and the political world who appreciate the contribution of science to humankind. For what is at stake in a sense is modernism itself. Unless corporate executives and those who wield political power recognize the central role that science and technology have played in the past four centuries, and can continue to play in the future, and unless science is defended, then I fear that the irrational growth of antiscience may undermine the viability of scientific research and the contributions of science in the future. The key is education—education within the schools, but education also within the media. We need to raise the level of appreciation, not simply among students, from grammar school through the university, but among those who control the mass media. And here, alas, the scientific outlook is often overwhelmed by violence, lurid sex, the paranormal, and religious bias.

The world today is a battlefield of ideas. In this context the partisans of science need to defend courageously the authentic role that science has played and can continue to play in human civilization. The growth of antiscience must be countered by a concomitant growth in advocacy of the virtues of science. Scientists are surely not infallible; they make mistakes. But the invaluable contributions of science need to be reiterated. We need public *re-enchantment* with the ideals expressed by the scientific outlook.

Chapter 3

Is American Business Ethical?

CURRENT CONTROVERSIES

Chapter Preface

The United States made tremendous industrial progress in the late nineteenth and early twentieth centuries, as it shifted from a predominately agricultural society to one of the world's most powerful industrial nations. Industrial development brought railroads, steel mills, and technological advances, which improved the qualify of life for many people and the economic strength of the country as a whole. But, as author Kenneth C. Davis writes, "Progress carries a price tag. . . . For every mile of railroad laid, every ton of coal or iron ore mined, thousands of workers died. Many of them were immigrants or war veterans, miserably underpaid, working in unsafe and unsanitary conditions, with little or no political voice. The new fortunes being made opened up an era of astonishing corruption."

Many corporate leaders seemed to have little concern for the welfare of workers, and few qualms about their corrupt business practices. "The business of America is business," as Calvin Coolidge said, and the primary goal of business was making profit, not concerning itself with ethical issues. Many factories employed children as laborers, paid low wages, exposed employees to health and safety threats, and polluted the nation's water and air.

In response, union organizers such as Eugene V. Debs and Mary Harris "Mother" Jones rallied workers to strike until working conditions and pay improved. Their efforts were aided by journalist "muckrakers," such as Ida M. Tarbell and Upton Sinclair, who exposed to the public the corruption in American business. The government was finally compelled to enact laws to protect workers, and gradually most businesses adopted the forty-hour work week, paid benefits for employees, and health and safety standards.

Those changes were pushed by labor and government, not by business. Yet recent decades have seen the evolution of a movement in which businesses are evaluating their actions in terms of ethics. Some companies, such as Ben and Jerry's Ice Cream, have been founded on the ethical principles of treating employees fairly and donating some part of company profits to charity. Other companies have found that employees are more productive and the public more responsive if the company shows itself to be one of integrity.

Whether this movement has improved the level of ethics in American business is one of the issues discussed in the following chapter. The contributors debate whether American business and businesspeople are ethical.

Businesspeople Are Ethical

by Edmund A. Opitz

About the author: *Edmund A. Opitz, an associate editor of* The Freeman, *served on the staff of the Foundation for Economic Education from 1955 until his retirement in 1992.*

A few years ago there was an immensely popular television series, named after Dallas. The central character of this show was a powerful and unscrupulous businessman who got that way by climbing over the backs of rivals, manipulating politicians, and wheeling and dealing with shadowy figures on the fringes of the underworld. J.R. Ewing finally got in the way of a bullet, and for months this nation was racked by the question: "Who shot J.R.?" But the civilized man could only wonder why the trigger man waited so long!

Bad Press

Business and the businessman have had bad press, almost uniformly. Do you remember the television show whose hero was a businessman? The show that portrayed this businessman as a person of integrity and vision, who labored long hours to produce a product that supplied a genuine need, which he marketed at prices people could afford? Who treated his employees with generosity and consideration, and his customers with unfailing courtesy? Who was a devoted family man, active in civic affairs, and a churchman? Who could recite Shakespeare by the yard, relaxed by listening to his fine collection of recorded symphony music, and could tell a Corot from a Monet? Do you remember that show? Perhaps it was a movie? Actually it was neither. Such a show was never produced; the subject is taboo, by today's mores.

The businessman has rarely if ever been treated fairly and accurately in drama or fiction. Is this because there are no men and women of superior intellect and high character in the world of business, industry, and trade? Not at all. Has the world of business no dramatic possibilities? Of course it has. But the fictional

Abridged from Edmund A. Opitz, "Ethics and Business," *The Freeman*, March 1993. Courtesy of the Foundation for Economic Education, Irvington-on-Hudson, N.Y.

businessman invariably turns out to be the villain. There is a reason why this is so; the businessman is portrayed as a scoundrel because there is an almost universal bias against business on the part of novelists and dramatists. Businessmen do not get a fair shake because novelists and dramatists—with rare exceptions—have an ideological axe to grind.

Television's Message

This is the impression that emerges from our casual contact with the world of popular entertainment, the world of television, films, and fiction. This impression is confirmed in an unpretentious little volume by Ben Stein entitled *The View from Sunset Boulevard*. Stein interviewed a number of Hollywood writers and producers of television shows in order to find out how they viewed the various aspects of American life. If a visitor from England were to spend a little time watching television, what image of America would he come away with? Stein deals with television's treatment of crime, the police, government, the army, the family, and other aspects of American life, including business. How do the people in Hollywood regard business? "One of the clearest messages of television," Stein writes, "is that businessmen are bad, evil people, and that big businessmen are the worst of all . . . the murderous, duplicitous, cynical businessman is about the only kind of businessman there is on TV adventure shows, just as the cunning, trickster businessman shares the stage with the pompous buffoon businessman in situation comedies." A well-known producer, Stanley Kramer, sees business as "part of a very great power structure which wields enormous power over the people." And beyond that, Kramer implies, there is an "arrangement" between business and organized crime: "the Mafia is part of the entire corporate entity now."

The warped feelings of wealthy and talented Hollywood writers and producers did not spring into existence unaided; it is one of the calculated end results of an intense propaganda effort that has been hacking away at the roots of Western society since the middle of the last century—attacking its religious origin, its values, and what is perceived as the last bastion of the bourgeoisie, business. A scholarly work which meticulously researched this vast literature appeared in 1954, by Professor James Desmond Glover of the

> *"The businessman has rarely if ever been treated fairly and accurately in drama or fiction."*

Harvard Business School, entitled *The Attack on Big Business*. Professor Glover writes: "In volumes upon volumes of testimony before Congressional committees, in popular novels, in learned treatises and textbooks, in poetry, in sermons, in opinions of Supreme Court justices, 'big business' and its works are seen as evil and attacked. The literature of criticism of 'big business,' and of the civilization it has done so much to bring into being, represents by now a perfectly staggering mass of material."

What is the rationale for this widespread antagonism toward the business system, otherwise known as capitalism? I don't profess to understand all the reasons for the anti-capitalistic mentality, but the root cause of the antipathy is surely the perception, the mistaken perception, that the relation between employer and employee is that of exploiter to victim. The employer may intend no harm, he may intend only good to those who work for him, but in the capitalistic mode of production—Karl Marx contended—the worker is denied the full fruits of his labor; a portion of every wage earner's product is garnisheed by his boss. To simplify Marxist theory, we might say that John Smith—who runs a machine in a shoe factory—punches the clock at eight o'clock in the morning and works till noon. During these four hours he produces six pairs of shoes, which represent his wage for the day. John Smith returns to his bench and works four more hours in the afternoon, but the shoes he produces during these four hours are expropriated by his employer.

> *"The root cause of the antipathy [for capitalism] is surely . . . the mistaken perception that the relation between employer and employee is that of exploiter to victim."*

Marx's Exploitation Theory

This is a summary statement of the surplus value theory, otherwise known as Marx's exploitation theory. It is a central contention of Marxism that labor alone creates value, the value of a commodity being measured by the quantity of labor normally necessary to produce it. But if it is labor alone that creates value, the value created should belong exclusively to labor. It does not, however; the lion's share is grabbed by the employer while the real producer is paid only a subsistence wage.

This theory overlooks the role of tools and machinery in production. The tool user in this generation is many times more productive than his counterpart of a few generations ago. Why is this? His naked labor power is no greater than that of people over the ages. The enhanced productivity of labor today is due to the tools and machinery at the disposal of every one of us—and those tools are the fruits of the labor of earlier generations. If today's "worker" retained the full product of his individual effort, and only that, the poor fellow would starve.

A contemporary of Marx, the celebrated Austrian economist Eugen von Böhm-Bawerk, demolished the surplus value theory in a book entitled *Capital and Interest*, published in 1884, the year after Marx died. The demolition job has been repeated many times since the appearance of Böhm-Bawerk's great book, and the consensus of opinion among independent economists is that the surplus value theory does not hold water. The exploitation theory has great propaganda value, however, and it is used unthinkingly by those who are acting out a grudge against business, which, in their distorted vision, keeps the poor locked in their poverty in order that others might be rich.

Ben Stein, in the book mentioned earlier, records a portion of his conversation with television writer Bob Weiskopf:

Q. Why are people poor in America?
A. Because I don't think the system could function if everyone was well off.
Q. What do you mean?
A. I think you have to have poor people in a capitalist society.
Q. Why?
A. To exploit. The rich people can't exploit each other. Consequently they always exploit the poor.

It is not only Hollywood script writers who profess to believe that the rich get richer only by making the poor poorer. The coordinator of the National Council of Churches' Anti-Poverty Task Force asserts that "Poverty would not continue to exist if those in power did not feel it was good for them." A moment's reflection will reveal this insulting accusation for the silly sentiment it is. We live in a commercial and manufacturing society. Our economy is featured by mass production, not only in factories but also in agriculture. The products of mass production flood our stores and supermarkets and showrooms, to be bought by the mass of consumers. Mass production cannot continue unless there is mass consumption; and the masses of people cannot consume the output of our mass production factories and fields unless they possess purchasing power—the money to buy the goods of their choice. To suggest that those who have goods and services to sell have some sinister interest in keeping their potential customers too poor to buy is sheer nonsense! If the president of General Motors wants to sell you a Cadillac or a Buick or a Chevrolet—which he does—then he wants you to be rich enough to buy. In the free economy, everyone has a stake in the economic well-being of every other person.

Who *Really* Uses the Poor?

It is in the immediate interest of business and businessmen that the masses of people be well off; people who are poor are poor customers, and business cannot survive without customers. Business has no stake in poverty; but there is a class of people who do need the poor, who do have an interest in keeping them poor.

> *"It is in the immediate interest of business and businessmen that the masses of people be well off."*

Permit me, in a slight digression, to offer you a few words on this point by the celebrated economist Thomas Sowell: "To be blunt, the poor are a gold mine. By the time they are studied, advised, experimented with and administered, the poor have helped many a middle class liberal to achieve affluence with government money. The total amount of money the government spends on its 'anti-poverty' efforts is three times what would be required to lift every man, woman, and child in

90

America above the poverty line by simply sending money to the poor."

Back now to the widespread animus against business, stemming from the false idea that labor is the sole source of value but is not allowed to keep what it produces. In the distorted vision of Karl Marx, business, industry, and trade—as these economic activities are organized in the free world—are intrinsically evil, and the businessman is a parasite and predator. Similar notions are entertained by many a man in the street who has never read a line of Marx, as well as by intellectuals who regard themselves as anti-Communists. Given this climate of opinion, the term "ethical businessman" is a contradiction in terms; it is the figure of speech known to English teachers as an oxymoron—a figure which juxtaposes incongruous terms like "virtuous thief" or "honest liar."

> *"There is no justification for the assumption that all businessmen are evil."*

Now, if businessmen are involved in activities which are intrinsically crooked, evil by their very nature, then it is pointless to discuss the ethical situations of business or the moral dilemmas businessmen sometimes face. It would be like instructing a thief on how to rob banks honestly! So I propose to spend a few minutes trying to understand the nature of the economic activities that engage businessmen, while touching upon some of the values that are implicated in the production of goods and services.

All Are Sinners

You have a right to know the direction from which I am coming at you, to know my bias. I have examined the catalogue of sins of which businessmen are allegedly guilty, and Lo! they are the very same sins exhibited by people in every other walk of life. We all break the Commandments now and then, every one of us. Businessmen have no monopoly on sin. My mind goes back to a conversation I had several years ago with a professor of economics with years of teaching behind him, who had also served for many years as the academic dean of a prestigious midwestern college. He said to me, "You know, Ed, a thoroughly dishonest man can last a lot longer in teaching or preaching than as a used car salesman." There may be some hyperbole here, but my friend has a point. There are good and bad in all walks of life, and there are very few saints anywhere; but in the eyes of the law all are equal. The law should mete out justice upon the guilty party with impartiality. It should punish those who harass, steal, defraud, breach a contract, assault, or murder. This is the rule of law in action.

There is no justification for the assumption that all businessmen are evil people who must therefore be regulated, i.e., adjudged guilty until proven innocent. There is no more reason for regulating businessmen than for regulating clergymen or teachers!

The free market economic system produces goods and services in abundance, and it rewards every participant according to his individual contribution—as his peers judge that contribution. "To the producer belongs the fruits of his toil" is an ancient bit of wisdom, as true now as when first uttered. The relation between an individual's effort and the eventual reward of his exertions is fairly clear in a simple situation like subsistence farming. You work by yourself, preparing the ground in the spring, seeding and tilling it, watering the furrows with your sweat during the heat of summer, reaping in the fall. The abundance of your harvest is directly traceable to your skills and the amount of work you put forth. The greater your effort the more ample your harvest—other things being equal. The harvest is your wage, and your wage in this instance is pretty much determined by your own skill and your own exertions; the more you put in, the more you will take out. What you take out is your wage, the economic equivalent of your contribution.

How is your wage determined in a complex division of labor society such as ours? Justice still demands that every participant in the economy be rewarded according to his contribution to the productive process. But how shall we identify each individual's contribution in order to reward him commensurately?

> *"The business of America is not business. It never was. The business of America is individual liberty."*

Economists from Adam Smith to Ludwig von Mises to F. A. Hayek and Milton Friedman have worked this question over and come up with an answer that is completely democratic and economically efficient, while encouraging every person in the full exercise of his lawful liberties. The answer provided by the economist is: Let the market decide what each person's contribution is worth and reward him accordingly. "The market" describes the process of social cooperation under the division of labor where free people specialize in a complex variety of tasks in anticipation of a consumer demand for the goods and services they produce— followed by multiple voluntary exchanges of these products in which persons give over something they value for whatever they value more. This market process will reward people unequally, but it will reward them equitably, compensating each person in a measure equal to his peers' evaluation of his services.

Market Forces

The eminent economist Frank H. Knight, founder of the Chicago School, put the matter in these words: "It is a proposition of elementary economics that ideal market competition will force entrepreneurs to pay every productive agent employed what his cooperation adds to the total, the difference between what it can be with him and what it would be without him. This is his own product in the only meaning the word can have where persons or their resources act jointly." In short, each person will get his fair share, defined as what others will voluntarily offer for his goods and services—provided there is general freedom.

Each one of us is judged by his peers; our offerings of goods and services are evaluated by consumers who give us what they think our offerings are worth to them, and not a penny more. This is a democratic judgment on the value of the products of our labor—one dollar, one vote—and it is made by consumers who are, as everyone knows, ignorant, venal, superstitious, neurotic, biased, and stupid. In other words, people just like us—because every one of us is a consumer! When it is a question of the wage we earn we are dependent on consumers, who couldn't care less that we are upright men of sterling character; their sole concern is: Do we have a product or service they want? If we do, they reward us handsomely. If we don't, it matters not that we have labored long and painfully over our brainchild; if the customers don't want it, we're stuck with it. This is consumer sovereignty.

> *"The market economy . . . channels the activities of energetic, ambitious, and competitive personalities into the production of goods and services."*

Consumers run the free economy; producers cater to their demands. It's their show. What kind of a show do they put on? Not always a good one, I'm sorry to say. But I'll say one thing for consumer sovereignty: it sure beats the alternative. . . .

The Market Economy

Human beings everywhere have engaged in trade and barter. There is some specialization and a division of labor even among primitive people, with a consequent exchange of the fruits of specialization. The voluntary exchange of goods and services is the market in operation, and the market is everywhere. But the market does not spontaneously or automatically transform itself into the market economy; the market economy emerges only when the moral, political, and legal conditions are right. This occurred under the Whig philosophy of men like Edmund Burke and Adam Smith, Thomas Jefferson and James Madison. These men drew up a frame of government whose main purpose was to secure each person in his life, liberty, and property. This political idea of limited, constitutional government is grounded on the religious conviction that we are God's creatures, possessing immortal souls. The conviction that persons are sacred is politically translated into our Creator-endowed rights to "life, liberty, and the pursuit of happiness." Adam Smith referred to his "liberal plan of liberty, equality and justice," with the free market as the economic counterpart to political liberty. The rule of law replaces the arbitrary will of rulers and personal freedom expands. It is significant that Smith's *The Wealth of Nations* appeared in the same year as the Declaration of Independence.

The discipline of economics as a separate subject matter was almost nonexistent prior to Adam Smith. Virtually starting from scratch, Smith created nearly the whole edifice of economics. Adam Smith presupposed the legal framework of the Whig jurists, where the law would eliminate force from the market-place, punish fraud, and enforce contracts. He also presupposed a high level of probity in the general population. Given these conditions, the market is self-start-ing and self-regulating; the buying habits of consumers guide producers, deter-mining how the entrepreneur will decide to combine scarce resources for the maximum satisfaction of consumer needs. There will be a harmony in these di-verse activities of millions of participants as if everything were directed by "an invisible hand." The market economy—dubbed "capitalism" by its enemies about a century after Smith—contained the promise of prosperity for the multitudes. These same masses composed a self-governing people. Political liberty expanded and people had lots of elbow room to pick and choose and plan their own lives.

The Declaration of Independence and the Constitution created the political frame for a people who aspired to the ideal of "liberty and justice for all." Politi-cal liberty assured freedom in economic transactions between employer and em-ployee, seller and buyer. The work ethic was enshrined in America and wages doubled, redoubled, and doubled again during the nineteenth century—an eight-fold increase in real wages. For the first time in history the masses glimpsed the possibility of pulling themselves out of poverty and creating new opportunities for their children. America's schools and churches sought to shore up the tradi-tional value structure of our culture and to orient the newly enlarged popular freedom toward virtue. Their success, needless to say, was only partial.

Was there ugliness in American life? Of course there was. Freedom was mis-used; the scramble for wealth was sometimes pretty crass. The newly rich were vulgar; plunderers bought and sold politicians, and fortunes were scooped out of the public treasury—all in violation of Whig theory and free market eco-nomics. But you cannot blame capitalism for the miscreants who refuse to abide by its rules.

Despite the gray and black areas in our history, there was still open opportunity on these shores, in comparison to what was available in other parts of the globe. Thirty-three million people told us so by coming here as immigrants during the half century before World War I. They came because life here—although far from perfect—was far better for them than life elsewhere.

> *"Business and the free economy beget a prosperous society."*

The business of America is not business. It never was. The business of America is individual liberty, with the law enforcing an even-handed justice among equal persons. When the law provides a free field and no favor—which was the original implication of *laissez faire*—the economic order is the free market.

The market economy does not carry any implication that business may act ir-responsibly with impunity. If, for example, industrial wastes are disposed of in such a way that persons are injured or property damaged, the law should punish those responsible and offer redress to the injured party. If a seller misrepresents a product, he is guilty of fraud and the buyer's injury should be redressed. If a businessman solicits and obtains a subsidy from government, or if government gives him monopolistic advantages over his competition enabling him to exact a higher price from his customers, he has forfeited his status as a businessman. A businessman as such has no power over anyone, his only leverage being the quality of his goods and the persuasiveness of his advertising. The businessman has the same rights and the same responsibilities as every other member of society, no more and no less.

Lord Acton's aphorism about power has been overquoted, but it is still terribly true. Power must be curbed if we will that people shall be free, and an independent economic order does put fetters on governmental power. People who control their own livelihood have little to fear from rulers; but political control of the economic life of a nation is totalitarian rule. The market economy curbs power in another way as well; it channels the activities of energetic, ambitious, and competitive personalities into the production of goods and services and away from politics. The rich in a free economy get that way because consumers appreciate the goods and services they offer; and if these few wish their descendants to enjoy this wealth the bulk of it must be invested in industries producing goods for the masses.

Let us give credit where credit is due; business, industry, and trade have made us into a prosperous nation. But our wealth has not made us a happy nation, or a contented one. We have proved once again—as if any further proof were needed—that prosperity and worldly success are, at best, a means to ends beyond themselves. Refine and improve a means as you will, it still remains only a means, needing a worthy end if it is to be meaningful. There is a discipline that deals with ends and goals, with the purposes that make life significant; it is called religion—though not everything bearing that label qualifies. But genuine Christianity is at a low ebb in the modern world; we have lost that vital contact with God and the moral law which energized our ancestors and made life for them an adventure in destiny. The decadence of Christianity is the root cause of the modern malaise; Plato argued two millennia ago that disorder in society is a reflection of disorder in the soul, that is, in our defective thinking and misguided loyalties. The work of renewal must begin here, with individual persons, and then go on to a restoration of the theological foundation necessary to a free society.

This is not the task of business, industry, and trade; the economic order has a more humble role to play. Business and the free economy beget a prosperous society which provides people the leisure they need to cultivate those goods which mark a high civilization: religion and worship, education and science, arts and crafts, conversation and play. These are the areas where people exercise their freedom most creatively, where they discover the goals proper to human life. Responsible freedom in the economic realm has the important role of supplying the indispensable means for these ends.

Business Is an Honorable Profession

by Tibor R. Machan

About the author: *Tibor R. Machan is a professor of philosophy at Auburn University in Alabama.*

Some time ago *Newsweek* ran a "My Turn" column by Professor Amitai Etzioni of George Washington University, who taught a term of business ethics at the Harvard School of Business. The author, who has written, among other works, a book, *The Moral Dimension: Toward a New Economics*, which is highly critical of neo-classical economics, spent the entire piece lamenting the meager interest his MBA students showed in the subject he was trying very hard to explain to them.

MBAs' Ethics

Professor Etzioni's main complaint in the *Newsweek* piece is that he "clearly had not found a way to help classes full of MBAs see that there is more to life than money, power, fame and self-interest." More specifically, the MBA students were disappointingly fond of business, including advertising. Some endorsed the idea of "consumer sovereignty," meaning that consumers pretty much have the chance to make up their minds as to what they will purchase, even in the face of the persuasive efforts of advertisers. Our author complained in the face of this belief, "But what about John Kenneth Galbraith's view . . . [which] argues that corporations actually produce the *demand* for their product, together with whatever *they* wish to sell—say male deodorants." The implication was that the idea of sovereignty is a myth; people are *made* to buy things by ads, not by their own considered judgment.

Another complaint advanced by Professor Etzioni was that Harvard's MBAs didn't wholeheartedly welcome his "ethical" criticism of corporate PACs. He notes that "scores of corporations encourage their executives to form political-action committees and use the monies amassed to influence both Congress and

Tibor R. Machan, "On Teaching Business Ethics," *The Heritage Lectures*, no. 253, May 1, 1990. Reprinted by permission of the Heritage Foundation.

state legislators. One student said he liked PACs: 'Last summer, I worked for a corporation that has one. Its PAC allowed me to advance my economic interest. And, I could use my vote in the ballot box, to support those who agree with my international ideas.'"

After he informs us of all these horrible goings-on, Professor Etzioni asks, "So it's OK for corporate executives to have, in effect, two votes, while the rest of us have one?"

Debunker Debunked

We could consider Professor Etzioni's substantive criticisms of business and its executives, of course, and find they aren't very telling. For example, although our professor never mentions it, there is a famous response to Galbraith's debunking of the consumer sovereignty doctrine. In a now well-known piece, only rarely used in business ethics texts, F.A. Hayek has argued that while, in a certain sense, desires are created, this is no different from how that occurs with all innovations—artistic, scientific, religious, or whatnot. When a new symphony is written, it "produces" a demand, yes. People take note of it and often find it preferable to what else they might listen to. Certainly, when a service or product is introduced on any front, it is hoped that it will meet someone's desires, someone who will see its point and judge it as having merit. Indeed, even male deodorants—a product Professor Etzioni snidely denigrates in his piece as an obvious case of trivial consumption—may have a point for some of us who are not, perhaps, as lucky as the professor.

Consumer Choice

Now no doubt there are consumers who will buy things for the hell of it and even waste their money on what is positively bad for them. But one may doubt Mr. Galbraith's—or even a business teacher's—competence to judge better than the consumers whether it is right for them to buy what they buy. It would be an especially hard judgment to make from Harvard or George Washington University's ivory towers.

Consider also the PAC case. What about the well-respected American public policy—part and parcel of any functioning democracy—for people "to petition the government for redress of grievances" (respecting, e.g., the double taxation involved in the corporate gains tax or being singled out as the bad guys in the fight for a clean environment)? Where does

> *"Business ethics courses . . . essentially involve demonstrating to the students that the very objective of the profession is something shady."*

Professor Etzioni's lament leave all the special interest groups that eagerly lobby in Washington for such noble causes as the protection of the snail darter, defense of animal rights, and the vigorous redistribution of the "nation's wealth"? What about all the Naderite PIRG [public interest research group] groups, the Sierra Club's constant pleading, etc., etc.?

In short, why should we decry PACs without also noting that in essentials these kinds of organizations, lamentable or not, are by no means unique to efforts by businesses to participate in the democratic process?

So, judging by the author's very own account of how he went about teaching his business ethics course, it is no wonder that his students responded with little enthusiasm. Evidently what our professor did was not teach business ethics but instead engage in that familiar academic pastime, namely, business bashing.

Denigrating the Profession

Professor Etzioni's approach to teaching "business ethics" is, sadly, typical. It is prevalent throughout the country's universities wherever such courses are taught. Such courses, all too often and rather ironically—considering that "truth in labeling" is one of those public policy matters urged during such courses—labeled as business ethics, are essentially concerned not with the subject matter of ethical conduct within the profession of business but with the denigration of the profession and the advocacy of public policy to reform it.

In medical ethics—and educational, legal, or engineering ethics—the objective is to take general and mostly familiar ethical theories and show how they might be made applicable to the problems that have to be tackled within these special disciplines. What would utilitarianism say about surrogate motherhood or the problem of

> *"[The pursuit of prosperity] could be well construed as a species of prudence, . . . the first of the cardinal virtues."*

honest communication in the case of fatal disease? How do we apply the tenets of Christian ethics or ethical egoism to the problems of risk aversion in the building of high-rise apartments or the production of automobiles?

Yet business ethics is presented entirely differently in most courses and text-books with that name affixed to them. Business ethics courses, as actually taught in most places, essentially involve demonstrating to the students that the very objective of the profession is something shady. Notice how eagerly Professor Etzioni recalls his student's justification of joining a PAC organization: it "allowed me to advance my economic interest." This, one may gather, had no ethical significance for our professor (who is well known as a severe critic of any kind of consequentialist ethics, the sort where good and right are identified by reference to some valuable results). For such philosophers and ethicists the pursuit of prosperity is by itself simply amoral. Never mind that there is a long tradition of ethical teaching wherein such pursuit could be well construed as a species of prudence, a trait of character that is, after all, the first of the cardinal virtues.

Instead of seeing business as the institutional expression of the virtue—the good deeds people engage in while carrying out prudent endeavors—business as a profession is something that is mostly mistrusted and denigrated in ethics courses and texts. By implication, of course, the only way to be ethical in business is essentially to abdicate. Short of that, which most people won't quite volunteer to do, one is at least required to wash one's hands clean after one has left the executive suite.

Admittedly, when business ethicists who denigrate commerce look to economists as the moral defenders of the institution and profession of business they find, apart from a few texts, very little that is of moral substance. No wonder, since economists seek only a technical understanding of the

"Business [is] the institutional expression of . . . the good deeds people engage in while carrying out prudent endeavors."

workings of business and make few assumptions about what generates business life in the first place. They do not dwell on moral issues—not at all unlike other social scientists, who are trying with all their might to remain value-free in what they take to be a scientific stance about their subject. (Some, unfortunately, extrapolate these assumptions to the rest of human life and thus pretend that their arid "science" can render all of human affairs fully understandable. But moral philosophers should not take advantage of economists' disregard for the moral dimensions of business life—and they usually do not when it comes to other social sciences, the politics and ethics of which they do not despair.)

Business Bashing

Instead of looking to economists to explain why business might indeed be an honorable activity, business-bashing ethicists should look to fellow ethicists—ones, however, who see in business activity a perfectly legitimate form of prudential behavior, aiming at the prosperity of the agents or their clients. And they should then try to come to terms with the arguments that try to establish the moral propriety of such prudential conduct.

Now, I'm painting a rather bleak picture. There might be others who teach this course, with a different perspective, who are more balanced in their approach than those I have been focusing on. Yet, if we consider the literature in the field—including major scholarly books and articles as well as textbooks used—the picture that emerges is very close to how I have been painting it.

For example, in the discussion of employment, the major objective of most business-ethics authors and professors is to demonstrate that there shouldn't be employment at will. Employers ought to be constrained forcibly—by government regulation or litigation—in their judgment as to whom they hire, fire, or promote in their particular endeavors. Nor can employees make certain kinds of decisions, for example, to work at higher risk than OSHA (the federal Occupational Safety and Health Administration) has allowed. If they wish to take the risk for higher pay, they are forbidden to do so by way of the government's imposition of certain standards on every business—never mind how new and how much in need of some initial cost-cutting it might be.

Or take another area, where the major objective of most business ethics professors now tends to be: how the role of subordination of most employees ought to be changed; how there are so-called employee rights that should cut down, if not totally eliminate, the position of management; and how the employer is a tyrant, an oppressor and an exploiter, and this needs to be countered with some effective legislation and court decision.

> *"Commerce has at least become legitimized."*

It does not matter at all that some employees may prefer working for others who take the bigger risks and are thus expected to reap the greater returns. Never mind that different business establishments might require different types of organization, and in some there might not be much room for shared management roles if they are to be run efficiently. All this is subordinated to the will of the state with the fervent approval of many who teach college students the ethics of business.

One vital question we need to ask is why is this such a prevalent phenomenon in university departments of philosophy, even in business schools? Why is it that business has such very bad press?

There is a fundamental reason underlying our cultural heritage why business has gotten such a bad rap. At least at the level of ideas, I think one has to admit this attitude comes from some of our most honored philosophers—Plato in particular and, to some extent, Aristotle. Indeed, many of the major philosophical figures in the history of Western and Eastern philosophy must take the blame. The basic intellectual underpinning of hostility to business is a form of idealism or, more particularly, a form of dualism.

Idealism in philosophy means, roughly, that the most important reality is ideas and not nature. Alternatively, it is the spiritual realm and not the natural that is of primary significance.

Dualism tends to mean that there are two major elements of reality: the natural or material element and the spiritual or intellectual element. In the history of philosophy, many of the major thinkers, when they did embrace a form of dualism of the two basic substances in the world, chose the intellectual or spiritual as the higher substance, as the more important one.

To the extent that they believe that human beings are composed of these two elements, these philosophers usually select for special treatment and honor the intellectual element of human life.

Happy Life

Indeed, in Aristotle's ethics—not entirely uncontroversially yet quite explicitly—the truly happy life is the life that is lived entirely in terms of one's intellect. This is the contemplative life. In Plato's philosophy, in his ethics as well as in his politics, at least at a first reading, one gets the impression that those people who specialize in the use of their intellect—who excel in that respect of their lives—are the more worthwhile people. And these, then, are the people who are excellent and who ought to be accorded the role of leadership and guidance in society.

This view of the intellectual or theoretical people is in contrast to how we should view those who are mostly concerned with mundane matters, including trade and business. Following this philosophical viewpoint, subsequent Western theology fell into line. This, in part, makes sense of why the Biblical claim—sooner will the camel go through the eye of a needle than the rich man gain entrance into the kingdom of heaven—has been taken to mean a denigration of wealth per se. And Jesus's extreme anger and even violence towards traders using the Temple also makes good sense in this context—one may be sure that churches were used by other professions—yet we don't know of Jesus ever resorting to violence against their members.

> *"The pursuit of prosperity here on earth is a worthwhile objective."*

These popular religious readings tend to be a denigration of prosperity and wealth seeking. The institution of usury, one that characterizes the tasks of most banking and lending establishments, was, for centuries, denigrated and found to be unnatural for human beings. This was and continues in some circles to be a normative point, namely, not that people don't charge usury, but that if they are to be true to their true selves they ought not to.

Generally speaking, the only time in Western philosophy that we escaped this kind of thinking was during a very radical and almost as extreme sway of the pendulum toward the other side. This came with Thomas Hobbes's complete materialism. Hobbes in the 16th century—following his enthusiasm with Galilean physics and science in general (which itself was given sanction through the reintroduction of Aristotle's work in Western culture by St. Thomas Aquinas)—basically completely denies the spiritual or intellectual realm. For Hobbes and his followers everything is matter-in-motion and the whole world can be understood pretty much in terms of physics. Hobbes's philosophy—roughly embraced by many others of that era (e.g., Francis Bacon)—was a kind of reaction, swinging from idealism or dualism over to pure materialism.

Base Activity

Suppose now that we find reality as well as the human being divided into two spheres. And suppose we designate the one sphere to be divine or spiritual—that is, a higher level of reality. It is then clearly not surprising that those who are concentrating their attention and work on supplying our natural needs and wants, the basis for our earthly existence—our worldly pleasures and happiness—will not be honored highly and may even be held in moral suspicion as human sexuality has been through the ages. It is a base sort of activity of human beings, necessary but not noble. It is certainly not deserving of honor or respect or to be held up high as something unambiguously respectable.

I think that a goodly portion of the attack on business can ultimately be traced to this attitude, with the additional factor in our time of the brief swing to the opposite extreme via the materialist philosophy of Hobbes and his followers—including the political economists of classical liberalism. In actual fact, business has made some gains, at least on the practical fronts and in those disciplines concerned with practical matters such as politics and economics. In short, commerce has at least become legitimized. Some of the more severe disdain toward it, which had once been expressed in outright bans of much of what now passes for business, is no longer institutionalized. Instead, what remains is a moral or ethical suspicion toward it which feeds into the law and has helped the institution of business fall into disrepute.

> *"We need to continue the trend of giving the profession of business much better press than it is getting in academe."*

Interestingly, with this attitude toward business, the West has lost the ability to teach the newly emerging Eastern European countries how they might recover from the socialist economic mismanagement. The moral high road for capitalism has been abandoned and only a half-hearted support can be heard. . . .

Fundamental Confusion

Yet none of this is new. It's not just today's *Newsweek* . . . or next term's business ethics courses that support this half-hearted attitude, a mixture of fascination and disdain. It is, as I have been suggesting, the fundamental confusion that human nature can be divided—that one part is far more noble and spiritual than the other lower material self, and that we are basically just waiting to get rid of this lower self and realize our nature.

Socrates put the theme of this fundamental confusion very well by saying that all of life is really just a preparation for death, and that death is the time when we join our truly spiritual selves and abandon our material and natural selves.

In that kind of dominant intellectual atmosphere it shouldn't be surprising that those who make a prosperous, successful, material, natural living possible for most of us—those who serve us in shopping centers, not in churches, not in laboratories—would not be looked upon as part of the class to be honored, to be respected.

It is interesting to notice, finally, some of the practical policy consequences of the widespread scorning of business. Just consider how throughout history the people who have been alien to the culture in which they found themselves and therefore couldn't participate in their own traditions often had no alternative but to join the business or financial class. Very often in Europe these were Jews, though elsewhere some other ethnic groups played the same role. These aliens were at first demeaned and later, when the practical value of their work could no longer be denied, were envied. In some cases, in the end they were liquidated.

Let me end by indicating two reasons the above considerations are of vital practical importance to anyone who is interested in human freedom and well-being.

First, the recently revved-up activism of environmentalists will only be checked by good sense if the privatization approach to that important social problem can be sold to the public. But that approach is not salable if profit making is deemed some kind of morally shady endeavor. If saving the environment can best be done by linking it with business—the private property rights system—then business must be morally vindicated.

Second, the recent reforms in Eastern Europe will not be long-lasting if free market solutions are not simply sold as efficient ways of saving nations from bankruptcy, but also as institutional arrangements for human beings to prosper. And for that it is necessary to explain that the pursuit of prosperity here on earth is a worthwhile objective, not something merely to be allowed for emergencies.

Business needs a good reputation. In the United States and Western cultures in general this reputation has, of course, been improving during the last several centuries. But now there is a backlash. If we are to improve our lives here on earth, we need to continue the trend of giving the profession of business much better press than it is getting in academe.

Businesses Are Increasingly Becoming Socially Responsible

by Mary Scott and Howard Rothman

About the authors: *Mary Scott and Howard Rothman are journalists and the authors of* Companies with a Conscience: Intimate Portraits of Twelve Firms That Make a Difference, *from which this viewpoint is adapted. Scott develops and implements social and environmental programs for corporations. Rothman has written seven books and contributed to nearly seventy publications.*

From Chicago's Stony Island Avenue, about nine miles south of the city's fabled Loop, you can see both the peril of urban America in the 1990s—and the promise of a new kind of American company.

On one side of the wide asphalt strip is Woodlawn, a section filled with burned-out buildings, debris-strewn lots, graffiti-scarred walls, and general despair.

On the other is South Shore, a section brimming with rehabilitated apartments, neat single-family homes, clean streets, and hope.

Worlds Apart

Stony Island physically separates these two adjoining neighborhoods in the heart of America's third-largest city—but in reality they are worlds apart. The difference between them is the Shorebank Corporation.

Formed in 1973, when Woodlawn and South Shore were equally experiencing early stages of urban decline, Shorebank is an unusual kind of community development organization. With a bank at its core—and a group of non-bankers at its helm—it is a multifaceted definitely-for-profit business created specifically to bolster the fortunes of South Shore.

By most measures—and particularly in contrast to the deterioration that ultimately destroyed Woodlawn—it is a remarkable success. Indeed, after the Los Angeles riots in the spring of 1992, Shorebank was often cited as *the* model for effectively distributing loans for small-business development and residential rehabilitation.

"People always ask me if that is risky," says Joan Shapiro, a senior vice-president at Shorebank's South Shore Bank. "But where have the losses in this industry been in the last 10 years? Not at a bank like South Shore. Our loan losses in 1991 were a little over 6/10ths of 1%, the year before that they were 46/100ths of 1%, and the year before that 42/100ths of 1%. Who has really taken the risks?"

A New Kind of Company

No wonder we found Shorebank, a financial institution, among more nationally familiar names like Ben & Jerry's (ice cream), Patagonia (clothing), Smith & Hawken (mail order), and Celestial Seasoning (herbal teas) when we set out to track leading examples of the new kind of socially responsible company that has surfaced in America.

They are driven by what Ben and Jerry call "caring capitalism"—an uncanny flair for business and an uncommon commitment to people. From visionary company founders like Yvon Chouinard of Patagonia to dedicated second-generation managers like Ms. Shapiro of Shorebank, the people who run these organizations combine a social worker's sympathies with an entrepreneur's instincts, an inventor's street smarts with an MBA's business savvy. They are interesting *to*, and interested *in*, those around them. And, fortunately for the rest of us, they are becoming the role models for successful corporate leadership in the '90s.

It was early in 1991 when we as writers began talking about the way corporate America seemed to be resetting its moral compass. We marveled at how the greed-is-good, house-of-cards economic engineering of the '80s was no longer in favor. And how the Michael Milkens, Charles Keatings, and Gordon Gekkos of the world—real-life Wall Street money men and cinematic West Coast power brokers alike—were suddenly and decisively out of fashion.

"The '80s were about style and life style," says clothing designer and entrepreneur Susie Tompkins of Esprit de Corp, headquartered in San Francisco. "The '90s are about soul-searching . . . about encouraging volunteerism. Before, we gave our employees French lessons, sent them on river trips—all of those personal things. Now, we're giving them character-building opportunities." To support employees' volunteer work, Esprit allows up to

> *"We saw evidence of the new-found ethical standard everywhere."*

10 hours per month of paid leave, to be matched by a similar amount of the employee's own time.

We saw evidence of the new-found ethical standard everywhere. Companies like Apple Computer and Wal-Mart were actively encouraging their employees and customers to recycle. Campbell Soup and H.J. Heinz were among those offering on-site day-care programs. Avon Products and General Mills were developing policies to help female and minority workers. Coca-Cola and 3M were investing heavily in community outreach efforts. Even General Motors released a packet of information called "General Motors and the Environment."

But we remained skeptical until we learned more. What we eventually found was a still small—but steadily growing—network of companies with a conscience. We decided to explore these companies as subjects for a book.

> *"What we eventually found was a still small—but steadily growing—network of companies with a conscience."*

The giants got the publicity, but we quickly discovered that smaller, often unknown companies really were the leaders in this nascent movement toward corporate responsibility. What's more, we discovered that many of these small- and mid-sized firms were actually making a regular and substantial profit.

We noted the mushrooming number of business schools requiring classes on environmental or ethical issues for the MBA degree. And we watched as companies like IBM began supporting major conferences on business ethics for their peers across the US.

"We're not trying to get people to stop consuming, we're trying to get them to cut back and consume better," says founder Chouinard of the Patagonia company.

Ms. Tompkins of Esprit de Corp recalls rewriting the company's mission statement: "We hired facilitators and we went over and over what we wanted to say." Finally the collective group of employees came up with three simple lines: "Be informed. Be involved. Make a difference."

Sharing Responsibility

Involving employees and decentralizing responsibility are tenets of the companies with a conscience. Alfalfa's Inc. of Denver, Colorado, is so successful (500 employees, $30 million gross in 1991) it had to decentralize by adding to its chain of natural-foods groceries.

"It has not been easy," admits Kashmir-born, London-educated Sahid M. Hassan, the firm's co-founder and CEO. "When I go into a store, I look at every shelf and every can and every display and every interaction, and I have an idea of how every one of those things should be to be perfect. It's not easy for me to acknowledge that I wouldn't do it the way that it's been done, but now it's essentially someone else's store. And if I want them to take complete pride in it, and to treat it like their own store, it isn't going to work if I constantly butt in."

To involve employees the management of Birkenstock Footprint Sandals Inc., a California-based wholesaler, shares projected sales and profits figures with everyone in the company. "Everyone feels that we are in on what was always a big secret," says Suzanne in the payroll department. "Once we learn what the company-wide goals are, each department works on an action plan on how to achieve those projections."

In addition, Birkenstock believes in paying for productivity. "We look at our location, our industry, and our position," says vice-president Mary Jones. "If there is a job we feel is especially important to us, then we will provide extra compensation." Among those positions considered essential is that of warehouse shipping clerk, and Birkenstock pays above the industry norm for it. "They are our vital link between the company and the customer," Jones explains.

Here are a few case histories of organizations with corporate and social responsibility:

America Works Inc. Dawn, a native of New York's South Bronx, had never been to Wall Street. A single mother to a three-year-old son, she was living at her mother's apartment and relying solely on public assistance. When she went to interview for a secretarial position with a prestigious Wall Street law firm, she didn't know what to expect.

"I was scared," she says. "I had graduated from high school and a business trade school, but when I had my son I couldn't keep up the job. Then, when I was ready, I couldn't find one. I was depressed and anxious."

Then Dawn learned about America Works Inc., a different kind of employment agency. After being placed on a three-month waiting list, she went through its one-week pre-employment session and three-to-five-week business lab. With the company's help, she eventually landed a job as assistant to a lawyer specializing in immigration law.

America Works, with offices in Hartford [Connecticut] and Manhattan, takes in $4 million annually by finding jobs in the private sector for more than 550 welfare recipients each year. Once a match is made, the newly hired employee works on a trial basis for four months. America Works pays a modest hourly wage while billing the employer a somewhat higher figure—depending on the wage for that particular position—to cover wages, benefits, and monitoring expenses. Typically, the cost to employers is about $1 an hour less than ordinary payroll costs. The employee receives reduced welfare benefits.

> *"Helping to provide a job is perhaps the central and most important thing I or society could do for a person."*

If the tryout proves successful, the employee then goes on the company's payroll at its going rate, and the welfare payments stop. If the employee stays on the job for a year, the employer can qualify for a federal tax credit amounting to more than $1,000. And each time an America Works client is fully weaned from welfare, the company charges the state—$4,000 in Connecticut, $5,300 in New York. To illustrate, a recent New York audit found that 80% of the employees are with the same companies after 2½ years.

"For $5,300 we guarantee the state doesn't have to pay $24,000 [the estimated cost of keeping a mother and two children on welfare]," says Peter Cove, founder of the company. He started it in 1985 and now runs it with his wife, sociologist Lee Bowes, who serves as CEO.

A veteran of several nonprofit efforts for the disadvantaged, Cove says: "I learned that . . . helping to provide a job is perhaps the central and most important thing I or society could do for

> *"Business in general can no longer function, and no longer be judged, solely on the basis of nets and grosses."*

a person. I also learned that the majority of people on public assistance would rather be working. And that's what America Works is all about."

Smith & Hawken. From a line of clothing made from cotton unpolluted by pesticides and processing chemicals to a brand of organic coffee grown and harvested by a collective of Mexican farmers, the Smith & Hawken mail-order firm practices what it preaches in a recent Christmas catalog:

"Because gifts we have long taken for granted—air, water, soil, natural and human diversity—are now endangered and need our attention, we try to create products that are restorative, natural, and beneficial to our society on many levels."

Founded in 1979 by Dave Smith and Paul Hawken (founder of the Erewhon natural-foods company in Boston in the 1960s), it now employs about 275 people in a series of old buildings in Santa Rosa and Mill Valley, California. Its products include recycled wrapping paper created by schoolchildren and packaged by disabled workers; silk socks made by former coca farmers in the Colombian Andes; clothing with buttons made of tagua nuts harvested from the Ecuadoran rain forest without destroying the trees; and shirts, jeans, and jackets to be colored with natural indigo dyes instead of toxic aniline substitutes. A portion of pre-tax profits goes to environmental causes.

Newman's Own Inc. These days movie stars are often as well known for their off-screen antics as their on-screen performances. One of the most famous, Paul Newman, is unique because his private-life fame comes partially from racing cars—and partially from his establishment of a multimillion-dollar food company. And partially because Newman's Own Foods—founded in 1982 by the author and his friend, writer A.E. Hotchner—gives away 100% of its pre-tax profits. The private company based in Westport, Connecticut, has donated $48 million to hundreds of charities—while selling more than $60 million in salad dressing, popcorn, lemonade, pasta sauces, and salsa in 1991 alone.

The two friends invested $40,000 to set up the company, with Newman as president, Hotchner as vice-president and treasurer, and the latter's wife, Ursula Hotchner, as second vice-president. To economize they furnished their offices with Newman's poolside furniture and a Ping-Pong table. Many of these furnishings are still used today.

Instead of spending hundreds of thousands of dollars on test-marketing and research—which is customary in the food business—Newman invited friends over for a tasting. Today the company remains lean. Only 10 employees work in the unpretentious headquarters. Goods are produced in 14 North American factories. The company keeps tight control over quality.

Each year Newman and the Hotchners go through thousands of grant requests and, according to Hotchner, "simply give to the neediest." Such recipients include a nun in Florida, who ran a school for the children of migrant farm workers. When her schoolbus broke down, she wrote Newman a letter and soon received a $26,000 check for a new one.

Aspen Skiing Company. Aspen may be best known as the ski resort for the rich and famous, but for more than a decade the former mining town in the heart of the Colorado Rockies has also been at the cutting edge of the environmental movement.

The commitment began in the late '70s, when Aspen Skiing—which operates the ski runs at Aspen Mountain as well as at nearby Buttermilk and Snowmass—started its free bus system for both employees and guests. This removed a large number of cars from the town's narrow streets throughout the winter, greatly diminishing automobile-generated air pollution.

> *"Today's bottom line encompasses more than just dollars and cents."*

During 1989-90 Aspen became the first ski area in the US to initiate an on-mountain recycling program, which created a system for handling all the glass, aluminum, and cardboard that was discarded at its 11 mountainside restaurants.

The program was expanded to recycling motor oil, computer and typewriter ribbons, and plastic toner containers, and purchase of a variety of recycled products such as paper for trail maps, brochures, business cards, letterheads, toilet paper, paper towels, and copy-machine paper.

In 1991 the company installed energy-efficient lighting and water-efficient bath fixtures at its base area and hotels. It also began working with the Pitkin County Waste Recovery Center on an experimental program to compost all waste from its mountain eateries—which quickly cut Aspen Skiing's refuse collection so dramatically that now less than 10% of it goes into the county landfill.

We could give many more examples. As the '90s wear on, it becomes increasingly apparent that business in general can no longer function, and no longer be judged, solely on the basis of nets and grosses. A positive impact on employees, customers, and the community at large has assumed an equal or even greater significance in the overall picture. Today's bottom line encompasses more than just dollars and cents, and corporations of all sizes and philosophical orientations are beginning to recognize this.

Businesses Are Becoming Less Ethical

by Kenneth Labich

About the author: *Kenneth Labich is on the board of editors for* Fortune *magazine.*

As this economic slowdown lingers like some stubborn low-grade infection, managers are putting the heat on subordinates. Many of the old rules no longer seem to apply. Says Gary Edwards, president of the Ethics Resource Center, a consulting firm in Washington: "The message out there is, Reaching objectives is what matters and how you get there isn't that important."

The result has been an eruption of questionable and sometimes plainly criminal behavior throughout corporate America. We are not dealing here so much with the personal greed that propelled Wall Street operators of the Eighties into federal prisons. Today's miscreants are more often motivated by the most basic of instincts—fear of losing their jobs or the necessity to eke out some benefit for their companies. If that means fudging a few sales figures, abusing a competitor, or shortchanging the occasional customer, so be it.

People lower down on the corporate food chain are telling the boss what they think he wants to hear, and outright lying has become a commonplace at many companies. Michael Josephson, a prominent Los Angeles ethicist who consults for some of America's largest public corporations, says his polls reveal that between 20% and 30% of middle managers have written deceptive internal reports.

The Harm Caused by Unethical Behavior

At least part of this is relatively harmless—managers inflating budget proposals in the hope of ultimately getting what they really need, for example. But a good share of it will almost surely hurt the people and the companies involved, in some cases grievously. The U.S. press, broadcast and print, has become increasingly adept at uncovering corporate misdeeds. Witness the frenzy of reports raising questions about Dow Corning's breast implants. The stock of

Corning Inc., one of the two corporate parents of Dow Corning, has declined by about 15% since the scandal erupted, even though the implants represented only around 1% of Dow Corning's revenues and its insurance coverage seems adequate to cover potential litigation.

The Justice Department has become far keener on catching and punishing white-collar criminals since the S&L crisis and the BCCI scandal. In November 1991 tough new sentencing guidelines for corporate crimes went into effect. Warns Josephson: "We are going to see a phenomenal number of business scandals during the 1990s. We are swimming in enough lies to keep the lawyers busy for the next ten years."

> *"The message out there is, Reaching objectives is what matters and how you get there isn't that important."*

The faint sign of good news is that many big U.S. companies have begun to respond to the crisis. According to a survey of *Fortune* 1,000 companies conducted by Bentley College in Boston, over 40% of the respondents are holding ethics workshops and seminars, and about one-third have set up an ethics committee. Some 200 major U.S. corporations have appointed ethics officers, usually senior managers of long experience, to serve as ombudsmen and encourage whistleblowing.

Regrettably, such actions won't put an end to ethical dilemmas—or to the current spree of shoddy practices. Dow Corning had a substantial ethics program in place for 18 years before the breast-implant scandal, but no questions about safety or testing of the implant materials were ever raised to the ethics committee.

The problem, says Kirk Hanson, a Stanford management professor and president of an ethics research group called the Business Enterprise Trust, is extreme pressure to perform. "Quite simply," he says, "the individual who isn't perceived as a top achiever is a candidate for a layoff." Under such circumstances, flirtations with impropriety are hardly surprising.

A Deeply Rooted Problem

Virtually every day we read about the hapless folks who get caught. Citicorp fires the president and senior executives of a credit-card-processing division for allegedly overstating revenues. American Express cans several executives for failing to write off accounts of customers who had filed for bankruptcy, as required by company policy. Alamo Rent A Car agrees to refund $3 million to customers who were overcharged for repair costs to damaged vehicles.

There is clearly quite a bit more iceberg down there. No one knows how many top managers are intentionally overlooking questionable acts because they are paying off. Josephson tells of a bank whose executives one day discovered that a large number of customers had been overbilled for mortgage payments. "There's no doubt what you ought to do in a case like that," says Josephson. "You come clean and you take your hit." That's what the bank eventually did—but only after regulators discovered the error.

Some practices born of competitive excess fall into a kind of gray area. In autumn 1991, Toys "R" Us managers sent employees to rival Child World stores around the country to buy up large quantities of heavily discounted items, which were then resold in their own stores. Misrepresentation? Other acts now taking place clearly cross the line. Gary Edwards tells of one struggling company that placed fake want ads in the hope of luring competitors' employees to job interviews where they might reveal trade secrets. Stanford's Hanson reports that three of his returning students were asked by summer employers to call up competitors and seek information under the guise of doing academic research.

Many top managers desperate for profits have turned to emerging markets overseas, a trend that presents a fresh set of ethical dilemmas. Far too often, a company will send off its team with no directive other than finding new business. Bribery and sloppy accounting may be a fact of business life over there, the customer base may be riddled with questionable characters, and yet the sales force is supposed to find its way with no ethical compass. Mark Pastin, an Arizona State University management professor who has consulted with many companies seeking to go global, suggests that the confusion overseas could later lead to problems at home. Says Pastin: "Don't forget that you eventually are going to reimport those managers. Once they've come back, do you think they're going to put on their old ethics like a new suit?"

> *"[There] has been an eruption of questionable and sometimes plainly criminal behavior throughout corporate America."*

As Pastin notes, ethics begin at home, in the nexus between employer and employee. The recent layoffs at many big companies carry a slew of ethical implications. Many job reductions have clearly been necessary, the result of lousy business. But at least some top managers have axed employees to pump up profits for the short term or impress Wall Street. Says Hanson: "Unfortunately, layoffs have sometimes become a way to buy a multiple." At such companies much of the work load may still be there, while many of the bodies are not. Middle managers end up pressuring the remaining employees to work unconscionable amounts of overtime. What are the ethics of that?

Compensation for top executives has become a hot-button ethical issue during this recession as well, especially at those companies where workers are being fired and the big guys' salaries appear excessive or unrelated to job performance. In such cases the old argument that companies need to bestow grand wealth on chief executives to prevent them from fleeing to a more beneficent competitor seems especially flimsy. The market for the overpaid chiefs of losing or minimally profitable enterprises is not a large one. In effect, the top dogs are isolating themselves—but not their employees—from the brutal realities of the marketplace. The basic injustice involved is obvious.

In tough times it's all the more important to remember that ethics pay off in the end, and on the bottom line. In 1982 James Burke, chief executive of Johnson & Johnson, put together a list of major companies that paid a lot of attention to ethical standards. The market value of the group, which included J&J, Coca-Cola, Gerber, IBM, Deere, Kodak, 3M, Xerox, J.C. Penney, and Pitney Bowes, grew at 11.3% annually from 1950 to 1990. The growth rate for Dow Jones industrials as a whole was 6.2% a year over the same period.

The case is probably easier to make in the negative: Doing the wrong thing can be costly. Under the new federal sentencing guidelines, corporations face mandatory fines that reach into the hundreds of millions for a broad range of crimes—antitrust violations, breaking securities and contract law, fraud, bribery, kickbacks, money laundering, you name it. And that's if just one employee gets caught.

Even if you don't land in court, you might find yourself on the front page or the evening news, which could be worse. In the past few years, most media have given much more coverage to business. Newspapers and magazines all over the U.S. now employ investigative reporters with MBAs and business experience to dig into the affairs of companies. The old advice is still the best: Don't do anything on the job you wouldn't want your mother to read about with her morning coffee.

Moral Rot

Even if a company's slippery practices go undetected, there is still a price to pay. Successful enterprises are inevitably based on a network of trust binding management, employees, shareholders, lenders, suppliers, and customers—akin to the network that Japanese call *keiretsu*. When companies slip into shoddy practices, these crucial relationships start to deteriorate. Says Barbara Ley Toffler, senior partner of a Boston ethics-consulting firm called Resources for Responsible Management: "The effects aren't obvious at first. People may feel bad about what they're doing, but they rationalize it somehow." Eventually a kind of moral rot can set in, turning off employees with higher personal standards and stifling innovation throughout the company. She adds: "People in these situations feel frightened, constrained. They are not in the proper frame of mind to take prudent risks."

"Outright lying has become a commonplace at many companies."

Companies that depend heavily on customer service are especially vulnerable. A company that jacks up prices unfairly, skimps on quality, or beats up on employees can hardly expect its salespeople to treat customers properly. Says Arizona State's Pastin: "You can put on a happy face for only so long before reality intrudes. I don't believe employees can deliver superior service if they don't think their company is

113

treating customers with respect." Ultimately, many of the most effective managers and most productive workers will find a way to work somewhere else. When the economy turns up again, companies with a sorry reputation for ethical behavior will have a harder time attracting top-quality people.

Among the scariest aspects of the current situation, ethicists say, is how unaware many top managers are of what is going on. Michael Josephson, who is usually called in after a company has landed in the headlines, begins by circulating questionnaires among top and middle managers to determine what's happening. More often than not, the CEO expresses shock and disbelief at the results of the anonymous survey. Adds Josephson: "There's very often a sort of 'kill the messenger' attitude, which may have led to some of the problems in the first place."

> *"We are going to see a phenomenal number of business scandals during the 1990s."*

Once the scope of the problem is clear, the next step is to communicate in no uncertain terms what is expected of managers and other employees. Hewlett-Packard, for example, works hard to ensure that all employees are familiar with its extensive standards for business conduct, which cover everything from conflicts of interest and accounting practices to handling confidential information and accepting gratuities. The standards are high; salespeople are instructed to avoid commenting on a competitor's character or business practices, even to refrain from mentioning the fact that a competitor might be facing a lawsuit or government investigation.

Innovative Ways to Promote Ethics

A little innovation helps in getting the message across. Citicorp has developed an ethics board game, which teams of employees use to solve hypothetical quandaries. General Electric employees can tap into specially designed interactive software on their personal computers to get answers to ethical questions. At Texas Instruments, employees are treated to a weekly column on ethics over an international electronic news service. One popular feature: a kind of Dear Abby mailbag, answers provided by the company's ethics officer, Carl Skoogland, that deals with the troublesome issues employees face most often. Managers at Northrop are rated on their ethical behavior by peers and subordinates through anonymous questionnaires.

More and more companies are appointing full-time ethics officers, generally on the corporate vice-presidential level, who report directly to the chairman or an ethics committee of top officers. One of the most effective tools these ethics specialists employ is a hot line through which workers on all levels can register complaints or ask about questionable behavior. At Raytheon Corp., Paul Pullen receives some 100 calls a month. Around 80% involve minor issues that he can resolve on the spot or refer to the human resources department. Another 10% of callers are simply looking for a bit of advice. But about ten times a month, a caller reports some serious ethical lapse that Pullen must address with senior management. Says he: "Most people have high standards, and they want to work in an atmosphere that is ethical. The complaints come from all levels, and they are typical of what you would find in any business: possible conflicts of interest, cheating on timecards, cheating on expense reports."

Some companies have been motivated to set up an ethics office after a spate of unfavorable publicity. Nynex took the step in 1990 following a series of scandals, including revelations of lewd parties in Florida thrown for suppliers by a Nynex executive. Later 56 middle managers were disciplined or discharged for allegedly receiving kickbacks, and the SEC [Securities and Exchange Commission] accused a former unit president of insider trading. The company has since been beating the drum about ethics, but Graydon Wood, Nynex's newly appointed ethics officer, says the job requires a realistic view of human behavior. Says he: "You have to recognize that even with all the best programs, some employees do go wrong. [In 1991] some marketing people didn't report properly, resulting in unjustified commissions. We fired them."

In the current crunch much deception and unethical conduct can be avoided if top managers make sure that the performance goals they set are realistic. Ethicists often cite a classic case that occurred at a GM light-truck plant several years ago. The plant manager got caught with a device in his office that periodically speeded up the line beyond the rate designated in union contracts. Confronted with the evidence, he pointed out that the company's production specifications were based on the line's running at maximum allowable speed 100% of the time. He was simply trying to make up for inevitable down time.

Managers must be sure that what they actually do fosters rather than impedes ethical conduct. One sure way to send the word is by rewarding admirable behavior. No code of ethics and no amount of cajolery by the chief executive will have much effect if promotions regularly go to the people who pile up big numbers by cutting corners. Says Kirk Hanson: "Senior management has got to find a way to create heroes, people who serve the company's competitive values—and also its social and ethical values."

These role models could be especially important for younger employees who are trying to survive in what seems to be an increasingly hostile business environment. Michael Josephson reports some dispiriting news about the start that the new generation are off to. He cites surveys of Americans 18 to 30 years old that show between 70% and 80% cheated in high school and between 40% and 50% cheated in college. And—are you ready for this?—between 12% and 24% say they included false information on their résumés.

Commenting on Americans' ethical standards in the 19th century, Alexis de Tocqueville declared that the nation had become great because it was good. He may have overstated a bit, but in pursuit of profits today we may indeed be losing an element vital to our long-term success tomorrow.

Executives Are Greedy

by Robert J. Samuelson

About the author: *Robert J. Samuelson is a regular columnist for* Newsweek *magazine.*

Don't look to Corporate America for moral leadership. Too many chief executives share the ethics of a welfare cheat. The welfare cheat breaks the law to chisel the government. Well, many a CEO twists company rules to raise his pay—and bilk the company. Welfare cheats probably need the money and grasp their wrongdoing. The CEOs don't need the money and are oblivious to their wrongdoing. Who's more honest?

The result is the great CEO pay boom. Between 1980 and 1990, cash compensation (not including stock options) of CEOs of major U.S. companies rose 156 percent, reports the consulting firm Sibson & Co. Meanwhile, the average compensation of U.S. workers rose 65 percent. A CEO of a big company now makes $1 million to $2 million in annual salary and bonuses. This is 50 to 100 times the pay of the average worker. In Japan, comparable CEOs earn 16 times the average salary, reports pay expert Graef Crystal.

Payouts are even more astounding when stock options are considered. In 1990, Steve Ross, the cochairman of Time Warner, was paid $74.8 million for his options in the merger of Warner Communications and Time Inc. Fair compensation, Ross says, for the value he created at Warner—and then he got new options to replace the ones he just sold. (Options give an executive the right to buy the company's stock at a fixed price. Once the stock exceeds that price, the excess is profit.) Typically, CEOs receive options annually worth 30 to 50 percent of their salaries.

Greed Fosters Discontent

What's wrong here is not the mere bilking of the company: for the firm, the extra payout is fairly small even though it is large for the CEO. (This, of course, is why abuse is widespread and easy.) The real harm is that CEO selfishness undermines U.S. business. To succeed, a company requires a sense of shared commitment among its workers. Instead, the CEO's message is: hey, I got mine. This spawns cynicism and indifference—even among would-be executives—that can hurt a company in dozens of ways from slipshod workmanship to unnecessary costs.

Consider a poll by *Industry Week* magazine of its readers, mainly middle managers. The survey found that 84 percent think U.S. CEOs are overpaid. "Executives should be willing to set examples," one middle manager said. "But instead they take bonuses while their employees lose jobs."

The CEO's great advantage is that he runs his own welfare department.

> *"Too many chief executives share the ethics of a welfare cheat."*

He doesn't have to break the rules, because he makes them. CEO pay is set by friendly boards of directors, usually following the advice of "compensation consultants" hired by the CEO. The consultant's role is to lend "objectivity" to a process that would otherwise seem totally self-serving. The consultants crank up surveys of other CEOs' compensation, and there's enormous pressure to interpret the data to justify higher pay.

"If the CEO wanted more money, and I didn't want to recommend [it] to the board . . . well, there was always a rival compensation consultant who could be hired," writes Crystal, who was a consultant for 20 years, in a new book (*In Search of Excess*). What results is a perpetual motion machine for higher pay. Most CEOs want at least their industry average—and many seek much more.

Watch how this works. Consider five CEOs in the same industry. One is paid $1.5 million annually, three receive $1 million each and the last is paid $500,000. If the CEO making $500,000 thinks he should be paid the average ($1 million), then the average will jump to $1.1 million. Now, the other CEOs will want raises to maintain their previous relative positions. So the average jumps again. We'd all like our pay to be set this way.

Low Mobility

The surveys are bogus. They presume that underpaid CEOs could easily jump to better-paying CEO jobs. Although a few could, most couldn't. First, openings are scarce. Second, many CEOs wouldn't be hired. Some are simply bureaucratic survivors; others have skills that are limited mainly to one company (its workers, customers and products). CEOs are not like baseball players or movie stars who have demonstrable moneymaking powers. Nor are they like engineers or secretaries whose compensation is set by a genuine market process. Higher pay isn't needed to entice people to head big companies. If IBM's chairman resigned tomorrow, plenty of qualified candidates would want the job—even at half the pay.

Boards of directors could bring sanity to this process by dispensing with the silly surveys. Instead, CEOs should submit a pay request that answers four questions:

1. What should you be paid? (If you want to hire a consultant, go ahead—at your expense, not the firm's.)

2. If you left the firm, what could you earn and where?

3. If you died today, who could take your place? (Is she or he well prepared? If not, why not?)

4. What is the lowest compensation you would accept? (Please attach a letter of resignation in case we offer less.)

This way, CEOs would have to put a price tag on their jobs—and risk dismissal if it were too high. They'd also have to face a basic question: have I groomed a successor?

Top executives ought to be well paid for good performance, but today's pay packages don't do that. Most stock options are giveaways that lavishly reward even mediocre performance and supplement excessive cash compensation. One remedy is to convert some of the boss's annual pay into restricted stock: shares that couldn't be sold for a number of years. The CEO's pay would be tied more closely to the company's fortunes, argues Seymour Burchman of Sibson & Co. As the stock rises or falls, so would CEO pay.

> *"The real harm is that CEO selfishness undermines U.S. business."*

"Every field has its abuses," says Bruce Atwater, the CEO of General Mills. His point is that some excesses don't merit branding every CEO a crook. True. But what he won't acknowledge is that most CEOs receive blatant favoritism, and the glaring excesses merely illuminate the system's basic flaws. There's no inclination to correct them. Lobbies like the Business Roundtable oppose steps that would make it easier for dissident shareholders to challenge the clubby ties between directors and CEOs.

This isn't surprising. If you ran the welfare department, would you surrender control? But it bodes ill for U.S. business. Companies increasingly ask sacrifices of their workers. It's hard to expect cooperation when the guy at the top, while preaching sacrifice, isn't practicing it.

Corporations Are Not Socially Responsible

by David Moberg

About the author: *David Moberg is a senior editor for* In These Times, *a liberal periodical of social and political thought and opinion.*

Who could possibly oppose "responsibility" and favor "irresponsibility"? As Lee Iacocca might say, it's a "no-brainer." Politically, it's easy enough to oppose teenagers' dropping out of school, getting pregnant at age 14, and shooting their neighbors randomly.

Responsibility

Yet most current advocates of responsibility who focus on urging the poor to be more upright and less of a problem to the rest of us offer an extremely truncated moral vision. We may reasonably ask people to be responsible—but we need also to explain to them what they should be responsible for, and to whom they should be responsible.

It is necessary but not sufficient for them to follow the laws and to do what they can to take care of themselves. Being responsible means caring about others around you—family, neighbors, fellow workers or anyone else that your actions may affect. It means being socially concerned and accountable, willing to own up to the consequences of one's actions.

If a young man fathers a child, then it is not unreasonable to expect him to support and nurture that child. There is little argument about that proposition. Yet if a corporate executive makes a decision to close an inner-city factory—a move that will make it more difficult for many young men to support their children—he is likely to be applauded as a wizard of corporate restructuring and rewarded with bonuses of millions of dollars. If he can get the same work done in Mexico for one-tenth the labor cost, he's simply a shrewd businessman.

Who will denounce him as irresponsible? In the Candidean world of free-market economics, his pursuit of narrow self-interest ultimately produces pub-

David Moberg, "Suite Crimes," *In These Times*, December 12, 1993. Reprinted with permission. *In These Times* is a weekly newspaper published in Chicago.

lic good. Why not see the runaway father's narrow self-interest in the same entrepreneurial light?

The rampant irresponsibility of many individual Americans is largely the product of a culture dominated by corporations that are themselves systematically irresponsible, except to their shareholders—and often not even [responsible] to them. Capitalism of yore assumed that the owner of a business was in some sense responsible for that enterprise, even if his power was used ruthlessly and

> *"Corporations . . . are themselves systematically irresponsible, except to their shareholders."*

against the social good. Now most owners have a distant, contingent and often fleeting relationship to the corporation—as blocks of stocks, options on stocks, or even financial futures based on the stock market are rapidly, incessantly traded. These investors don't want to take responsibility for business even in the conventional capitalist sense.

America has always been an extremely individualistic society, but the individualism of the yeoman farmer or mechanic assumed a vision of a relatively egalitarian, democratic society resting on a base of hardworking, independent producers. In practice, there were also many forms of cooperation and mutual support. The contemporary consumerist culture—built up over the past century with credit, advertising, assiduous marketing and the creation of identities through purchases—breeds a much narrower, self-obsessed individualism. At most, the consumer's responsibility is to pay the minimum balance on the credit card bill.

Irresponsibility at the Top

The general culture reflects the irresponsibility at the top. In terms of values, it is not clear that much of the middle and upper middle class is so much more morally responsible than the poor. Is profiting from the revolving door between business and government morally superior to resorting to welfare?

Members of the upper middle class have more opportunities and more money, but that is not entirely a result of their being more responsible. Likewise, the limitations placed on the poor are not all a result of their being irresponsible. If there is proportionately more social irresponsibility among the poor—and given that charitable giving as a percentage of income tends to be greater among the poor, that's not immediately evident—we can find it simultaneously understandable, unfortunate, undesirable and inexcusable.

The gross irresponsibilities of some of the poor—especially street crimes—are more immediate and comprehensible menaces than the suite crimes of some corporate executives. In both cases, it is possible to explain the actions of individuals in large part by looking at the social and economic forces that shape their lives—and still expect them as citizens and moral agents to take responsi-

Ethics

bility for what they do with their lives. But, unlike the irresponsible poor, the executive or owner of a corporation often can escape legal responsibility for his actions, hiding behind the corporate shield.

If we really want to make people more responsible, we must start with the most powerful influences on society. In recent years, we've witnessed auto companies calculate the cost of lost lives from their faulty cars and decide it's cheaper to kill innocent people than to redesign their vehicles. We've seen a pharmaceutical company market a drug for animals to humans and jack up the price a hundredfold. Corporations, often with taxpayer assistance, have closed plants and fled overseas to politically repressive regimes. Though workers have the legal right to organize and act collectively, corporations typically do everything they can—including breaking the law—to crush the faintest sign of workplace democracy.

Three-fourths of manufacturers in 1991 made no effort to prevent pollution and reduce toxic chemical usage, according to a recent study of toxic waste releases by the Citizens Fund, the research arm of Citizen Action. "Companies talk a good game about preventing pollution," Citizen Action environmental director Ed Hopkins says, "but when it comes to actually doing something, pitifully few take any responsible action."

Corporate irresponsibility has its immediate harms—unsafe or unaffordable products, dangerous or alienated work environments, unemployment and growing inequality, ravaged urban centers, widespread pollution. Yet it also sets the tenor for society: political democracy is deeply corrupted and the idea of a social compact becomes laughable. Why should workers be responsible when their bosses aren't? Why should the poor be responsible when their legislative representatives aren't?

> *"We've witnessed auto companies calculate the cost of lost lives from their faulty cars and decide it's cheaper to kill innocent people than to redesign their vehicles."*

A Social Covenant

When Bill Clinton began campaigning, he talked about the need for a new social covenant, about responsibility from corporations as well as from workers and welfare recipients. But in office, the Clinton administration has shown little stomach for demanding corporate responsibility. True, taxes on the rich were raised. But the revenue from those tax hikes was committed to reducing the debt and making the bond traders happy, not to public investments that might lead to jobs.

Clinton did not lay the groundwork for a social covenant when his administration negotiated a labor side agreement to NAFTA [North American Free Trade Agreement] that did not protect the right to organize unions. Citizens were not encouraged to assume more responsibility when Clinton's Environmental Protection Agency permitted the operation of a hazardous waste inciner-ator near a school and homes in East Liverpool, Ohio, even after it had failed government tests.

Corporate Rights Must Be Restricted

Writers Richard L. Grossman and Frank T. Adams, advocates for both the en-vironment and workers, argue that Americans must resurrect an old political tradition to insure greater corporate responsibility. In a recent pamphlet entitled "Taking Care of Business: Citizenship and the Charter of Incorporation," Grossman and Adams observe that corporations operate on the basis of charters that are granted by state governments. In the early 19th century, citizens de-manded strict definitions of charters. These terms included limits on the length of a charter and clauses reserving the right to revoke it. There was widespread distrust of corporations, which were seen as threats to democracy and to work-ing people.

During the late 19th century, as corporations increased their influence over state legislatures, the states "gave corporations limited liability, decreased citi-zen authority over corporate structure, governance, production and labor, and ever longer terms for the charters themselves," Grossman and Adams observe.

Far worse, the courts began to expand corporate privileges: judges gave some corporations the right to take private property with minimal compensation. Courts also eliminated jury trials to determine harm and damages from corpo-rate actions. And through the doctrine of "the right to contract," judges stripped legislatures of much of their powers over corporations. Moreover, the courts re-duced corporate liability, and the liability of individual corporate officers, and gave management the power to stop civil rights at the plant gate.

In 1886, the Supreme Court ruled that a private corporation was a natural per-son with the same rights as an individual under the Bill of Rights or the 14th Amendment, which guarantees due process under law. Courts began to rule that many laws took corporate property without due process, a line of argument re-cently expanded by the free market "law and economics" ideologists. They ar-gue that virtually any federal social or regulatory legislation, including most of the New Deal and its legacy, represents unlawful "takings" of pri-vate property.

"Corporate irresponsibility . . . sets the tenor for society: political democracy is deeply corrupted and the idea of a social compact becomes laughable."

Grossman and Adams argue for a new movement to challenge the charters of corporations that have demonstrated social irresponsibility. Community groups have in recent years used bank charter laws and, in particu-lar, the provisions of the Community Reinvestment Act, to challenge the expan-sion plans of banks that have miserable lending records to minorities and poor neighborhoods.

Despite some remaining state charter laws that open interesting political opportunities, Grossman and Adams' idea would be best pursued by demanding national chartering of corporations. More than a decade ago, Ralph Nader promoted a Corporate Democracy Act as part of such national chartering. Corporations, he argued, should be forced to abide by broad responsibilities to workers, communities, the environment and to the well-being of the national economy if they are to be entitled to any privileges—including the right to exist.

Greater corporate social responsibility is essential for any significant increase of individual responsibility to society. Contrary to the holy text of irresponsible competition, both the experience of many successful national economies and recent theoretical work even in economics demonstrate that cooperation and social responsibility can improve national economic performance. If there is a growing clamor for more personal responsibility, then reasserting society's power to create and control corporations is the responsible move to make.

Chapter 4

Do Ethical Business Practices Benefit Society?

Chapter Preface

Throughout America's history, many American companies have paid little formal attention to how ethics might affect their day-to-day business. For most businesses, profit has traditionally been the primary goal. Ethics has largely been considered appropriate for individuals and scholars, but not for money-making ventures.

Although profit is still the main goal of most companies, many business leaders have begun to consider the role ethics plays in business. Companies are incorporating ethics into their policies in a variety of ways. Many donate a portion of company profits to charitable causes. Others, such as Lotus, AT&T, and Olivetti, make socially responsible investments—for example, investments that benefit the environment, or promote peace. Still others offer courses in ethics to their employees. As journalist James Srodes writes, "Ethics has become big business. Universities are racing to set up ethics courses the way they once vied for rocket scientists. Big Eight accounting firms, trade associations, the Business Roundtable and the Conference Board all offer competing boxed sets of ethical commandments and credos." Srodes estimates that more than two thousand American corporations have drafted ethics codes for their employees.

Most critics applaud these measures and believe that applying ethics to business benefits everyone: corporations, their employees, and their clients. For example, a waste-reduction program introduced by Northrop benefited the environment and saved the company $20 million in hauling, disposal, and raw material costs over three years. Douglas Ades, cofounder of the Beacon Fund for Human Service Enterprises, a socially minded investment firm, reflects the attitude of many ethically oriented businesspeople: "What we're attempting to do is hold together two seemingly but not necessarily contradictory principles: that you can do well financially and do good socially."

But some critics are skeptical of the new relationship between ethics and business. Corporations may donate to charities or be "ethical" in other ways simply to improve a tainted reputation. For example, environmentalist Jack Doyle cites Du Pont as an example of a company that has attempted to improve its public image by portraying itself in commercials as an ethical, environmentally aware corporation. According to Doyle, Du Pont is in reality the single largest corporate polluter in the United States. Cases such as this make some critics fear that companies will use ethics as a front to hide harmful actions.

Many businesses today are changing their policies and practices to reflect higher ethical standards. The authors in the following chapter evaluate how businesses are introducing ethics into their companies, and whether these changes benefit or harm corporations, employees, and consumers.

Ethical Business Practices Strengthen the Economy

by Dexter F. Baker

About the author: *Dexter F. Baker is chairman of the executive committee of the board of directors of Air Products and Chemicals, Inc., a company that produces industrial gases, chemicals, and equipment.*

If America is to lead the world in a resurgence of economic growth, the business foundation upon which that future must be built is a commitment to ethical conduct. . . .

If we are to be a leader in the 21st Century, then those responsible for our nation's business firms upon which the national economic well-being depends must be dedicated to insure that their stewardship of American enterprise is based upon a strong sense of ethical and moral values. . . .

Competition for Supremacy

The competition of the 1990s and beyond will not be over ideologies. We have won that war. The competition now is for supremacy in the global marketplace. Those companies, industries, and nations who invest the most, who best train and educate their work forces, who commit themselves to create, produce, and market quality products through the world, will be the leaders in the 21st Century.

Government leaders, business leaders, and community leaders must constantly remind ourselves that each of us is held accountable to a higher authority to conduct our affairs in an ethical and moral way. Each day we are tempted to take short cuts and to compromise our moral and ethical standards either through expediency or the promise of some economic or political gain.

I believe we in the business community as stewards of our nation's wealth-creating processes have a special responsibility to ensure that the value systems upon which our business operates are based upon the highest ethical standard we can conceive. The economic well-being of our nation depends upon it.

From Dexter F. Baker's speech "Ethical Issues and Decision Making in Business," *Vital Speeches of the Day*, January 15, 1993. Reprinted by permission of the author.

Webster says ethics is about dealing with good and bad, with moral duty and obligation. A system of moral values. Principles of conduct that govern our daily decisions.

That's pretty basic and down to earth—moral values, principles of conduct that help mold our judgments, and guide our decisions.

As I recall, back in the late '40s and early '50s, when I was in college, I did not spend much time thinking about moral judgments. I did think a lot about getting a good job that offered strong career opportunities. I believe I probably took ethics for granted in my day also.

> *"Each of us is held accountable to a higher authority to conduct our affairs in an ethical and moral way."*

But now, with almost 40 years of valuable hindsight, I truly believe that students yesterday, or today, or tomorrow would be well served by a clear understanding of the super-critical role that a strong character plays in any individual's ultimate success regardless of his or her career choice.

Based on my experience in the business world, I would urge you to accept as gospel that the strength of your character, which feeds the quality of your judgment, is openly displayed day in and day out via the ethical values you live by in your business and in your personal lives. The quality and consistency of your ethical practices will play a major role in determining the level of professional or business success you ultimately attain.

You cannot be one kind of person at work or play and a different kind of person at home or in church. Your consistent adherence to high ethical standards in business and in private life will help secure for you the firmest foundation for success—your self-respect and the key to the Kingdom of God.

The CEO Sets the Tone

I believe it is the responsibility of the chief executive of a corporation or any organization to set the moral and ethical tone of the organization. If he or she is firmly determined to conduct the business of the organization on the highest possible ethical standards, others will follow because that is what is expected of all employees.

On the other hand, if half truths are tolerated, gift-taking and -giving accepted, less than top-quality products supplied, less than safe operations permitted, a sloppy environmental performance tolerated, then that will become the corporation style and standard.

Emerson once wrote, "What you are stands over you the while and thunders so that I cannot hear what you say to the contrary." It follows that, "If you would not be known to do anything immoral, then never do it." In other words, our "actions speak louder than our sayings."

At every level in any organization, almost no day, certainly no week, passes free of the responsibility of thinking through and applying ethical judgments in ways that promote or protect the character of our company or the well-being of our people and those we serve in the external world.

Real issues that we in business face every day [include]:

• How we treat people, employees, applicants, customers, shareholders, and the folks who live near our facilities.

• Are we free of systemic, or individual, practices of discrimination?

• How do we spend our shareholders' money on our expense accounts as an institution and as individuals?

• What is the level of quality that goes into our products—do we meet our customers' expectations for quality? Do we meet our own high standard for our products?

• What is our concern for safety, not only of our employees, but also our customers and our neighbors in communities in which we operate?

• How ethically do we compete?

• How well do we adhere to the laws of the locales, regions, and nations in which we do business?

• How ethically do we work with governments?

• What is acceptable gift-giving and gift-taking?

• How honest are our communications to our employees and our public advertising?

• What are our corporate and personal positions on public policy issues and how do we promote those positions?

And the list goes on. But hopefully my point is clear—taking actions or making decisions, large and small, based at least in part on ethical grounds, is a way of life for any successful businessman or -woman. And the quality of the ethics applied will in the short and long term impact the success of the institution and individuals involved.

> *"It is the responsibility of the chief executive . . . to set the moral and ethical tone of the organization."*

It is my belief that ethical judgments are based in part on instinct, learned values, and experience. I am convinced that the practice of ethical values requires consistent and frequent exercise, just as our bodies require regular and relevant exercise and just as hitting that little white ball takes a lot of practice. . . .

Beware a Soft Backbone

When we start to shave or compromise our ethical standards, our backbone of conviction that allows most of us to make quality judgments, well, that backbone begins to soften. Do not let that happen to you.

Practice in ways that strengthen your character and stiffen that backbone you rely on when you face situations which call for sound ethical judgment. Make those tough choices with a full recognition of the ethical standards by which you want others to remember you.

Furthermore, sound ethical standards is not just a pious way to conduct one's affairs, it is also the most remunerative in the long run. Nobody likes doing business with a sharpie, a corner cutter, someone you just can't trust, to deliver quality products and services, honestly priced, all the time. The world is rapidly dividing into two parts—those who believe in and produce quality products and services based upon sound ethical values—and those who do not. Those who do practice high ethical standards will eventually only deal with other like-minded firms, organizations, and individuals. All others will have to do business with the sharpies.

Ethical Business Practices Can Help the Environment

by Fred Krupp

About the author: *Fred Krupp is the executive director of the Environmental Defense Fund, a nonprofit education and advocacy organization that seeks solutions to a wide range of environmental and public health problems.*

Management expert Peter Drucker once wrote that there were only two basic functions of business—innovation and marketing.

Drucker's observation . . . sums up for me the environmental challenge for American business in the years to come. Innovation and marketing good products are the keys to developing the new approaches we need to solve our toughest environmental problems.

These new approaches would rely on market incentives to help solve problems which threaten the long-term survival of our planet. Instead of using heavy-handed regulations with detailed and restrictive mandates, market-based approaches would give businesses the incentives and opportunities to develop the actual technology or process innovations.

Innovation and Marketing

We would have business, in other words, do what it does best—innovate and market.

But we would hold business more accountable to achieve fundamental innovations and improvements—not just superficial marketing tie-ins with environmental organizations, or sham "green" products. We need the active, serious, full engagement of business to meet the challenge of survival.

Let me describe for you some of those challenges:

- In the 1970s and 1980s, we added 1.6 billion people to the world's population. An increase of nearly a billion more people is in store during the 1990s—with huge new demands on our natural resources.
- Untold thousands of species of plants and animals have become extinct.

From Fred Krupp's speech "Business and the Third Wave," *Vital Speeches of the Day*, August 15, 1992. Reprinted by permission of the author.

They no longer exist. Like the canaries used to detect poisonous gases in coal mines, these dying species are trying to tell us something.

- The ozone layer which protects us and all life forms from the sun's damaging ultraviolet radiation is now developing vast holes over populated areas of the Northern Hemisphere, not just at the North Pole.
- Finally, the excessive production of greenhouse gases by burning fossil fuels promises global warming with profound implications for our survival.

Not Doing Enough

These and many other losses tell us that we cannot continue business as usual without endangering our very survival on earth. They have demonstrated both our power to alter nature, and our carelessness.

As that great social critic, Pogo Possum, summed it up a few years ago, "We have met the enemy, and they is us." The science fiction future of a dying planet is no longer that unthinkable.

Further, these losses are noteworthy because they happened during two decades of major efforts to protect our environment.

They show that what we have done has not been enough. The damage our world is sustaining is stark testimony to the fact that you and I—all of us—are simply not doing enough to ensure our survival.

But more important, these losses tell us that the answer is not just more of the same. The tasks we face are so immense, the challenges so huge, that business, government, and environmentalists cannot continue to work against each other anymore.

We need instead to embark on what I call the Third Wave of Environmentalism. This Third Wave would use market forces to set up price signals on the playing field with the difference to construct an economy that provides prosperity without environmental degradation. It would build on the two earlier waves which have accomplished so much.

The First Wave of Environmentalism was the Conservation Movement, which began at the turn of the century under the leadership of President Theodore Roosevelt. He saw the necessity of protecting vast tracts of lands as national parks and forests, preserving them for their natural beauty and useful resources.

> *"We need the active, serious, full engagement of business to meet the challenge of survival."*

The Second Wave of Environmentalism began in the 1960s with a surge of citizen activism to protect the environment, which created the impetus to adopt new laws to reduce pollution and protect natural resources. Awakened by the voice of Rachel Carson, people realized not just Yellowstone, but the environment in their own backyard, was at risk.

The Clean Air Act, Clean Water Act, and a host of others became law during the 1960s and '70s, with governments at all levels establishing large environmental agencies to enforce them.

Litigation by environmental organizations and individuals became a key part of this Second Wave. Courts stepped in to enforce laws when executive agencies or legislatures were slow to respond to critical problems.

The Environmental Defense Fund (EDF) was part of that Second Wave. We began in 1967 at a living room gathering of citizens concerned about DDT [an insecticide] use on Long Island, which had virtually stilled reproduction of the osprey. We've since grown to include a staff of over 130, including scientists and economists, lawyers and engineers, supported by over 200,000 members, and an annual budget of some $18 million.

The Necessity for a Third Wave

The progress made by this Second Wave is undeniable, and we have much to show for three decades of environmental regulation.

But the challenges which remain require new approaches which can come only from a Third Wave of Environmentalism.

These challenges call on us to raise our sights to attack global environmental problems with solutions which are truly global in scale. Only with worldwide programs to alter some of our most basic consumer products and industrial processes can we expect to slow down and ultimately

> *"We cannot continue business as usual without endangering our very survival on earth."*

reverse the damage already done. And while we have already taken steps to eliminate such problems as the use of ozone-destroying chemicals by the United States and many industrial nations, we must have a coordinated effort by all nations to produce the needed results.

We cannot stand by and do nothing while developing nations make the same mistakes we have made to raise living standards. We need only to look at the wholesale poisoning of the land, water and air of Eastern Europe and former Soviet Union to see what the future holds if developing nations industrialize without regard to the environmental costs.

In short, there has never been a greater challenge to the ingenuity, wisdom and spirit of humanity than today.

Not the least of our challenges is the notion that we must choose between efficiency and environmental protection.

A typical statement of this notion comes from Charles DiBona, president of the American Petroleum Institute. In a recent speech, he criticized new environmental regulations as "stupid" and declared,

> There may have been times in the past when U.S. economic supremacy allowed this country to indulge in costly, inefficient diversions, but there won't be such times in the highly competitive world that lies ahead.

DiBona continued, "Inefficient regulation does hurt U.S. industries and working people. Plants will be driven elsewhere. Good jobs will be harder to come by."

This refrain will sound familiar to veterans of the environmental movement— and it may appeal to more people than usual during this recession. But it has no more validity today than it did decades ago.

The factories of Eastern Europe didn't pollute because they were efficient. They were grossly inefficient.

> *"The science fiction future of a dying planet is no longer that unthinkable."*

If U.S. environmental regulations are a competitive burden, then why have so many foreign manufacturers built an unprecedented number of new factories and other facilities here in the last two decades?

These new foreign-owned factories in America produce everything from chemicals and computers to automobiles and tires. They comply with the same environmental regulations—the so-called "inefficient diversions" Mr. DiBona complains about. Yet these foreign-owned factories often out-produce and out-compete U.S. firms.

Vexed by a Lack of Imagination

The plain truth is that pollution is the most visible sign of inefficiency and waste and short-sighted management. Our main competitive handicap is not environmental regulations—it's a lack of imagination.

In turn, our real competitive opportunity is not to subordinate environmental goals but to fuse them with our drive for a more efficient, more prosperous, and less polluting economy. That is why Japan has a 21st century plan to produce new products the world will need to answer the global warming challenge.

That requires business to change, but also for our regulatory approach to change. In many cases, we have reached the point of diminishing returns in the use of rigid mandates for specific anti-pollution technologies, which is the way many regulations have been.

We cannot regulate our way out of every environmental problem; we have to innovate our way out—and that innovation has to come from the marketplace.

To the environmental ethic we must add the entrepreneurial spirit. To harness that spirit will take finding and using the power of economic incentives.

At a time when one centralized economy after another has collapsed in Eastern Europe and the former Soviet Union—and these nations are seeking to establish market economies—we must make a similar effort to adapt market solutions to environmental problems.

Entrepreneurial Spirit

I liken the current challenge to what took place at the turn of the century, when we developed the first automobile efficient and economical enough for average Americans to own one.

There was no central laboratory that produced such a car. Instead there were literally a thousand small shops around the country experimenting with a myriad of different ways to design and build a practical automobile. Henry Ford was one of them, and he went on to produce the first mass-market automobile. He and other pioneers provided the entrepreneurial spirit and talent similar to what we need today to find the best solutions to our global pollution problems.

That's the kind of spirit and talent we need today. From everyone involved in environmental issues, we need a positive vision and constructive spirit.

Environmentalists must recognize that, behind the waste dumps and dams and power plants and pesticides that we oppose, there are legitimate social needs—and that long-term solutions depend on more than just confrontation. Environmentalists can and should help to find alternatives which are both efficient and effective.

And businesses must look beyond quarterly earnings reports to appreciate how they add to our global problems—and how they can solve them efficiently.

True efficiency, after all, is productive economic activity without waste and pollution. And true innovation requires us to think positively about how we can meet legitimate needs and sustain life on earth.

McDonald's Success

The Environmental Defense Fund used such an approach recently with the McDonald's Corporation to reduce the amount of materials used and solid waste generated, and to provide a model for other fast-food companies. With that goal in mind, we approached McDonald's and formed a joint effort of McDonald's executives and EDF solid waste experts.

McDonald's allowed our experts unprecedented access to its internal operations. We paid our own expenses, by the way, and accepted no compensation from McDonald's, not even a free burger. The result was a plan which can reduce solid waste by 80 percent, with gains that include new efficiencies and cost savings.

With over half its business in take-out, McDonald's realized that attempting to recycle polystyrene might have sounded environmental, but would not have been environmentally sound.

> *"The plain truth is that pollution is the most visible sign of inefficiency and waste and short-sighted management."*

Simply by replacing its Styrofoam "clamshell" box with new paper wrapping for burgers and sandwiches, McDonald's found it retains heat better, weighs less, and costs less.

The plan includes innovations in the areas of source reduction, re-use, recycling, and composting. McDonald's will re-use its shipping containers, try starch-based cutlery to replace plastic, use unbleached and recycled paper products, and experiment with composting food scraps. It will also lean on its suppliers to use recycled paper and come up with further reductions.

This effort to reduce McDonald's solid waste by 80 percent not only has great symbolic value, it is a major advance in itself. On any given day 18 million Americans eat at a McDonald's—1 out of every 14 Americans.

> *"To the environmental ethic we must add the entrepreneurial spirit."*

McDonald's has not only reduced its waste, it has helped create new markets for recycled goods. Paper products they recycle are turned into corrugated cardboard to use again, closing the garbage loop.

The McDonald's experience also provided some lessons.

First, it shows how a genuine effort to improve products, and only a genuine effort, can yield results. There are all-too-many examples of clever but insincere new or repackaged products. One example is the supposedly disposable diaper that could be composted as "soil enhancers"—which in reality includes small bits of plastic. It is a little like selling Astroturf for cattle feed.

The second lesson is people are much more sophisticated about products than ever before. That's partly because people are better educated today. And because the news media are better at discerning between the hokey product and the genuine article.

What Good Managers Can Do

The third lesson is that businesses which come up with innovative environmental solutions are also the best managed companies. Good managers can figure out how to save or even make money while meeting environmental goals. One recent example is the computer equipment manufacturer who switched from plastic foam cushioning to ship his products. By using repulped newsprint, much like paper egg cartons, he not only recycled waste paper, he cut the cost of packaging by two-thirds.

Businesses that reduce waste, conserve energy, and cause less pollution also tend to be the most profitable and successful in the long term. No wonder McDonald's is one of the most admired and profitable companies in the world.

There is another Third-Wave effort that I want to describe—the use of air pollution offsets to reduce power plant emissions. These will help reduce by half the total output by power plants of sulfur dioxide, the main precursor of acid rain.

Incidentally, I remember what Senator Ed Muskie said in the 1970s when utility officials proposed to reduce pollution by what they called "intermittent controls," which consisted of waiting until a good wind comes along, then blowing pollution out a tall smokestack. Muskie called this "the rhythm method of pollution control."

The Environmental Defense Fund broke a ten-year stalemate by developing an approach using tradeable air emission permits. We got the White House to support the proposal, and it became law in 1990—the toughest Clean Air Law in our history. It accomplishes deep reductions in pollution by creating new market incentives to stimulate innovative air pollution abatement methods.

Under this new system, regulators tell power companies to cut emissions in half. Pollution-monitoring equipment on each smokestack will measure the emissions continuously.

The companies are free to reduce emissions to the allowed level however they want to, as long as they meet local air quality standards. The technical solution is up to them. If they reduce emissions below the required level, they can sell their extra reductions to other power plants which need credits to meet requirements.

The sellers thus have the financial incentive to aggressively reduce emissions far below the allowable level. The buyers have a similar incentive to reduce emissions as much as possible to reduce the amount of credits they need to buy.

This is a dramatic improvement over the conventional regulatory schemes which specify what technology to use, and provide no reward for doing better than prescribed levels, and thus discouraging what might be more promising innovations.

Environmental Innovations

The new market incentives have already inspired dozens of entrepreneurial inventors to develop new, cheaper ways to remove sulfur emissions. The chairman of Pacific Gas & Electric, Dick Clarke, reports that when Congress was expected to dictate a single solution—scrubbers—no one had an incentive to develop other ways. But now entrepreneurs both inside and out of the company are rushing to find new ways to lower sulfur dioxide emissions.

The new technology that comes from this can be marketed to other utilities, other industries—even other countries—all the while making PG&E more profitable and the United States more competitive.

These two examples of EDF's working with companies and using market incentives to solve these pollution problems—helping McDonald's reduce solid waste, and reducing power plant emissions with tradeable credits—are but two examples of a growing and much-needed Third Wave of Environmentalism.

> *"Businesses must look beyond quarterly earnings reports to appreciate how they add to our global problems."*

Let me suggest another application for market incentives—to wean ourselves from coal and oil to produce less carbon dioxide and thus reduce the threat of global warming....

Scientists advising the United Nations predict that the present buildup of greenhouse gases will increase the earth's average surface temperature by three to eight degrees Fahrenheit by the end of the next century. The results would be ecological catastrophe—rising sea levels, a shift in agricultural zones, and more disruptive droughts.

To reverse the buildup of greenhouse gases in our atmosphere, we need to get investors and entrepreneurs stimulated to develop new, lower-cost, alternative energy technologies. And the emphasis must be on lowering the costs, otherwise the challenge will not be met.

An international CO_2 offset system could also provide an exchange of funds by which industrial nations could pay such countries as Brazil to preserve their tropical rain forests as global sponges for carbon dioxide.

The use of tradeable permits could be expanded, as well, to a whole range of industrial and commercial enterprises—allowing them to come up with new combinations of pollution reduction, energy conservation, and alternative energy sources.

I've provided these examples to illustrate an approach—not to claim the ultimate wisdom of the Environmental Defense Fund. We don't have all the answers.

That's the great promise of the Third-Wave approach—to push decision-making and innovation down to the ground level—to decentralize and stimulate innovation.

The Third Wave I have outlined offers us tremendous new opportunities to solve some of our most intractable pollution and energy problems.

They do not take the place of the successful applications of Second-Wave regulations and litigation. There are still chemicals like CFCs [chemicals widely used in manufac-

> *"We must have solutions which reconcile environmental imperatives with economic needs."*

turing that are believed to cause stratospheric ozone depletion] we must ban outright, just as we banned DDT a generation ago.

For our part, the Environmental Defense Fund will continue to sue governments which fail to enforce laws. We will continue to promote new, higher regulatory standards where they make sense. All of us must continue to press for strict regulation of pollution and conservation of our natural resources.

In fact, we do not see the Third Wave as a repudiation of the progress made by regulations in the Second Wave—any more than the regulatory actions of the 1960s and '70s were a repudiation of the First Wave of the Conservation Movement.

We are simply recognizing that the market offers us powerful new tools to harness an entrepreneurial spirit that has long distinguished us as a nation.

Environmental vs. Economic Needs

If we are to succeed in saving our planet—and we are degrading it at an accelerating rate—we must have solutions which reconcile environmental imperatives with economic needs.

We are all in this together, and we must all take part in the solutions.

Adlai Stevenson years ago said something which provides me new meaning and inspiration each time I read it. I can't think of a better way to express the urgency and importance of our work as environmentalists. He said,

> We travel together, passengers on a little spaceship, dependent on its vulnerable reserves of air and soil; all committed for our safety to its security and peace; preserved from annihilation only by the care, the work and, I will say, the love we give our fragile craft.

I think we can do this, and I call on you to join in this Third Wave of innovation today. It is our opportunity to become architects of the future, not just critics of the past—to have a positive vision of what we are capable of doing to overcome these challenges.

Socially Responsible Investing Benefits Society

by James B. Goodno

About the author: *James B. Goodno is a staff editor for* Dollars & Sense, *a magazine of liberal economic and political opinion.*

Like other financial institutions, Chicago's South Shore Bank takes deposits and offers loans. But SSB is a bank with a difference: It places social concern before maximum profits. Since its founding in 1974, SSB has issued about $175 million in loans to business and homeowners in Chicago's depressed and mainly black South Shore and Austin neighborhoods, areas traditional lenders avoid.

SSB is one of the most visible achievements of a growing movement of socially responsible investors. An increasing number of Americans are breaking ranks with Wall Street's avaricious business practices to invest in what Ben & Jerry's pop philosophers have dubbed "caring capitalism." According to Joan Kanavich, associate director of the Social Investment Forum, a Minneapolis-based trade organization, the volume of socially responsible investments (SRI) grew from $40 billion in 1984 to $625 billion in 1992.

"People recognize that economic activity needs ethical, moral, and human dimensions," says Ritchie Lowrie, a sociology professor at Boston College and publisher of *Good Money*, a social-investment newsletter. "Take out the human dimension and you're left with a hollow shell."

Ethics and Social Change

For centuries, many religious groups practiced an older form of SRI, shunning the "sin trades" of tobacco, alcohol, and gambling. Foes of the Vietnam War gave birth to its modern equivalent, establishing mutual funds that avoided the armaments industry and organizing shareholders to fight distasteful corporate behavior. Today, SRI reflects familiar activist concerns: opposition to apartheid, nuclear weapons, and atomic power; support for the environment, workplace democracy, and minorities' and women's rights.

James B. Goodno, "Caring Capitalism," *Dollars & Sense*, January/February 1992. *Dollars & Sense* is a progressive economics magazine published ten times a year. First-year subscriptions cost $16.95 and may be ordered by writing *Dollars & Sense*, One Summer St., Somerville, MA 02143 or by calling 617-628-2025.

SRI now encompasses three forms of investing. Lowrie categorizes them as ethical, alternative, and social investing:

- *Ethical investors* direct their investments away from companies involved in unacceptable practices. They practice the least political form of SRI.
- *Alternative investors* purposefully put their money into underfunded and socially useful activities, like low-income housing and businesses situated in poor communities. Alternative investors started SSB.
- *Social investors* play a more active political role in "their" companies, frequently working together to raise issues of concern with the board, other shareholders, and con-sumers. To do so, they might own shares in companies ethical investors shun.

> *"Investments made by public and private institutions provide people without money an opportunity to use [socially responsible investments] as a political weapon."*

SRI's most influential players are institutions—state, county, and local governments, churches, pension funds, and some universities. Government entities account for more than $400 billion of socially screened investment; other institutions add another $100 billion. [Before apartheid was abolished], these institutions screened virtually all of their money to eliminate investment linked to South Africa. Many institutional investors apply other screens as well. Some pension funds, for example, rule out anti-labor firms, and a few city governments refuse to invest in Northern Ireland.

Investments made by public and private institutions provide people without money an opportunity to use SRI as a political weapon. As Robert Zevin, a Boston banker who helped found SSB, points out, activists can urge their unions, universities, and local governments to screen investments and join corporate campaigns. In fact, he suggests that by influencing institutional investors, citizens, union members, and students can have more impact than more prominent individual investors.

Individual investors can choose from a variety of socially responsible mutual funds, money market accounts, and investment advisers. Investment houses like the Calvert Group, Progressive Asset Management, and the Pax World Fund offer various multi-purpose and environmentally oriented funds. New York's Interfaith Center for Corporate Responsibility manages $30 million for activist "social investors." And with SRI's increasing popularity, many mainstream investment houses—such as Merrill Lynch, Dreyfus, and Prudential/Bache—have developed SRI funds despite professional skepticism about the profitability of bringing social concerns to financial markets.

How Does SRI Perform?

SRI's industry critics make a simple point: Applying social standards to corporations and to investment precludes participation by socially responsible investors in some of the most profitable investments. While this is true, well-managed socially responsible portfolios actually perform as well as, and sometimes better, than their unscreened counterparts. For example, the Pax World Fund performed better than any other balanced-growth fund between 1985 and 1990. The Calvert-Ariel Growth Fund earned close to 3% more than the average small growth fund in 1989, and the Calvert and Working Assets Money Market funds performed only slightly below the average of 275 similar unscreened funds during the year starting June 30,1989.

Financial managers measure SRI's profitability in a variety of ways. In the late 1970s, Lowrie created the "Good Money Industrial Average" (GMIA). This index compares the stock market performance of corporations screened for an array of social practices with that of the corporate community as a whole. Since 1976, no companies on the GMIA have been replaced for performance reasons. According to Lowrie, the value of the 30 GMIA stocks rose by 646.6% (from 28 to 207) between 1976 and 1989. During the same period, the Dow Jones Industrial Average rose by 174.1% (from 1005 to 2753). Similarly, Kinder Lydenberg Domini, an investment advisory house, uses the Domini Social Index to follow 400 ethical stocks. Between April 1990 and April 1991, the Domini 400 gained 19% compared to 18% for Standard & Poor's 500.

Social Impact

Some on the left criticize SRI by exposing the scams run in its name (some environmental funds have no qualms about investing in waste-disposal firms with dubious track records), highlighting the bad decisions made by industry headliners (Pax World Fund, for example, has invested in the World Bank), and questioning the social responsibility of some of the companies touted by SRI advocates (companies like 3M and McDonald's). As Lowrie readily concedes, no corporation is a saint; some companies, however, behave better than others. He argues it's worth making distinctions, both to support "good" companies and to pressure "bad" ones.

> *"No corporation is a saint; some companies, however, behave better than others."*

Motivated investors can easily find which supposedly socially responsible investments are dubious, and concerned investors can steer clear of the particular investments that trouble them the most. But how far, beyond making its practitioners feel good, does social investing go?

According to Zevin, socially responsible investors are trapped by their role as investors. "They think what gives them leverage is [their being] investors," he says. "As investors, they're trying to think, 'How much can I tear the system down and [remain] an investor?' Not that much. They're inclined to [imagine] a sort of liberal, moral, well-behaved corporate capitalism, in which the problem is to change . . . people and not the institutions." As such, Zevin suggests, SRI encourages illusions. Instead of adapting a rigorous analysis of our economy and its problems, many socially responsible investors join what he calls suspect campaigns for "corporate democracy" and "corporate citizenship."

Nevertheless, Zevin and others remain committed to using SRI as a tool for change. But not all types of SRI are effective tools. If, for example, an ethical investor simply sells stock in a "bad" company to buy existing stock in a "good" company, then the impact is minimal. Massive selling of "bad" stock would drive the value of a company's stock down and could lead corporate managers to change policy. However, with only 5% to 10% of all equity being screened for social reasons, ethical investing alone does not take place on a large enough scale. Nor does purchasing existing stock make a difference "to the good firm," since it does not infuse fresh capital into it.

> *"SRI's role in combating apartheid demonstrates the need to combine individual ethical investing with more pointed political action."*

By buying new stock or providing venture capital, an investor exerts a much larger impact, allowing a "good" company or bank to expand, create jobs, and compete more effectively with its "bad" counterparts. Activist managers of SRI funds do seek viable new investments and some of these—like the creation of the South Shore Bank—have affected society.

"[The founders of SSB] had a real strategy for empowering people who lived in the increasingly poor and black ghetto on the South Side of Chicago," Zevin observes. According to Zevin, SSB worked because it supported education and training programs, community organizing, and local planning. Its investors' decision to earn less on their invested capital also contributed to SSB's success.

Shareholder activism also has a decent, though limited, record for advancing social change. Activists have shaped corporate behavior by bringing issues before boards of directors and into the public eye through shareholder resolutions. Shareholders have wrung concessions from companies afraid of adverse publicity and consumer response on issues ranging from excessive power plant construction to unfair labor practices. Unfortunately, most socially responsible investors take a passive rather than active approach to their investing, choosing to get out of "bad" companies rather than sticking around to fight for change. As Zevin suggests, "They like the feeling of having their hands clean."

Lessons from South Africa

SRI's role in combating apartheid demonstrates the need to combine individual ethical investing with more pointed political action. Between 1984 and 1989, the number of U.S. companies investing directly in South Africa fell from 317 to 124. The anti-apartheid movements used SRI as one weapon in the battle against corporate involvement in South Africa. But mass divestment from companies doing business in South Africa came only after students campaigned for university divestment; union members for pension-fund withdrawal; and African-American, civil rights, and progressive groups for government sanctions against corporations doing business in South Africa. State and federal sanctions crowned these efforts, which resulted in the massive disengagement of institutional America from South Africa.

Shareholder activism and voluntary divestment contributed to the movement's growth, but a sophisticated and many-sided political effort made the movement effective. Many SRI advocates are aware that a multifaceted approach to social change is needed. As such, the SRI industry itself is trying to develop an environmental counterpart to the anti-apartheid movement. Leaders of the SRI industry believe the environmental activist's arsenal should include SRI. They also believe a pro-environment campaign can keep their industry growing and their vision of caring capitalism alive.

Some activists will find that vision and strategy limited. SRI can't substitute for an industrial policy that would restrict financial speculation and direct even bigger money into productive activities. But one needn't buy the vision or the more outlandish claims of some SRI advocates to use it as a part of a comprehensive strategy for social change.

Corporate Charity Harms Society

by Menlo F. Smith

About the author: Menlo F. Smith is chairman of the Sunmark Capital Corporation in St. Louis and founder of the Sunmark Foundation.

I do not consider myself to be any kind of authority on the subject of corporate charity. Yet, I do have some ideas on the matter and I'm happy to share them, to the extent they may have any value.

We are all familiar with the cliche "social responsibility of business." I have, in vain, talked to the heads of many major corporations who have used the term, and I've asked them to define it for me. None has been able to give me what I would consider to be a cogent or even logical explanation. As far as I can determine, the social responsibility of business is simply a term that's used in the same way that Willy Sutton used to describe his endeavors in robbing banks: "Because that's where the money is."

The basic purpose of business, I think, was most clearly summarized by the economist Benjamin J. Leeming, who said the aim and purpose of all legitimate business is service, at a profit, with a risk. I don't think it was coincidental that he put service first. I think that if any corporation is going to succeed meaningfully, it has to put service first. Profit is not the primary objective; it is a by-product of serving effectively and efficiently.

Corporate Irresponsibility

This being the case, a corporation, or any other business for that matter, is in business to provide valued services to customers in exchange for livelihood for its employees and benefits to its shareholders. In the process, it must preserve its resources. A very anti-social action for any corporation would be to squander its resources or use them in ways that are inimical to the interest of the business and its shareholders. Too often, I think corporate social responsibility gets translated into irresponsible corporate giving. Corporations are economic enti-

Menlo F. Smith, "Can Corporations Be Charitable?" *Philanthropy*, Spring 1993. Reprinted by permission of the author.

ties. They have an obligation to their owners and to society to utilize their resources for business purposes and to avoid failure.

Over the years it has been, and still remains, the philosophy of The Sunmark Companies to insure all of our assets against those risks which we would be unable to absorb directly. We happen to consider the free-enterprise system, of which we are beneficiaries, the most important asset we have in our business. Unfortunately, we can't buy an insurance contract to ensure that the free-enterprise system prevails, so

> *"Too often, . . . corporate social responsibility gets translated into irresponsible corporate giving."*

the principal corporate giving we do supports the activities of organizations that devote themselves to the preservation of the free-enterprise system. We feel that any expenditure by a corporation that does not have a direct business purpose is an inappropriate one.

Giving, in the charitable sense, really should be done by the shareholders. After all, the resources of the business belong to them. Because our shareholders will always have different charitable interests, we concluded long ago that any giving done by Sunmark should have a very direct business purpose, and that if it does not, the giving should then be done individually by the shareholders, and not the corporation.

Many times we find officers or managers of corporations pursuing with corporate resources objectives (often social objectives or charitable objectives) that have little to do with the direct interests of the business. I suggest that this is wrong. If a manager or officer of a business appropriates funds of that business to pursue his own personal, charitable objectives, he is appropriating funds of that business for his own purposes, not those of the owners of those funds. I would call that largess, not charity.

Supporting Anti-Capitalism

The Capital Research Center's work has now shown that corporations give approximately twice as much to organizations and efforts that are anti-capitalist as they give to organizations that support the free-market system. That is not charity. It is not even responsible, in my view. More than that, it adds a destructive, irresponsible dimension to corporate giving because it is not in the interest of the shareholders, nor is it in the interest of their employees, and ultimately, I would suggest, it is not in the interest of society.

The social responsibility of business, in my view, is to render a service to the public in the form of a useful and valued product, period. Beyond that, the corporation must concentrate on being a good corporate citizen. As we have loaded social tasks on business, we have produced a good deal of corporate giving that is not charitable at all.

When a corporation or government assumes the role of benefactor, they do several things. First, they drive out individual beneficence. Second, any charitable content to the effort is lost, and instead the process tends to become politicized. In the case of government, givers are replaced by coerced taxpayers. In the case of the corporation, givers are replaced by coerced employees and deprived shareholders.

The standard of living in this country is diminishing as corporate America is distracted from its basic purpose. Society becomes bent upon gaining and giving entitlements rather than charitable endeavors and, in the process, our love for one another diminishes in proportion. We become a society of ill will, rather than goodwill. Without a correct concept of the role of corporations in responsible giving, and a view of charitable giving as a voluntary matter for individuals, I think man will continue to be the only animal to insist on fouling his own nest. The process finances its own destruction.

Corporate Involvement in Environmental Causes Is Harmful

by Brian Lipsett

About the author: *Brian Lipsett is organizing director for Environmental Background Information Center, which provides information on corporations involved in activities potentially harmful to the environment. He is the former editor of* Everyone's Backyard, *published by Citizen's Clearinghouse for Hazardous Wastes.*

Corporations never give away money for nothing, but always for gain. The corporations get a good return from their contributions to environmental causes. In fact, dollar for dollar, the investment can't be topped. Beyond public relations dividends and tax deductions and even increased business opportunities, corporate sponsorship fractures internal consensus within recipient groups, divides grantees from other environmental groups, blunts criticism from grantee groups, and creates openings for future influence by securing corporate representation on the groups' boards of directors.

Protecting People from Abuse

The environmental movement, like the labor movement, has from its earliest days been engaged in a struggle to protect people from the abuses of powerful corporate interests. In 1970, on the occasion of the first Earth Day, civil rights leader George Wiley told a crowd at Harvard University, "If you are a serious movement, you must be prepared to take on the giant corporations who are the primary polluters and perpetrators of some of the worst conditions that affect the environment of the country and, indeed, the world." Denis Hayes, an organizer of the first Earth Day, said, "If we want [corporations] to do what is right, we must make them do what is right."

This fundamental notion, widely held in the environmental movement, that

Brian Lipsett, "'Dirty Money' for Green Groups?" *The Workbook*, vol. 18, no. 1, Spring 1993. Reprinted by permission of the Southwest Research and Information Center, Albuquerque, N.M.

the public has the right to force corporations to change their behavior, strikes a blow at the constitutional protections enjoyed by corporations. In 1886, the U.S. Supreme Court refused to hear an appeal in the *Santa Clara v. Southern Pacific Railroad* case in which a lower court had ruled that corporations had the right to protection under the 14th Amendment *as a person.* With personhood, corporations have been able to solidify other constitutional protections under the First, Fourth, and Fifth Amendments to the Constitution. These protections limit the ability of government to regulate corporate behavior.

The environmental movement, by forcing governmental regulatory intrusion into corporate activities, poses a direct threat to a corporation's supposed right to do what it pleases with its own property. It should come as no surprise that corporations respond with a vast array of tactics and strategies to combat this challenge. Funding of environmental causes is only one of these strategies.

The Rise of Corporate Environmental Philanthropy

Corporate philanthropy has been around much longer than the environmental movement, and controversies surrounding the ethical dimensions of corporate charity predate it as well. According to Matthew Josephson's *The Robber Barons* (1934), J.P. Morgan, J.D. Rockefeller, and Andrew Carnegie cultivated influence during the early 1900s through large donations to churches and universities. The violent union-busting and monopoly-building practices of these tycoons provoked moralists to charge that Rockefeller's church donations were "tainted money." One cleric responded, "People charge Mr. Rockefeller with stealing the money he gave to the church . . . but he has laid it on the altar and thus sanctified it." (Rockefeller claimed simply, "God gave me my money.")

Like religious values, environmental issues are deeply embedded in the American psyche today. As any number of recent polls indicate, the American public is deeply concerned with the destruction of the environment and the role of corporate misbehavior in that destruction. The polls suggest the public supports increased government intervention and even criminal prosecution of corporate environmental crimes. In order to counter this public concern, corporations have gone "green," proudly advertising their newfound environmental consciousness while donating large sums of money to environmental causes.

> *"Corporations get a good return from their contributions to environmental causes."*

One need only examine the financial reports of private corporate foundations to see that corporate environmental giving has skyrocketed. And the financial reports of America's largest environmental groups reveal just how dependent they have become on corporate largess. Groups like the National Wildlife Federation, National Audubon Society, Sierra Club, Environmental Defense Fund, and World Wildlife Fund now actively solicit corporate donations, and the corporations are responding, as environmentalism has become a new altar for corporate money. In difficult economic times, it is not easy to raise enough money to sustain a large environmental organization. But the heavy reliance on corporate funding by the large environmental organizations is being challenged by smaller groups.

The Challenge to Corporate Environmental Funding

As the large environmental groups have replaced protestors with lobbyists and picket signs with legislative drafts, smaller groups have risen in their wake. These groups reflect a different constituency, of blue-collar workers, housewives, minorities, and a convergence of labor, social, and racial justice interests. These groups frequently and quite openly condemn organizations that rely on corporate funding.

The smaller organizations do not, and cannot, rely on corporate funding. Many, particularly small grass-roots groups, lack the coveted Internal Revenue Service "501(c)3" tax-exempt status necessary for qualification as a recipient of a charitable grant or donation. Grass-roots organizations and associated support groups have a fundamentally different set of needs and principles than those of the large environmental organizations. But more importantly, these groups are so deeply involved in direct fights with large corporations that they would as soon accept corporate money as sign a pact with the devil himself. To the grass-roots group fighting for environmental justice, any individual or group that takes such "blood money" becomes aligned with the enemy either directly or implicitly, and so they cannot be trusted.

"The entire 20th Anniversary Celebration of Earth Day [was] 'a commercial mugging' led by polluting industries."

The larger regional and national organizations that work with the grass-roots groups know well that if they are to maintain their own credibility, they must hold the same high ground when it comes to corporate funding.

How the Public Became Informed

Beginning in the mid-1980s, small grass-roots journals within the environmental community began reporting on the issue of corporate environmental funding. In 1987, The Citizen's Clearinghouse for Hazardous Wastes and the Environmental Research Foundation published reports on the financial and board interrelationships between Waste Management Inc. (the world's largest handler of hazardous wastes, which has paid more than $60 million in fines and settlements of environmental and anti-trust civil and criminal charges) and the National Wildlife Federation (NWF). These exposés led to complaints from a number of NWF members to NWF director Jay Hair about Waste Management CEO Dean Buntrock's position on the NWF board. Hair's response, circulated in a February 1988 form letter, read: "We feel that Waste Management Inc. is conducting its business in a responsible manner." This endorsement of one of the worst operators in the environmental field left many NWF members angry and unsatisfied.

A *Multinational Monitor* March 1990 article, "Environmental Board Games," expanded the coverage, showing a widespread pattern of "penetration," as corporate executives follow their donations onto the boards of environmental groups. The article reported that of the "Group of 10" national environmental organizations, all of whom rely heavily on large corporate donations, six had corporate executives as board members, trustees, or council members. The *Multinational Monitor* story included a statement by Gayle Bingham, vice president of World Wildlife Fund, that Exxon Chemical president Eugene McBrayer's presence on WWF's board was "a good thing" because McBrayer "cares about the environment, too. . . . It's in our interest as an environmental organization to help corporations engage in their economic activities in a more sound environmental manner." But WWF lobbyist John Welner admitted that the group "pretty much" stayed clear of oil spill legislation efforts following the Exxon Valdez oil spill in Alaska.

> *"Corporate funding has engendered internal divisiveness and driven a wedge between grass-roots activists and larger environmental organizations."*

Bill Gifford's "When Environmentalists Are Good for Business," published in *Legal Times* in May 1990, revisited the issue of WMI's presence on the board of National Wildlife Federation. NWF vice president William W. Howard told Gifford, "We have found [WMI CEO Dean Buntrock] a strong supporter of our environmental programs. In no instance has he attempted to influence the Federation's environmental policies in any way that contradicts the policy resolutions adopted by our affiliates or the programs and activities of staff."

NWF's Jay Hair added, "you don't change [corporate] behavior by kicking people in the shins all the time." But in 1989, Hair had not only refrained from shin-kicking, he had also figured at the center of the "Breakfast with Buntrock" scandal. Hair set up a meeting so Waste Management CEO Dean Buntrock could lobby then EPA (Environmental Protection Agency) chief William Reilly to pressure Southern states to lower barriers to out-of-state hazardous waste imports, a direct contradiction of Federation policy. Hair subsequently admitted that his involvement in the affair, which resulted in a congressional probe, was probably a mistake.

A "Commercial Mugging": Earth Day 1990

Earth Day 1990 served as a high profile watershed for the issue of corporate funding of environmental causes. The tremendous level of corporate sponsorship of Earth Day events and the limp casting of the issues—"if everyone recycles we'll solve the environmental problem"—combined to deepen the rift within the environmental movement and force the issue into major newspapers. The conflict was represented in miniature on the Washington, D.C., Mall one week before Earth Day festivities were to begin.

Greenpeace, Citizen's Clearinghouse for Hazardous Wastes (CCHW), U.S. Public Interest Research Group (PIRG), and several other environmental groups joined in a press conference to denounce EarthTech '90, a symposium set up to show off corporate environmentalism. The groups blasted the symposium as an attempt to "greenwash" the poor environmental records of many of the more than 100 corporations sponsoring the event. When questioned by reporters, EarthTech spokesman Charles Miller as much as admitted that the fair was a public relations ploy, saying, "I think you'd have to be naive not to think so." *Time* magazine would later eulogize the entire 20th Anniversary Celebration of Earth Day as "a commercial mugging" led by polluting industries.

Audubon for Sale?

In 1991, an AP wire story picked up the issue again. Dave Kalish reported that Waste Management Inc. representative William Brown openly allowed that WMI's donations to environmental causes, which totaled $1.1 million in 1990, were good for business. Brown told Kalish, "We certainly potentially could gain business by helping companies subject to those laws manage their waste better and comply with the law." Kalish went on to report that the National Audubon Society (NAS) received about $60,000 to help in its efforts to support stronger federal regulation of industrial waste discharges.

Shortly after the article appeared, WMI president Philip Rooney joined the board of NAS. This led Florida Audubon members to claim that the Society was for sale—and the price was $60,000. Critics also pointed to National Audubon's campaign to win regulation of oil-field waste, funded by WMI, as another example of how corporate funding co-opts environmental groups to the benefit of a corporation. WMI is well positioned to take over and profit from the disposal of the more than 200 tons of oil-field waste generated in this country by oil companies each year.

> *"A few corporate executives have openly admitted that funding of environmental groups improves business opportunities."*

The article described the concerns of Sue Greer, an Indiana grass-roots activist fighting WMI, who remarked, "I don't see [NWF] having a big attack on Waste Management while they're taking $55,000 a year in the form of funding." Kalish added, "Greer's resentment is hardly isolated. As environmental groups increasingly steer away from adversarial relationships with business, controversial alliances with Waste Management and other corporations are resulting in a deepening rift in a once tightly knit movement. Grass-roots, low-budget environmental groups like Greer's are voicing growing concern about such close associations."

Kalish's AP article was carried widely, demonstrating the newsworthiness of the controversy within the environmental community. The subject has subsequently shown up in *Outside Magazine, Buzzworm,* and *World Policy Journal.* A *Washington Post* May 3, 1992, article, "Squabble in Margaritaville," described an attempt by Florida-based Save the Manatee Club to secede from National Audubon Society. Jimmy Buffett, a pop singer who acted as spokesperson for the club, claimed that Audubon had become a corporate shill and so the Manatee Club would no longer be associated with Audubon. Audubon officials responded by changing the locks on the Manatee Club's doors and firing its executive director. The *Post*, paraphrasing Kalish, added, "The clash between Buffet and the Florida Audubon Society points to a growing tension between large, established environmental groups and their smaller cousins that operate on a grass-roots level."

In light of such events, it is apparent that some of what may be regarded as "paranoid" concerns about corporate funding of environmental groups holds true. Corporate funding *has* engendered internal divisiveness and driven a wedge between grass-roots activists and larger environmental organizations. National Audubon and National Wildlife have been rocked by the controversy, and so has the Sierra Club. To suppose that corporate funders themselves are unaware of their role in provoking such divisions is to deny credit to their intelligence.

> *"A corporation's civil and criminal environmental violations fall within a larger set of legal and ethical considerations."*

There is also evidence that grant recipients tend not to bite the hand that feeds them. In addition, a few corporate executives have openly admitted that funding of environmental groups improves business opportunities. All in all, the news media have characterized the situation in such a way as to undermine the credibility of the large environmental organizations.

Implications for the Funding Community

Foundations that routinely finance environmental issues have not escaped the growing tumult over corporate donations to environmental causes. First of all, most of these large foundations (i.e. Rockefeller, MacArthur, Ford, Mott, and numerous others) owe their starts to corporate magnates to whom they also owe their names. These philanthropies now have little direct connection with the corporations that are their progenitors, although they may continue to have stock investments in the founding company.

On the other hand, some corporations operate charitable foundations that receive money only from the company. Some corporations also hand out money directly from their own bank accounts. In either case, the corporation earns a tax write-off because the funds are donated to charitable organizations.

This distinction between independent and corporate foundations is not well understood by the public, and a few capitalize on the ignorance. In Pennsylvania, for example, a corporate-sponsored counter-organization charged that the Citizen's Clearinghouse for Hazardous Wastes was tainted by money it received from the Mary Reynolds Babcock Foundation.

> *"Grass-roots groups will continue to condemn organizations that take money from corporations that violate the law."*

During a meeting sponsored by a local community environmental organization, the counter-group circulated a flyer which read in part, "If you think that CCHW is truly interested in protecting public health and savings lives, ask them why they eagerly accepted money from the Mary Reynolds Babcock Foundation—a foundation that derived its wealth from the tobacco industry." And an article appearing in *In These Times* (Oct. 28–Nov. 10, 1992) alleged that the National Toxics Campaign fired a veteran grass-roots organizer in order to secure a grant from the Pew Charitable Trust Foundation, "originally established by the founders of the Sun Oil Company to counter the influence of the civil rights movement within the Presbyterian Church."

The issue is becoming increasingly important to grantmaking foundations. In 1988, WMI tried to join the Environmental Grantmakers Association, a coalition of environmental funders. WMI was rebuffed by EGA's membership, which collectively declared in an EGA internally circulated letter, "it is readily apparent that Waste Management Inc. has engaged in a pattern of abusive corporate conduct involving repeated violations of both criminal and civil laws." But EGA eventually adopted a membership policy that allowed WMI to be reinstated. EGA's current policy, adopted after a long and vigorous debate, affirms:

> EGA membership is open to any foundation or corporate giving program that chooses to join with the sole exception of one that during the past five years has been convicted of a felony offense directly related to environmental degradation or whose employee in the course of employment or whose majority-owned subsidiary has been convicted of such an offense.

Maybe We Just Don't Get It

The narrow legalistic framework of this policy, while clearly well-intentioned, reflects the myopia affecting a large segment of the environmental community. Grass-roots environmental activists do not share this affliction. They are not simply concerned with a corporation's *criminal* environmental record, they are concerned about *civil* environmental violations as well. Equally, these activists don't stop with environmental laws. They frequently confront corporations for violations of child labor, workplace safety, truth in advertising, anti-trust, food and drug, product safety, campaign finance, and any number of other laws governing corporate misbehavior.

The logic held by grass-roots activists goes far beyond simple ethical and tactical considerations. While corporate behavior is regulated by a vast array of state and federal regulatory agencies with specific mandates, the crimes have a common element: they are all economic in nature and the victims are real people, often whole communities of individuals. A corporation's civil and criminal environmental violations fall within a larger set of legal and ethical considerations.

Many in the environmental community don't seem to get it. The only people who seem to understand are the victims. These people have been organizing in their own neighborhoods, across the nation, across traditional issue boundaries, and even across national borders to fight back—while the large environmental groups have abandoned the notion that environmental issues are social justice issues.

There is a profound difference between lobbying and legislating, on the one hand, and organizing and empowering people, on the other, to protect our democratic heritage. Perhaps this is the difference between environmentalism and environmental justice. Grass-roots groups will continue to condemn organizations that take money from corporations that violate the law. Large environmental groups will continue to justify their fundraising activities. Perhaps this is what will finally divide us, what will make us go our separate ways—social justice down one route, a pristine wilderness down the other.

Socially Responsible Investing Is Ineffective

by David Vogel

About the author: *David Vogel is a professor at the Walter A. Haas School of Business at the University of California, Berkeley.*

Adam Smith wrote in *The Wealth of Nations*: "It is not from the benevolence of the butcher, the brewer, or the baker, that we expect our dinner, but from their regard to their own self-interest. We address ourselves, not to their humanity but to their self-love, and never talk to them of our own necessities but of their advantages."

These often-quoted lines capture the moral contradiction that lies at the heart of capitalism, in which morally dubious intentions combine to produce morally beneficial results. On the one hand, we do get the food that we need to survive—certainly no mean accomplishment in a world in which hunger was once commonplace. But on the other hand, the way we achieve this happy outcome is by paradoxically assuming that the providers of food are indifferent as to whether or not we are actually fed.

The Ethics of Capitalism

If one judges the ethics of capitalism by its results, then the system deserves our unequivocal moral approbation. By any conceivable criterion, appealing to the self-interest of humanity "works": market economies have produced more wealth and greater economic security for more individuals than even their most ardent eighteenth- and nineteenth-century defenders thought possible. Capitalism's improvement in the quality of life is equally impressive. And no other economic system has proven even remotely so compatible with liberty and democracy.

However, the issue of motives constitutes the moral Achilles heel of capitalism. This is because of the appeal to self-interest that is at the core of a market economy. Notwithstanding capitalism's impressive results, many remain uncomfortable with a system in which economic action is motivated by selfishness.

Numerous scholars have tried to address this moral issue, without much success. In *The Passions and the Interests*, Albert Hirschman presents the ideas of a number of eighteenth- and nineteenth-century thinkers who argued for the ethical superiority of capitalist motives. They favorably contrasted a society in which people sought to maximize their interests with one in which people were ruled by their passions. As Montesquieu wrote in praising market economies, "[It] is fortunate for men to be in a situation in which, though their passions may prompt them to be wicked, they have nevertheless an interest in not being so."

Now it may well be the case, to cite Samuel Johnson's famous epigram, that "there are few ways in which a man can be more innocently employed than in getting money." Certainly, when one compares the profit motive to the homicidal and genocidal passions that have motivated so much human behavior, the moral case for the profit motive is clear. John Maynard Keynes' judgment is surely correct: "It is better that a man should tyrannize over his bank balance than over his fellow citizens."

Audacious Capitalism

The last few centuries, however, have also demonstrated that far from calming men's passions, the pursuit of money can just as easily inflame them. Writing in *The Predator's Ball*, Connie Bruck portrays Michael Milken [a junk-bond trader who was convicted of illegal trading practices] as a man driven less by the rational pursuit of self-interest than by megalomania; he is hardly the kind of individual that Montesquieu had in mind, one presumes.

Moreover, while the pursuit of material self-interest may be preferable to some motives, it is hardly superior to all of them. Much of the ethical appeal of socialism in the West has derived precisely from the moral superiority of the motives that it would substitute for the pursuit of material self-interest. It remains far more uplifting to exhort people to "love one another" than to "maximize utility," even though the latter may in fact be more socially beneficial.

Perhaps the most audacious effort to reconcile the motives of capitalists with the results of capitalism can be found in George Gilder's *Wealth and Poverty*. Gilder argues that capitalism begins not with material self-interest, but with "giving." Because the investor has no guarantee of return on his investment, his investment effectively constitutes a gift to the community. And like the gifts of the South Sea Islanders, it is given in the hope that it will be reciprocated. This argument has persuaded no one: as one of his numerous critics put it, Gilder's attempt to equate giving and investing is as likely to give philanthropy a bad name as capitalism a good one. Yet at the same time, his analysis—perhaps unwittingly—also helps make sense of both the pervasiveness and widespread public appeal

"Many remain uncomfortable with a system in which economic action is motivated by selfishness."

of corporate philanthropy. In fact, corporate philanthropy fits Gilder's model far better than does business investment. Philanthropy clearly involves giving, with no guarantee of return.

Yet at the same time, the gifts given by corporations are commonly understood to be motivated not simply by altruism, but by the firms' long-term interests. They thus represent a kind of happy medium between a genuine gift, whose primary purpose is to improve the welfare of the recipient, and an investment, whose only purpose is to maximize the wealth of the investor.

> *"Far from calming men's passions, the pursuit of money can just as easily inflame them."*

Not surprisingly, corporate philanthropy has been criticized from both the left and the right. One set of critics has attacked it for failing to serve the objectives of the firms' stockholders; they argue that too much corporate philanthropy goes to organizations and institutions that are hostile to business. Another group of critics attacks it for precisely the opposite reasons: they claim that its real purpose is to improve the image of the company, so that it is misleading to describe it as philanthropic. The paradox of corporate philanthropy is that the more the public perceives it as altruistic, the more effectively it serves the self-interest of the company that provides it.

Michael Novak's *The Spirit of Democratic Capitalism* represents another contemporary effort to improve the moral status of capitalism by redefining the motives that underlie it. Novak notes that "like prudence in Aristotelian thought, self-interest in democratic capitalist thought has an inferior reputation among moralists." He argues, however, that it is misleading to equate "self-interest" with greed or acquisitiveness. Rather, self-interest also encompasses "religious and moral interests, artistic and scientific interests, and interests in peace and justice," as well as concern for the well-being of one's family, friends, and country.

Self-Interest or Selfishness?

But while it is certainly true that much behavior in capitalist societies is self-interested in Novak's broader sense, this is decidedly not true of economic behavior proper. The predictive power of neoclassical economics rests precisely on the fact that consumers, investors, and employers do define their self-interest primarily—if not exclusively—in pecuniary terms. It is possible to deplore the extent to which our economic system rests on economic self-interest; it is not, however, appropriate to deny it.

The doctrine of corporate social responsibility can also be understood as part of the ongoing effort to reconcile the intentions and results of capitalism. It does this in part by fudging the issue; no small part of the nearly universal appeal of corporate social responsibility rests on the doctrine's ambiguity. Proponents of corporate social responsibility do not deny the legitimacy of the profit motive; instead they redefine the profit motive to encompass other, more public-spirited purposes. The notion of the "corporate conscience" represents an attempt to humanize the firm, to endow its managers with a range of motivations that transcend the selfish pursuit of wealth. Likewise, speaking of "enlightened" self-interest is clearly meant to soften self-interest, which itself is employed as a euphemism for selfishness.

But the term "enlightened self-interest" begs a critical issue. What happens when a manager's concern for the welfare of society conflicts with the material interests of his company's shareholders? Supporters of the free market believe that society is best served when executives try to maximize the interests of their shareholders. Thus an important conservative criticism of corporate social responsibility is precisely that it gives businessmen "credit" for serving society only when they are engaged in activities that are not primarily motivated by shareholder interests—thus undermining a central moral *raison d'etre* of a market economy.

The response of the advocates of corporate responsibility is to deny that there is a tension between intentions and results: common to virtually every exposition of the doctrine of corporate social responsibility is the belief that in the long run the interests of "society" and of business converge, so that those firms that intend to do good also wind up doing well, and vice versa.

This is also the position of the movement for socially responsible investment: much of the popularity of "socially responsible" investment vehicles rests on their claim to resolve the tension between "bad" intentions and "good" results that characterizes a market economy, by enabling investors to hold on to their good intentions without sacrificing their rate of return. Much of the claim for the need to instruct businessmen in ethics rests on a similar social vision.

What Is the Point?

Appealing as this position evidently is, unfortunately it is not terribly persuasive. If corporate social responsibility amounts to nothing more than enlightened self-interest, why would anyone need to devote special effort to understand it or to urge others to pursue it? For that matter, what would be the point of teaching ethics to present or future managers? Why not simply teach them how to become more intelligent or sophisticated profit maximizers? Likewise, if socially responsible funds offer their investors a market rate of returns, then why is it praiseworthy to invest in them?

The fact that so much effort is devoted to preaching to both executives and investors about their social and moral responsibilities suggests that we are still uncomfortable with an economic system that relies so heavily on the motive of selfishness to achieve its goals—however laudable they may be. The moral paradox that Adam Smith so insightfully described more than two centuries ago remains with us; we are no closer than he to resolving it.

Chapter 5

Are Modern Biomedical Practices Ethical?

Overview: The Birth of Bioethics

by Albert R. Jonsen

About the author: *Albert R. Jonsen is professor and chairman in the department of medical history and ethics at the University of Washington School of Medicine, Seattle.*

On 23-24 September 1992, "The Birth of Bioethics," held at the University of Washington, Seattle, gathered many of the "pioneers" of the new ethics of medicine to review its history and project its future. A pioneer was defined as one whose name had appeared in the first edition of the *Bibliography of Bioethics* (1975) and who had continued to work in the field. Some sixty persons made the cut and, of these, forty-two came to Seattle.

Who Lives? Who Dies?

The occasion of this conference was the thirtieth anniversary of the publication of an article in *Life* magazine, "They Decide Who Lives, Who Dies" (9 November 1962). That article told the story of a committee in Seattle whose duty it was to select patients for entry into the chronic hemodialysis program recently opened in that city. Chronic dialysis had just been made possible by [the work of] Dr. Belding Scribner. It quickly became apparent that many more patients needed dialysis than could be accommodated. The solution was to ask a small group, composed mostly of nonphysicians, to review the dossiers of all medically suitable candidates and sort out those who would receive the lifesaving technology. Thus, the committee was faced with the unenviable task of determining suitability on grounds other than medical. Should it be personality? finances? social acceptability? past or expected contribution? family dependents and support? While the committee was anonymous, word of its existence appeared in the *New York Times*. *Life* correspondent Shana Alexander travelled to Seattle to cover what she described at the "Birth of Bioethics" as "the most fascinating story of [her] career."

As professor of ethics in medicine at the University of Washington, I thought that the thirtieth anniversary of the appearance of that article was worth commemorating. My university would claim a birthright and, more seriously, those who had worked for some years in bioethics could reflect on the origins and the evolution of our work. Quite shamelessly, I entitled the event "The Birth of Bioethics" although, as any decent historian knows and as many of the conference participants declared, dating the time and place when any social movement begins is perilous and near impossible. Still, the interesting events in Seattle were worth recalling, and the features of those events that presaged the full-grown bioethics movement were worth pointing out. Whether the Seattle events were a birth, a conception, or merely a gleam in someone's eye, I thought it a good time for the early workers in the field to gather, reminisce, and perhaps, begin to make a history.

> *"Bioethics has matured into a minor form of moral philosophy practiced within medicine."*

Bioethics has matured into a minor form of moral philosophy practiced within medicine. Today, soundly reasoned articles on a variety of ethical questions appear regularly in the major medical journals. In almost every American medical school, students study, in one form or another, the new medical ethics. Twelve thousand persons subscribe to the *Hastings Center Report* [a publication covering ethical issues in medicine and science]. Ten "special government employees" of Hillary Rodham Clinton's Health Care Task Force were identifiable as bioethicists. The effect of these developments on medicine and health care has been remarkable. The first historian of the bioethics movement, Professor David Rothman of Columbia University, writes in his *Strangers at the Bedside:*

> The record of bioethics' influence . . . makes a convincing case for a fundamental transformation in the substance as well as in the style of medical decision making.

Where did this new ethics of medicine, or bioethics, come from? What events occasioned its origins? What form has it taken? Who elaborated it? Who pays attention to it? What is its significance for modern medicine, health care, and health policy? Those who work in this new field are only now beginning to reflect on these questions. . . .

Rothman describes bioethics as a movement. Movement takes place because from time to time an impetus is imparted to an inert body. The issue in the debate over the Seattle committee was the contemporary echo of an ancient Hippocratic phrase: "into whatever houses I enter. . . ." The modern nephrologist, armed with the new expensive dialysis machine, could not enter every house where help was needed. What standards should determine the choice of houses? The standard that had often served in the past, namely, the quality of the neighborhood and the wealth of its inhabitants, seemed no longer appropriate. Amer-

ica in the 1960s had become acutely aware of discrimination as a social problem. Why should a new medical advance create a new medical discrimination?
Who should set the standards? The authorities of the past, namely physicians,
seemed inadequate. Fairness in selecting candidates for medical treatment is
not, in itself, a medical skill. Laypersons, it was thought, would do it as well, or
as poorly, perhaps even better than physicians, since they would be free of bias
in favor of one's own patients.

Thus, starting in the early 1960s, a radically new problem appeared. It stimulated unprecedented public interest and engaged the attention of persons hitherto remote from medical discussions, who began to create a literature about the
problem. Finally, it led to a radically new solution: the delegation by physicians
to laypersons of decisionmaking power about admission to a medical treatment.
Rothman writes, "a group of physicians, in unprecedented fashion, turned over
to a lay committee life-or-death decisions prospectively and on a case-by-case
basis. A prerogative that had once been the exclusive preserve of the doctor was
delegated to community representatives."

The Problem Created by Science

The dialysis events of the early 1960s were an early impetus that nudged the
world of medicine toward a realignment of its values. A second impetus came
several years later. Henry Beecher, professor of anesthesia at Harvard Medical
School, published an article in the *New England Journal of Medicine* entitled
"Ethics and Clinical Research." In it he accused of unethical design and conduct
twenty-two biomedical research studies that had appeared in leading journals.
The article stirred up a hornets' nest. However, like any impetus, prior pushes
had set the ball rolling. The Nuremberg trials in 1945 had revealed the terrible
abuses, called medical experimentation, perpetuated by Nazi doctors on concen-
tration camp prisoners. But, horrible as these were, the problem posed by medical research was deeper. It was not the maliciousness and callousness of scientists but the very nature of modern biomedical science that created the problem.

Modern biomedical science is by
its nature innovative. It moves from
observation and discovery to fresh
observations and further discoveries
by canons of evidence and statistical

> *"Modern biomedical science is by its nature innovative."*

methods that require the manipulation of data. In addition, it works within a social milieu that demands of scientists constant productivity and consistent origi-
nality. The experiments of Buchenwald and Dachau took place, in part, because
the scientific zeal of the perpetrators, aggravated by their racist arrogance,
found "human material" at hand for their manipulations. Scientific research in
its ordinary course is neither vicious nor racist, but it can find "human material"
at hand in the vulnerable sick. Slowly, researchers began to sense, and the public began to demand, that studies be conducted in ways that not only advance

science, but protect the rights and welfare of human subjects as well [that is, that subjects be treated with respect and consideration, and not be thought of as "Guinea Pigs"]. Within four years of Beecher's article, the syphilis experiments carried on over several decades by the U.S. Public Health Service in Tuskegee, as well as several other research projects, made this clear. The Congress established the National Commission for the Protection of Human Subjects of Biomedical and Behavior Research to recommend policies that would guide researchers in the design of ethical research. That commission, which sat from 1974 to 1978, engaged the help of a wide variety of scholars from many disciplines and solicited public opinion on many issues. Perhaps more than any other impetus, its work brought into being a discipline of "bioethics," with a literature filled with concepts such as autonomy of patients, standards for informed and proxy consent, and the equilibration of risks and benefits.

A third impetus came from the public response to another dramatic medical advance. In 1967, Christiaan Barnard transplanted a human heart from a dead (or dying) person into a patient with terminal cardiac disease. The world was astonished, but some wondered about the source of the organ. Was its source truly dead? Was the heart taken without regard to the wishes of its source while living? One leading medical editor wondered how we should think about "the use of borrowed organs." Kidney transplantation had been underway for some fifteen years, but heart transplantation pressed these questions more urgently. CIBA Founda-

> *"Bioethics is a native-grown American product."*

tion in England held a ground-breaking conference, "Ethics in Medical Progress with Special Reference to Transplantation." Almost all participants were physicians and scientists. Within a few years, such a conference would be unthinkable without philosophers and theologians. After all, these scholars could say, our disciplines have meditated on life and death long before modern science was conceived. By 1968 a Harvard Medical School committee, headed by Beecher, proposed a definition of "brain death" to close a question that Pope Pius XII had called open in 1958. A theologian sat on the Beecher committee. I myself, a college philosophy teacher, first entered the medical world when invited to sit in on a similar "brain death" committee at the medical school of the University of California, San Francisco.

Theology and Ethics

Several prominent theologians had not been oblivious to these developments in medical science and health care. One very prescient figure, the Episcopal theologian Joseph Fletcher, had written a book in 1954, entitled *Morals and Medicine*, unlike any previous book on that subject. While Catholic theologians had long discussed such questions as euthanasia and abortion, Fletcher departed from the usual theological analysis to stress the freedom and authority of the patient. This viewpoint led him to expound remarkably liberal positions about euthanasia, truth-telling, and patients' rights. In 1970 another theologian, Methodist Paul Ramsey, was curious enough about the changes in medicine to spend a year in the clinics and on the wards of Georgetown University Hospital. His book, *The Patient as Person*, was an insightful (though dense) analysis of the ways in which the new medicine was modifying the moral dimensions of the relationship between patient and physician. If we think of bioethics as an academic discipline rather than a popular movement, we might choose a work of scholarship as its origin. That work would certainly be Ramsey's book.

The definition of death by brain criteria was novel and somewhat contentious, yet it won quick public approval because of its utility: it promised more organs for lifesaving transplantation. Death captured the public's attention in yet another way. The near death of a young New Jersey woman named Karen Ann Quinlan in 1975 became a public spectacle. Karen Ann's parents, convinced that their daughter would never recover consciousness, asked that life support be removed. Their plea, rejected by doctors and hospital, eventually was sympathetically heard by the New Jersey Supreme Court. In the first legal case about life support ever adjudicated, the court recognized the problem posed by the new life-support technologies that had evolved over the past twenty years: organic life may continue, but human living "in a conscious, sapient condition" may be forever lost. Other cases, both similar to Karen Ann's and, even more agonizing, about tiny premature infants kept alive only by machinery, began to be debated. Again, the philosophers and theologians contributed wise words to the debate. Hospital policies about orders not to resuscitate, public law about advance directives [in which a patient decides the extent of their treatment before hospitalization], and the endorsement of hospice care for the dying came out of that debate.

Quality of Life

Again, the echo of the Hippocratic phrase could be heard, "I will enter only to benefit the sick." This ancient admonition, followed by good doctors for centuries, had become difficult to apply in the setting of modern medicine. The respiratory, renal, and cardiac technologies that had come into being during the postwar era could produce wondrous physiological effects. It was not always clear, however, that those effects were benefits for the patients in whose body they were produced. The debates over the artificial heart, first implanted in the Seattle dentist Dr. Barney Clark in 1982, made that paradox clear to everyone concerned. Prolongation of life is too simple a measure of benefit. The difficult concept of "quality of life" cried for recognition, yet the

"Our response to the fear of technology beyond control has been the fashioning of new technologies, such as the living will, to save us."

discriminatory potential latent in its application made even the experts hesitate. Indeed, the ill-advised "Baby Doe Regulations" issued by the government to regulate the care of newborns rejected the concept totally, categorically ordering (and wishfully thinking) that "medical treatment decisions are not to be made on the basis of subjective opinions about the future 'quality of life' of a retarded or disabled person."

By the beginning of the 1980s, the bioethics movement was well underway. Professorships had been established in many medical schools. Many health professionals had become amateur bioethicists by sitting on institutional review boards and hospital ethics committees, and by attending workshops and seminars. Courts acknowledged the ideas and arguments crafted by bioethicists. Bioethics was a creation of the times. It was conceived as a response to the new technologies in medicine, but it was gestated in a culture sensitive to certain ethical dimensions, particularly to the rights of individuals and their abuse by powerful institutions. Health care had become a powerful institution, with powerful technologies. The needs and preferences of patients had to be asserted vigorously. The first decade of bioethics as a movement and discipline did just that.

The Future of Medical Ethics

Whether its birthday was 9 November 1962, the date of the *Life* article about the Seattle committee, or 16 June 1966, the day Beecher's article on the ethics of research appeared in *New England Journal of Medicine*, on 31 March 1976, when the New Jersey Supreme Court rendered its decision *In the Matter of Karen Ann Quinlan*, all these events pushed medical ethics out of its past into its future. Whether its conception was in Joseph Fletcher's fertile brain in 1954 or in Paul Ramsey's mighty intellect in 1970, or in the inspiration that struck Dan Callahan and Will Gaylin in 1969 to start The Hastings Center and, almost simultaneously, struck Andre Hellegers to start the Kennedy Institute for Bioethics in Georgetown, the ideas for bioethics were waiting to be heard.

"Medical progress goes on, and the perils of progress must be heeded."

Callahan said at the Seattle conference, "Bioethics is a native-grown American product." Modern bioethicists react to medicine, medical technology, and health care services with peculiarly American concerns about the rights of individuals, fairness and equity in access to benefits, and secularized reflections about death, abortion, suffering, and aging. Additionally, as Callahan also noted, the resolution of many of these problems had been peculiarly American, namely, the devising of regulations and guidelines. Medical historian Stanley Reiser also noted that our response to the fear of technology beyond control has been the fashioning of new technologies, such as the living will, to save us. Medical historian Dan Fox went further, suggesting that the "history of arms control is to the defense sector of our country what the history of bioethics is to health care. . . . Arms control intellectuals and bioethicists have been mediators between the ideologies and the technical fantasies of the professionals on the one hand, and the most adamant, uninformed advocates of civilian control on the other." In a uniquely American style, we create a class of mediators to fashion a mean between the extremes.

> *"Modern medicine . . .*
> *cannot afford to work in*
> *secrecy and silence."*

The mediators came, almost all of them, from the traditional disciplines of theology and philosophy. There were a few physicians, a few lawyers, and an occasional social scientist, but early bioethics was fashioned out of bits and pieces from moral philosophy and moral theology. By now, modern bioethics has shown medicine the utility of philosophical thought about ethical problems. At the same time, the style and content of American philosophy has been changed by its encounter with medicine, as the philosopher Stephen Toulmin's provocative title, "How Medicine Saved the Life of Ethics," announced. Philosophy no longer gazed impassively and imperiously on the confused world of medical decisionmaking. It entered that world and struggled to shape the logic of moral judgments. Its theories about the nature of morality and moral reasoning were revivified. At the same time, philosophy realized that it had no answers to the questions asked by physicians and patients. Rather, it began to speak with them about the larger, wider dimensions of what they saw as their problems. It helped place them, as we often say, "in a context" of personal needs, preferences, and rights, as well as of social constraints and possibilities. This became a program of spelling out in detail the implications of seeing "the patient as a person," badly needed when the patient had become "an organ," or a "statistic," or even a "consumer."

A Friendly Force

Many of the pioneers who gathered at the Seattle conference commented on the success of bioethics as, in Callahan's words, "a friendly, not hostile force within medicine." Yet, many of the attendees also worried about this. Had the critical edge that Ramsey honed in *The Patient as Person*, warning about the moral dangers of unreflective acceptance of medical advance, become only the moral enthusiasm about medical progress manifested in the thinking of Joseph Fletcher? George Annas wondered whether bioethics has been coopted by medicine. Has bioethics, in Rothman's words "rather heroic" in its early days, slipped into, as Arthur Caplan colorfully phrased it, "sway-bellied middle age, looking pretty institutional, with its people talking ex cathedra and flexing their expertise"?

It would be a shame if that were so, because so much remains to be done. Medical progress goes on, and the perils of progress must be heeded. Jay Katz, physician, law professor, and ethicist, who heroically pulled the ethical problems of human experimentation into the light of critical scrutiny in the 1960s, praised "the vigorous and vociferous inquiries into bioethics that can only cheer a person who long ago tried to pierce the silence." Critical, analytic, and even prophetic voices must greet each innovation in medical science and practice, lest the silence descend again. Modern medicine, as personal service or public enterprise, cannot afford to work in secrecy and silence. If it were to try to revive that comfortable secrecy, the silence would be broken perforce by threatening, destructive voices.

Today, bioethics as a discipline and a movement takes on the even newer medicine. The scientific changes in medicine that will come from the mapping of the human genome will raise unusual ethical questions. Those questions had been already raised less urgently by the evolution of genetic science and the development of screening and testing. They will become more pervasive and complex as we move toward the molecular medicine of the future. The early questions about fairness in selecting patients for the scarce resource of dialysis have been transformed into broad questions about justice in access to health care in general. The new forms for delivery and financing of health care services that are emerging from policy and politics have ethical implications about rationing, prioritizing, and the patient-physician relationship that cannot be ignored. The reproductive technologies that can modify traditional views of parenting and even of personhood require careful scrutiny. Today, unlike the days when the Seattle committee met for its fateful deliberations, concepts and methods, together with scholars and students, exist to help us undertake these examinations. Patients, physicians, and the public will demand these examinations and appreciate their open, reasonable, and fair resolution.

Many New Reproductive Technologies Are Unethical

by Ellen Goodman

About the author: *Ellen Goodman is a nationally syndicated columnist.*

It's been 15 years since Louise Brown's birth was flashed across the globe in headlines announcing the arrival of the first "test-tube baby." In retrospect, her conception in a petri dish from her mother's egg and father's sperm seems relatively natural.

Today, a man's sperm can meet a woman's egg for a one-night stand in a laboratory. The genetic offspring of these strangers can then be placed in a second woman's womb, and given to yet another couple for raising.

In the years between Baby Louise and Teenager Louise, we learned to subdivide the very word mother into functions: genetic mother, gestational mother, birth mother, social mother. We spawned an entire generation of ethical worries about reproductive science and human nature.

Fetus Farming

Now, from Europe, comes the next generation of these fertile questions. They have arrived, unexpectedly, carrying uncomfortable little identification tags that read "retirement babies" and "fetus farming."

In Italy and England, women who were infertile for the most natural of all reasons—they had passed menopause—have been impregnated as late in life as 59 and 62 years old. With the egg from a young woman and the sperm from a younger husband, with hormones pumped in and dollars freely spent, they have broken the biological barrier.

In Scotland, a researcher announced in a calm scientific voice that within a few years, we will be able to "harvest" eggs from an aborted female fetus. He raised the specter of children whose own genetic mothers were literally never born.

I don't think there are thousands of women eagerly waiting for the chance to cash in their Social Security checks for maternity clothes and diapers. Nor do I think that a woman who chooses to have an abortion would want her female fetus to become a mother. I cannot imagine that the same woman who decides not to be a birth mother, for example, would consent to becoming a birth grandmother.

But these cases raise deep anxieties about the choices that science now offers and human beings now have to make. And they are by no means the last nor most unsettling options.

> *"The notion of taking eggs from aborted fetuses is grotesque."*

In January 1994, for example, the French government proposed banning the use of donor eggs for the in vitro fertilization of postmenopausal women. But what if these eggs belonged to the women themselves? A few years ago, before soldiers went off to the Persian Gulf War, a number banked their sperm. If women want to beat the biological clock, will they deposit their eggs in some holding tank for future use?

The notion of taking eggs from aborted fetuses is grotesque. But how long is it before someone suggests filling the "shortage" of eggs in other ways? Will brain-dead or dying females become egg donors the way they are now kidney and liver donors? Will we harvest eggs to conceive our own grandchildren?

Ethical Stop Signs

We need some ethical stop signs. One stop sign goes up at the idea of using fetal eggs at all. Another stop sign should go up at the sight of the dollar sign. In no way should eggs or sperm be bought and sold in the marketplace.

Will such stop signs make it harder for infertile couples to have children? Maybe so. Every step on this reproductive hi-tech-way, from in vitro fertilization to cloning, has been defended as a way to help with the real pain of infertility.

But how much of a help is it? For every woman who eventually delivers a child, how many others are led further and further down paths of false hope that don't have to end now until death?

Even if this technology does produce a picture-perfect baby for some couples, it's fair to ask how much we should sacrifice in moral and scientific terms for that portrait. In the end, this may be the toughest ethical issue.

We live in a world that is bursting at the seams with children. We cannot count the unwanted and the underfed, those in need of families. In such a world, how much should be devoted to the problems of infertility?

Before Baby Louise began life in a petri dish, we depended on nature, the life cycles, the human body, to determine our limits. Now we must depend on the heart and the brain. At times, they seem like much less reliable organs.

Organ Donation from Anencephalic Infants Is Unethical

by Paul A. Byrne, Joseph C. Evers, and Richard G. Nilges

About the authors: *Paul A. Byrne is a neonatologist at St. Charles Hospital in Oregon, Ohio. Joseph C. Evers is an associate clinical professor of pediatrics at Georgetown University School of Medicine in Washington, D.C. Richard G. Nilges is an emeritus member of the neurosurgery staff at the Swedish Covenant Hospital in Chicago.*

A Fort Lauderdale infant with anencephaly [a condition in which an infant is born without most of the brain], Theresa Ann Campo Pearson, was recently the subject of many newspaper articles, television shows, and medical and legal discussions. Her parents had filed a petition in a Florida circuit court for the "right" to authorize the excision of Theresa Ann's unpaired vital organs. The petition sought a judicial determination that anencephalic infants be considered legally dead for the purposes of organ transplantation. The trial court's order denying the petition was summarily upheld on appeal. The Florida Supreme Court affirmed, thus rejecting an expansion of Florida's common law to include anencephaly within the legal definition of death.

In this viewpoint, we will consider the case of Theresa Ann in the context of the brain death controversy. We will show how the attempt to declare death in a living baby with anencephaly is but another step in the growing acceptance of something less than actual death as legal death for the purpose of acquiring transplantable organs.

The Case of Theresa Ann

Theresa Ann was diagnosed antenatally as having anencephaly. Soon thereafter, plans were made to remove her organs for transplantation following her birth. After she was born, Theresa Ann was intubated and received ventilatory support. The ventilator was removed after about one week. Theresa Ann then breathed on her own for a period of time, clearly indicating that the brain stem function governing spontaneous breathing was intact. Other brain stem functions that control heart rate, blood pressure, salt and water balance, pituitary-endocrine organ functions, as well as many other organs and systems, were presumably also intact and functioning in Theresa Ann's body.

> *"Despite widespread acceptance, brain death is still controversial."*

At least some of the physicians treating Theresa Ann knew, and made others aware, that her brain was functioning. Based on this, the Florida Supreme Court ruled that Theresa Ann could not be "brain dead" under Florida law.

Anencephaly results from a failure of the neural tissue to completely close at the cephalic end. Even though anencephaly literally means the absence of the brain, functioning neural tissue is always present. The telencephalon is usually absent, but the brain stem is present. Absence of the cranium (acrania) is a constant finding. . . .

Brain Death Law

The Uniform Determination of Death Act (UDDA) was recommended for adoption in all jurisdictions of the United States by the 1981 President's Commission for the Study of Ethical Problems in Medicine and Biomedical and Behavioral Research. The UDDA reads as follows:

> An individual who has sustained either (1) irreversible cessation of circulatory and respiratory functions, or (2) irreversible cessation of all functions of the entire brain, including the brain stem, is dead. A determination of death must be made in accordance with accepted medical standards.

The Florida Supreme Court affirmed the lower court's ruling that Florida state law "[does] not permit a determination of legal death so long as the . . . brain stem continue[s] to function." Since Theresa Ann had obvious functioning (or functions) of her brain, the statutory criteria of irreversible cessation of all functioning (or functions) of the entire brain had not been fulfilled.

When so many patients today are being legally declared brain dead in the presence of some brain stem activity, why was the same not permitted for Theresa Ann? The answer lies in the second sentence of the UDDA, which states that "[a] determination of death must be made in accordance with accepted medical standards." Whereas Theresa Ann's case presented the question of whether a certain class of infants should be considered legally dead by definition, these other patients are declared brain dead on a case-by-case basis under more ambiguous and flexible criteria, i.e., accepted medical standards.

Like the Florida court justices, many people are not aware that accepted medical standards may include the presence of some functions of the brain when a determination of brain death is made. For example, it was reported that ten out of ten organ donors at a leading university hospital showed a dramatic rise in blood pressure and heart rate as soon as the scalpel was applied during organ removal and that such an occurrence "appears to be common during organ harvesting" [according to Randall C. Wetzel et al.]. Is there any way that this could have happened in ten out of ten patients without a functioning brain stem? The reflex centers for control of cardiac and hemodynamic functions are in the brain stem. How could Judge Moriarity be expected to know that, under current medical practice, it is "acceptable" to declare brain death in the presence of some brain functions, when the law so clearly requires the cessation of *all* functions of the *entire* brain?

Thirty Ways to Be Declared Dead

What has society accepted in brain death? Death is a fact, but is it fulfilled when brain death is declared? Before the acceptance of brain death as legal death, the criteria for the determination of death were based on the definition of death in *Black's Law Dictionary:* "The cessation of life; the ceasing to exist; defined by physicians as a total stoppage of the circulation of the blood, and a cessation of the animal and vital functions consequent thereon, such as respiration, pulsation, etc."

With the emergence of organ transplantation research and technology came the recognition that only living organs were viable for transplanta-

> *"A prediction of death is not the same as death."*

tion. This realization culminated in a 1968 report by the Ad Hoc Committee of the Harvard Medical School, which introduced the medical community to the concept of brain death. It addressed the problem of irreversible coma and, in defining this entity, offered criteria for its recognition. The Harvard Criteria, as they are now known, were published under the title "A Definition of Irreversible Coma," but in the article *coma* was translated into *brain death*. The article was published without any patient data or any basic science research or references.

The 1971 Minnesota Criteria for brain death were developed from a study of twenty-five patients. An electroencephalogram (EEG) was done on only nine of these patients. Two of the nine had "EEG activity at the time of brain death" [according to A. Mohandas and Shelley N. Chou]. Their conclusion: no longer is it necessary for the neurosurgeon to use the EEG in making a determination of death.

The British criteria also do not include the EEG for diagnosis. The *British Medical Journal* reported that doctors in Great Britain were considerably influenced by the doctors in Minnesota who do not require the EEG.

The National Institutes of Health (NIH) Criteria were derived from a study known as the Collaborative Study. The NIH Criteria were recommended for a larger clinical trial, which still has yet to be done. By 1978 there were more than thirty nonidentical sets of criteria already published. A physician is free to use any one of these thirty sets. Thus, a patient could be determined to be dead by one set but not by another. Furthermore, the President's Commission indicated that "[t]he 'functions of the entire brain' that are relevant to the diagnosis are those that are clinically ascertainable." In one sentence, the commission reduced whatever diagnostic stringency there may have been to no more than what is "clinically ascertainable."

Criteria for Determining Death

In the case of Theresa Ann, clinically ascertainable functions of her brain were easily observed. Those wanting to take her organs were willing to go to the state supreme court in an attempt to include anencephaly within the meaning of death or to ask for a ruling that the criteria required by the Florida brain death law deprived the parents of Theresa Ann of *their* right to donate *her* organs.

At the time of the report by the President's Commission, it was stated that "[p]hysicians should be particularly cautious in applying neurologic criteria to determine death in children younger than five years." Since then, a task force has published *Guidelines for the Determination of Brain Death in Children.* In these guidelines, there is a requirement that "[t]he patient must not be significantly hypothermic or hypotensive for age" when the determination of brain death is made. When body temperature is normal without control by environmental warming or cooling, and when the blood pressure is normal without control by pressor drugs, the brain *must be functioning.* The diagnosis of brain death despite the observation of these normal vital signs (temperature and blood pressure), and despite the possibility of the presence of nonevaluated and non-tested brain functions, has been medically and legally acceptable at all other ages as well. Since the publication of the guidelines, it has become not only acceptable but is now *required* that these vital signs of normal temperature and normal blood pressure be present when making a determination of brain death in children. No wonder there is, and has been, confusion regarding the use of the anencephalic infant as a source of vital organs!

Absence of brain stem functions is determined by the lack of response of some brain stem reflexes. When the patient is unconscious, unresponsive, and on a ventilator, and pupillary, corneal, oculocephalic, oculovestibular, cough, and gag reflexes are absent, the patient may be taken off the ventilator to observe the presence or absence of spontaneous breathing. If there is no breathing apparent, in

> *"As long as there is doubt about the fact of death, one should not take any lethal action."*

some circumstances for as short a time as thirty to sixty seconds, the patient is considered brain dead even though the patient has a normal temperature, normal blood pressure, normal heart rate, normal salt and water balance, normal thyroid and adrenal functions—all of which depend on a functioning brain.

Despite widespread acceptance, brain death is still controversial. A. Earl Walker wrote "Based upon the findings of the Collaborative Study, from *8* to *40%* of persons meeting different sets of clinical criteria for brain death . . . had biological activity in their electroencephalograms." Was the "progress" of medicine in the area of brain death based on adequate, valid scientific data? We think not.

Stuart J. Youngner et al. reported, after interviewing physicians and nurses involved in organ procurement, that "[o]nly . . . 35% correctly identified the legal and medical criteria for determining death . . . [and] 19% had a concept of death that was logically consistent with changing the whole-brain standard to classify anencephalics and patients in a persistent vegetative state as dead." The latter is a standard that is not legally recognized in *any* jurisdiction. The Youngner article was accompanied by an editorial that stated,

> [T]he whole-brain concept reflects no fact about the patient's status as living or dead. Whole-brain death is . . . an aid to decision making in intensive care and transplantation. On the conceptual level it makes less sense than either of its chief rivals: the traditional heart-lung concept and the higher brain definition, which defines death as the loss of those brain functions that support awareness and cognition.

Why is there confusion in this serious matter of brain death? The answer lies in the distinction between the brain's "functions" and its "capacity to function." The UDDA and all the laws in this matter call for absence of brain function, functions, or functioning. The observation of *nonfunctioning* of a reflex is then considered as the absence of *capability* of function. However, absence of functioning, or nonfunctioning, may simply show that the function is idle. In current practice, the absence of only certain tested brain stem functions is considered to satisfy the statutorily required absence of *all* functions of the entire brain. Needless to say, far too much is and has been concluded from what is observed.

Furthermore, brain death criteria confound loss of function with physical destruction. Consider the following analogies: an unplugged computer is nonfunctioning, but an electrical current can restore its functions; a parked automobile is nonfunctioning, but a driver with a key can restore its functions. Similarly, during sleep there is some loss of brain functions that recover on awakening. Narcotics and toxins also result in temporary cessation of many functions; an antidote can restore these functions. Destruction includes alteration of the basic structure, that is, *structural* or *organic* change resulting in the loss of the *capacity* to function. Contemporary brain death criteria only consider the cessation of functioning. None of the criteria is designed to diagnose the destruction of the brain, or even part of the brain, much less the destruction or death of the organism.

> *"The baby with anencephaly is a human being. . . . That baby is alive."*

Death is a fact. After death, what is left of the body is referred to as "the remains." During life, there is an interdependence of organs and systems resulting in the oneness or unity of the person. To observe an absence of only certain tested brain stem reflexes and an absence of breathing when taken off the ventilator, then to conclude that brain death has occurred without evaluating other brain functions or considering that organs and systems of the body are still functioning, is contrary to the facts of death.

Brain Death

The Uniform Determination of Death Act accepts two separate, readily distinguishable, clinical situations as death: cessation of circulatory and respiratory functions or cessation of brain functions. Both of these "deaths" can be manifest sequentially in the same individual patient. The diagnosis of brain death can vary depending on which of the more than thirty, nonidentical sets of criteria are used to determine "irreversible cessation of all brain functions." Once the diagnosis of brain death has been made, current practice is such that the patient's ventilator will often be continued until it is convenient to perform organ transplantation. Prior to the removal of unpaired vital organs, anyone in attendance can witness the intact circulatory system by auscultation or the oscilloscopic display of the beating heart, as well as by a recordable blood pressure. The normal color of the skin indicates an intact respiratory system. The exchange of oxygen and carbon dioxide can be verified by determining blood gases. The continued interdependence of circulatory and respiratory systems can be observed by applying pressure to the skin, resulting in blanching followed by a normal color within a few seconds after removal of the pressure. With more sophistication, an intact endocrine system (pituitary, thyroid, and adrenal hormone production) can often be demonstrated. Detoxification by the intact liver can be documented through appropriate testing. If the individual declared brain dead is pregnant, the mother and the fetus can often be maintained until the fetus matures and can be delivered.

"One should presume . . . that anencephalic babies are no less aware or capable of suffering than some laboratory animals."

Clearly, there are many signs, including the vital signs, that both physicians and laymen are accustomed to associating with being alive. When ventilator support is gradually reduced or, more often, when it is abruptly turned off, everything else may stop, or sometimes the individual resumes spontaneous breathing. On the other hand, whether or not the support is gradually reduced or abruptly stopped, if the beating heart is excised and no substitute is implanted, the other set of criteria acceptable under the UDDA—the cessation of circulatory and respiratory functions—will be fulfilled, and the individual will manifest the symptoms more universally identified with the fact of death. Are we not, then, being asked to accept two medically, clearly distinguishable situations as being equivalent and identical?

We know when a body is, in fact, living. There are activities required for a living body to continue living. We also know when a body is, in fact, dead—at least there are certain activities that are acceptable only with regard to a dead body, e.g., burial or cremation. However, if there is doubt about whether a body is alive or dead, may one take action, such as cutting out the still-beating heart? Does one become dead merely because someone says he/she is dead? Rather, isn't there a factual state of death that should be fully ascertained *before* permitting a pronouncement of death to be made?

> *"A prediction that death will occur soon is not the same as being already dead."*

The issues involved in taking an unpaired vital organ from an anencephalic baby are not new to the discussion of brain death and death. Some postulate that absence of function of the cortex (e.g., the parts of the brain that support awareness and cognition) is sufficient for death. Others say that the so-called whole-brain standard, i.e., irreversible cessation of all functions of the entire brain including the brain stem, is required. Still others hold that absence of function, in itself, is not sufficient for acceptance of factual death. This latter position recognizes that a prediction of death is not the same as death and that, as long as there is doubt about the fact of death, one should not take any lethal action, such as cutting out the beating heart, until the doubt has been removed.

Confusing Laws

The laws, including the UDDA, have not been helpful in resolving these issues. The UDDA states that an individual who has sustained either (1) irreversible cessation of circulatory and respiratory functions or (2) irreversible cessation of all functions of the entire brain, including the brain stem, is dead. Thus, the pronouncement of death can be done by (1) or (2), but in view of the looseness of the criteria for brain death, neither is really required. . . . Furthermore, already by 1978 there were more than thirty sets of criteria (and there have been many more sets introduced since then) for the determination of death. Thus, there exist at least thirty-one different ways to be pronounced dead (when the traditional cardiopulmonary standard is included). Together, these factors have only enhanced the confusion that currently surrounds the issue of the determination of death.

Many proponents of brain death, including the President's Commission, acknowledge that a patient with autoregulatory functions is not dead. Yet, in its 1981 *Guidelines for the Determination of Death*, the President's Commission did not require, or even suggest, that the autoregulatory functions be tested.

The baby with anencephaly is a human being. When he/she has a beating heart, a recordable blood pressure, some movement, and many functioning internal organs and systems, that baby is alive. While the prognosis for long-term survival is not good, some anencephalic infants live for a considerable period of time. One report found that more than forty percent of live-born anencephalic infants survive longer than twenty-four hours; of these, roughly fifteen percent survived more than three days, and five percent lived longer than seven days. There are reports of an anencephalic baby living five and one-half months, and another, fourteen months. Anencephalic babies may die because of lack of protection of the brain from trauma and infection (since the scalp and skull are partially absent). If the brain were sufficiently protected, life could be prolonged for years.

Difficulties in Diagnosing Anencephaly

D. Alan Shewmon has reviewed the issue of anencephaly and organ transplantation. His reviews include some of the difficulties encountered in accurately diagnosing anencephaly. (It is less accurate by sonographic examination than by direct clinical examination of the infant.) In reviewing the topic of consciousness in anencephalic babies, he points out many differences between the functions of the brain of an adult and those of the brain of an infant. In response to those who declare the anencephalic infant insentient based on the absence of an upper (or "higher") brain, Shewmon states,

> It simply begs the question to state categorically that [anencephalic babies] lack conscious awareness because they lack cerebral hemispheres. Much less is there any logical or physiological basis for the claim of some that an anencephalic infant can neither feel, nor experience, pain 'by definition.' For practical purposes, one should presume, at the very least, that anencephalic babies are no less aware or capable of suffering than some laboratory animals with even smaller brains, which everyone seems to feel obliged to treat 'humanely.'

Those [such as Michael R. Harrison, quoted in the following passages], who propose taking organs from the anencephalic infant have one or more of several attitudes toward the infant: (1) "[T]he anencephalic baby is a product of human conception incapable of achieving 'personhood' because it lacks the physical structure (forebrain) necessary for characteristic human activity. . . ." In response, this is merely a philosophical postulation based on the premise that unless there is sufficient physical structure for rationality and self-awareness, the living human organism is not a human being. Yet, an infant with anencephaly is as much a

> *"Every infant—including one with anencephaly—has a . . . moral claim to our care and protection."*

human being as a monkey with anencephaly is a monkey and a dog with anencephaly is a dog. (2) "[T]he anencephalic [baby] is a dying person and . . . death is inevitable at or shortly after birth because of the brain [abnormality]." However, to state the obvious, a dying person is still alive. Death is inevitable for all of us, including the baby with anencephaly. A prediction that death will occur soon is not the same as being already dead. This contention, then, is true for everyone, not merely the baby with anencephaly. (3) "[T]he anencephalic [baby is] . . . brain absent." In response, the anencephalic baby always has some brain tissue. Death may be caused by trauma, nonfunction, or dysfunction of the brain that is present and/or by infection.

A Greater Moral Claim

The infant with anencephaly is a living human being who has a congenital abnormality that usually is not associated with long-term survival. If the infant with anencephaly is dying but not yet dead, he/she is still a living person. Being inherently vulnerable, every infant—including one with anencephaly—has a greater moral claim to our care and protection than an adult who is otherwise healthy and self-sufficient.

After an unpaired vital organ has been excised from an infant with anencephaly, death inevitably follows just as surely as it would for anyone else from whom an unpaired vital organ is taken. To create a fictional category of death for anencephalic infants in order to obtain their vital organs is not only medically dishonest but is, in the final analysis, morally reprehensible.

Cloning Is Unethical

by Leslie Bond Diggins

About the author: *Leslie Bond Diggins is a writer for the National Right to Life News, the newsletter of the National Right to Life Committee, a pro-life organization in Washington, D.C.*

In a move that has given rise to Frankensteinian specters of mass-produced humans, test tube babies grown for spare parts and "super-embryos" genetically engineered and sold to the highest bidder, two medical researchers announced in October 1993 that they had "cloned" human embryos.

Dr. Jerry L. Hall and Dr. Robert J. Stillman, both of the George Washington University School of Medicine in Washington, D.C., made their announcement without fanfare at the annual meeting of the American Fertility Society in Montreal. But as soon as word of the human experiment reached a wider audience, a vociferous debate erupted among doctors, bioethicists, columnists, and the general public—with all but a few expressing concern and alarm about the controversial research.

Far from Science Fiction

Media reports cited bioethicists and others raising specters of "cloned" human embryos being frozen for later use as organ donors, or mass-produced and sold at high prices by marketers who could point to the desirable characteristics of a child resulting from a genetically identical embryo. Others pointed ghoulish pictures of identical twins being raised years apart and embryos being duplicated so that genetic testing could be done—killing the duplicate in the process and allowing the "original" to be discarded as well if it "failed" to meet certain specifications.

Far from being "science fiction," human embryos produced through *in vitro* fertilization have already been subjected to genetic testing—and thrown away if found to be "imperfect."

The experiment that gave rise to the furor took place "in recent months," according to media accounts, at the In Vitro Fertilization and Andrology Laboratory at the George Washington University School of Medicine in the nation's capital. There, a team of researchers headed by Hall and Stillman took 17 living

Leslie Bond Diggins, "Human 'Cloning' Sparks Fierce Ethics Debate," *National Right to Life News*, November 5, 1993. Reprinted by permission of the author.

human embryos, varying in development from two to eight cells, and created 48 distinct living human embryos from them.

The researchers' first step was to chemically remove each embryo's "zona pellucida," a hard, shell-like covering which nourishes and protects the developing baby. Next, the researchers separated each embryo into individual cells, called blastocytes.

The 48 resulting blastocytes were then coated with a synthetic substance made to mimic the zona pellucida and placed in a solution conducive to embryonic development. The blastocytes did, in fact, begin to divide and grow, developing into distinct human embryos, each genetically identical to the original embryo from which it was taken.

> *"The procedure was . . . not a 'breakthrough' but rather a 'breakdown' in both morality and intelligence."*

The new embryos developed to stages varying from two to thirty-two cells each. Researchers planned to discard the embryos after seven days, but all died on their own within six days.

(Calls by *NRL [National Right to Life] News* to Hall were referred to the university's public relations office, and repeated calls there were not returned, leaving unanswered numerous basic questions. For example, reportedly, the embryos used for the experiment had been fertilized with more than one sperm, an abnormality making them unacceptable for implantation. However, it is unclear whether these embryos were intentionally fertilized with multiple sperm specifically for the purposes of the experiment, or if the multiple fertilization occurred accidentally during attempts to create embryos for implantation. In either case, there is no indication whether the parents of the embryos—the women who produced the eggs and the men who produced the sperm—gave permission for their offspring to be used in the experiment.)

Technically, what the researchers did is not properly called "cloning," but rather "artificial twinning." True cloning involves taking a cell from a fully developed person or animal and creating a genetically identical twin from that cell. In artificial twinning, the cells of an embryo—which have not yet differentiated into various types of cells, such as skin, brain, heart, etc.—are separated and then grown into distinct, though genetically identical, individuals.

A Breakdown in Morality

Researchers claim the experiment was done in an effort to improve *in vitro* fertilization techniques, by creating multiple embryos for implantation without having to stimulate the production of multiple eggs by the woman seeking to become pregnant.

But far from being a scientific breakthrough, artificial twinning has been done in animals for a decade, stressed internationally renown physician and pro-life lecturer Jerome Lejeune, M.D. The novelty of Hall's and Stillman's work, Lejeune told *NRL News*, was that the procedure was carried out on *human* embryos—a fact which is not a "breakthrough" but rather a "breakdown" in both morality and intelligence.

Artificial twinning is rarely used in animal reproduction these days, he explained, "because it doesn't improve efficiency." Many of the embryos created by the process die before they can be implanted and many that are implanted do not "take." To take a procedure which does not work well in animals and apply it to human beings makes no sense, he emphasized.

Researchers who would follow such a course "believe human beings at these early stages of development are animals," he said. "This is absolutely wrong. We are always human beings, from the moment of conception."

Numerous other ethical issues were raised by Andrew Kimbrell, policy director for the Foundation on Economic Trends, a Washington-based biomedical watchdog organization.

"My primary objection is that the whole 'cloning' process will lead to even more disrespect for life, and will further lead to the commodification of life—treating human beings as machines," Kimbrell told *NRL News*. The result will be a very dangerous program of "commercial eugenics," he warned, in which researchers attempt to come up with the "perfect embryo" and then sell copies of it to parents seeking certain traits. Embryos found to have "undesirable" traits will be discarded in a process that encodes society's prejudices for certain characteristics—and against others—into the very genetics of the next generation.

> *"We are always human beings, from the moment of conception."*

Once "superior" embryos were created, Kimbrell added, researchers could further dehumanize them by attempting to patent them, to prevent others from copying "their" embryos.

And the ability to duplicate human embryos would result in more applications than attempts to create "perfect" children, Kimbrell stressed. For example, researchers who now perform experiments with human embryos could remove numerous variables and obtain more consistent results by using genetically identical embryos. Further, he said, some scientists already are predicting the use of frozen embryos to provide organs and tissues.

No Sense of Uniqueness

In addition to these concerns, Kimbrell stressed that "no one has any idea of the impact it would have to know you are a 'clone.'" People's sense of individuality—an important part of who we are as human beings—could be in serious jeopardy, he stressed.

This concern was echoed by Cynthia Cohen, Ph.D., head of the National Advisory Board on Ethics and Reproduction. "I'm concerned about making a duplicate of an individual human being," she said in a telephone interview with *NRL News*. "Do we *want* to manufacture human beings in this manner?" she asked. "Is there a concern about what this does to the meaning of being human?"

But some seemingly had no qualms about the procedure. Norman Fost, a medical ethicist at the University of Wisconsin, told the *New York Times* he believed it was the parents' right to decide what to do with their embryos. He said he started "with a presumption of privacy and liberty, that people should be able to live their lives the way they want and to make babies the way they want."

Taking issue with these views was Arthur Caplan, Ph.D., director of the Center for Biomedical Ethics at the University of Minnesota. "I think that the marketplace ethics and pounding the autonomy drum are not sufficient when it comes to decisions of how to make future generations of children and their descendants," he told the *Times*. Saying that the issues raised were more than a matter of privacy, he added, "There is room for governmental and societal debate and, perhaps, prohibitions and control and restraints."

No friend of the unborn on the issue of abortion, Caplan acknowledged that under the right-to-life perspective, the embryo is a human being deserving full legal protection. "But whether others agree on this or not, obviously the embryo has *some* rights," he said in an interview with *NRL News*. "It's human tissue, potentially a person, and society has an interest in those potential people."

A similar sentiment was expressed by Cohen. Although Cohen's group is in direct conflict with pro-life organizations over such issues as the use of fetal tissue procured from induced abortions, she expressed some concern for the human embryos in question.

"No matter what position you take on the moral status of embryos, if they are frozen for later implantation, you are talking about a child-to-be," she told *NRL News*. "I think sometimes we lose sight of that."

One of Cohen's primary concerns was the fact that researchers went ahead with their experiment with virtually no prior ethical discussion. "We were surprised," Cohen told the Associated Press. "We had been assured that this sort of experiment wouldn't be done in this country. We haven't discussed this issue at all."

In fact, the first notice Cohen's group received that the experiment had taken place was when Hall and Stillman made their presentation at the American Fertility Society meeting.

Kimbrell said the Foundation on Economic Trends has petitioned the National Institutes of Health to put a moratorium on the funding of all such experiments on human embryos, and to cease funding any institution which supports such research. Further, Kimbrell said, the Foundation plans to work toward passing laws forbidding the cloning, sale, or patenting of human embryos.

"This is a technology with no redeeming value," Kimbrell stated emphatically. "Whatever minimal benefit there might be [from cloning] to reproductive technologies, they can never be balanced" by the inherent wrongness of the procedure, he said. "It is antithetical to human rights."

182

Maintaining the Bodies of Brain-Dead Pregnant Women Is Unethical

by Joel E. Frader

About the author: *Joel E. Frader is an associate professor in the department of pediatrics and the department of anesthesiology and critical care medicine at the Children's Hospital of Pittsburgh and the University of Pittsburgh School of Medicine. He is also the associate director for consultation at the Center for Medical Ethics at the University of Pittsburgh.*

There has been considerable media attention focused on a few cases [of brain-dead women giving birth] and considerable political energy spent on passing "incubator clauses" in state living-will legislation. [But] one has to wonder whether this is much ado about a very rare phenomenon. In the vast majority of cases, the condition affecting the mother will result in the death of the fetus long before the philosophical debate [over maintaining her bodily functions] can even commence. . . .

Dead Bodies Are Dead

Why should we discuss this problem as if the dead body were not dead? According to Jay E. Kantor and Iffath Abbasi Hoskins, the approach "will help to shed light on the ethical issues." Does it? It isn't clear. We do have systems for ascertaining the wishes of those who have died: donor cards, wills, and so forth. This approach could apply to the brain-dead pregnant body as well. Kantor and Hoskins suggest that a woman's clearly expressed desire for body functions to continue in order to sustain the pregnancy probably should carry substantial moral weight. But this suggestion poses several problems. How often will a healthy, pregnant woman let others know her thoughts on this matter? Probably not very often. It seems inappropriate for ignorance of prior wishes alone to provide a moral warrant for ignoring her death and pretending she lives on.

From Joel E. Frader, "Have We Lost Our Senses? Problems with Maintaining Brain-Dead Bodies Carrying Fetuses," *Journal of Clinical Ethics*, vol. 4, no. 4 (Winter 1993), ©1993 by the Journal of Clinical Ethics. Reprinted with permission.

Why not deal with the reality, including the tragedy and the attendant concerns about appropriate respect due dead bodies? . . .

A Gruesome Problem

One could argue that continued "treatment" of the cadaver is, in and of itself, undignified and even gruesome—regardless of any "interests" one may wish to attribute to the fetus. Surely the moral sentiments—not to mention the raw emotions—of doctors, nurses, and respiratory therapists who would have to minister to the body require some attention.

The more one thinks about this kind of problem, the more one must wonder what modern medical science and technology have wrought. Instead of fussing about theoretical problems, like how many angels can dance on the head of a pin, we now confront real but terribly distorted situations involving the stuff of horror movies and distasteful science fiction. We argue about when bodies are "dead enough" to justify removing organs or whether a body is sufficiently "undead" that we should administer fluids, nutrients, hormones, vasoactive substances (substances affecting the degree of relaxation or contraction of blood vessels), and oxygen, to bring yet another motherless child into the world. . . .

Our technical capacity to manipulate physiology seems less and less grounded in either reality or good sense. Should we stop for a minute to think about the implication of keeping the body of a brain-dead pregnant woman functioning so that an embryo or fetus can grow or develop, no matter what the *former* prospective

> *"No consideration . . . allows me to feel wholesome about sustaining dead bodies to 'grow' fetuses."*

mother might have wanted? A fetus near term, assuming it has not been severely damaged by whatever injury killed the mother, can probably survive with immediate delivery. Beyond this already uncommon circumstance, no material or symbolic meaning I try to assign to a dead woman's enduring interests, the putative interests of a preterm fetus, or the interests of the father or other family members, and no consideration of resources allows me to feel wholesome about sustaining dead bodies to "grow" fetuses.

Pregnancy has special biological, cultural, and religious significance; indeed, it has great political import in our society. But then, so does death. I do not believe that we want to say that the remote possibility of continuing a new life should sweep aside the ways we have come to deal with dead bodies—especially our belief in the value of relatively prompt burial or cremation and the accompanying mourning rituals. We must resist technologic tyranny, despite our fascination with the philosophical conundrums it produces.

Cloning Is Ethical

by John A. Robertson

About the author: *John A. Robertson is Thomas Watt Gregory Professor of Law at the University of Texas in Austin.*

Accustomed though we are to advances in medical technology, a 24 October 1993 news report that human embryos had been cloned astonished many persons. A *New York Times* story, "Researcher Clones Embryos of Humans in Fertility Effort," was the feature that Sunday morning in many newspapers throughout the country. Media coverage continued for several days, with debates about cloning on editorial pages, *Nightline*, and *Larry King Live*.

Within a week the issue had faded from media consciousness, aided in part by *Time* and *Newsweek* stories that stressed the huge gap between the reported research and the *Jurassic Park*-type fears of cloned human beings that initially spurred national coverage. Bioethicists and lawmakers, however, must still contend with the ethical and policy issues that even limited cloning of humans presents. Should researchers be free to continue cloning research? May infertile couples and their physicians employ cloning to form families? Or should government prevent cloning research or discourage some or all of its later applications?

As with many biomedical developments, these questions present a mix of issues that need careful sorting. They involve, among others, questions of the propriety of embryo research, the validity of deliberately creating twins, and the importance of nature versus nurture in forming human beings. They also raise slippery slope concerns: should otherwise seemingly valid uses of a new technique be stopped to prevent later undesirable uses from occurring? To address those issues we must first describe the cloning research that has touched off the furor and the concerns that it presents.

Two Types of Cloning

The research that put cloning on the public agenda was a long way from Huxleyian fantasies of identical babies, mass produced in laboratories, and did not involve cloning as conventionally understood at all. To clone means to create a genetic copy or replica. Perhaps due to science fiction fantasies, it has been assumed that cloning would occur by removing the nucleus from the cell of one person, placing it in an egg that has had its nucleus removed, and then implanting it in a laboratory incubator or a woman who would bring to term a child with the identical genetic characteristics of the person providing the cell nucleus. Although this procedure has worked with frogs, it has never succeeded with mammals and appears highly unlikely to be accomplished in even the mid-range future. If this form of cloning were possible, scientists could fabricate as many copies

> *"The actual birth of children as a result of embryo splitting might well occur in the next two to five years."*

as one wished of any available human genome, subject only to the limits of uterine or artificial gestation.

A second and more limited way to create clones is to split the cells or blastomeres of an early multicelled embryo before the cells have begun to differentiate. Because each blastomere at this stage is in theory totipotent (that is, capable of producing an entire organism itself), the separated cells can become new embryos, all of which will have the same genome. This form of cloning is now practiced to some extent in the cattle industry. Cloning by blastomere separation is limited to the number of cells that can be separated before cell differentiation, which destroys totipotency, occurs.

Embryo Splitting

The study that generated the recent interest in cloning involved a small but essential step toward cloning human beings by embryo splitting. Researchers at George Washington University Hospital in Washington, D.C., separated cells or blastomeres from seventeen two- to eight-celled preembryos and showed that, to a limited extent, they would divide and grow in culture. The cells had been obtained from polyspermic embryos that had no chance of implanting in the uterus and that ordinarily would have been discarded. The separated blastomeres were coated with an artificial zona pellucida [a hard covering that protects the developing fetus] and placed in the culture medium used for in vitro fertilization (IVF).

The researchers obtained forty-eight blastomeres from the seventeen polyspermic embryos (eight two-cell, two three-cell, five four-cell, and two eight-cell), or theoretically forty-eight new totipotent embryos. A similar percentage of embryos cleaved for each stage of the embryo from which they were taken. While morulas (thirty-two-celled embryos) were achieved when blastomeres from two-celled embryos were cultured, blastomeres from four-celled embryos developed only to the sixteen-cell state, and no blastomeres derived from the eight-cell stage grew past eight cells in culture. These results suggest that splitting embryos at the two-cell stage appears to be more conducive to further development than does separation at the four-cell or eight-cell stage. However, the maximum stage at which a single blastomere can be reprogrammed to exhibit totipotency by itself or with cellular materials transplanted from other cells is unknown.

The study thus demonstrated that experimental cloning or twinning of human embryos is potentially feasible as an aid to relieving infertility, though much additional work remains before offspring are produced, and there is uncertainty whether the technique will ever work at all. To produce a child by this method would first require showing that excised blastomeres from normal embryos would grow in culture to the point at which transfer to the uterus would ordinarily occur. Such research should also show the optimal stage for splitting normal embryos. It would then be necessary to place embryos that appear to be developing normally from split blastomeres into the uterus to show their potential for implantation and a successful pregnancy.

Some experts, however, are dubious that infertile couples would ever benefit from cloning by blastomere separation. They view the higher pregnancy rate after transfer of several embryos as due to the genetic heterogeneity of the embryos transferred, not to numbers alone. On this view, placing several genetically identical embryos in the uterus will not increase the chances of pregnancy if one embryo with that genome would not have implanted. If this view is correct, there will be little incentive to use blastomere separation to treat infertility, and the ethical issues discussed below will have little practical significance. The following discussion, however, assumes that blastomere separation could provide certain advantages in treating infertility, and examines the ethical and policy issues that then arise.

Fears and Concerns

Some commentators saw nothing particularly unethical or disturbing in the George Washington research. This was simply another step toward improving the efficacy and efficiency of IVF, particularly for those couples who produce too few eggs or embryos to initiate pregnancy.

Many news reports, however, highlighted the disturbing or possibly unethical features of cloning and quoted ethicists who found the practice troubling. They described hypothetical scenarios in which embryos would be cloned for sale or to produce organs and tissue for existing children who needed transplants. One ethicist [Michael Waldholz] termed cloning

"The most likely uses of cloning are neither so harmful nor so novel that all research and development should now stop."

as "contrary to human values"; others [such as Gina Kolata] saw it as "an opportunity for mischief" that called for "governmental and societal debate and, perhaps, prohibitions and restraints." The Vatican newspaper termed it a step into "a tunnel of madness," while the United Methodist Church called for an executive order banning cloning in all federally financed institutions. A poll a week after the first story reported that 60 percent of Americans opposed cloning.

The fears and concerns about cloning have several strands. Some of them arise from the artificial nature of assisted laboratory reproduction. Others are tied to discomfort with the manipulation and destruction of embryos that cloning research, if not the procedure itself, will inevitably cause. The most prevalent ethical concern, however, arises from the dangers that intentional creation of identical twins or multiples of one genome might pose to resulting offspring. The fear is that cloning will violate the inherent uniqueness and dignity of individuals, as well as create unrealistic parental expectations for their children. It also opens the door to identical embryos being created and sold because of their genetic desirability, as cattle embryos now are sold to increase animal yield and profitability. A worst-case scenario envisages the mass production of identical embryos to be sold to persons seeking desirable children. Finally, there are fears that embryos will be created to provide organs and tissue for existing children who need transplants.

> *"Cloning embryos . . . poses no greater harm to embryos than other IVF practices."*

Despite these reservations, research into the feasibility of splitting embryos will undoubtedly continue. Cloning by blastomere separation is basically a mechanical procedure that requires only the ability to micromanipulate fertilized eggs and embryos and a few hundred dollars' worth of culture medium. No DNA analysis or genetic expertise is necessary. It is likely that the next research steps—separating and culturing single blastomeres from normal embryos and then placing those that grow well into the uterus—and the actual birth of children as a result of embryo splitting might well occur in the next two to five years. As micromanipulation of eggs and embryos is a rapidly growing practice, the ability to excise blastomeres from an embryo will easily be within the reach of many IVF physicians and embryologists. If shown to be safe and effective, physicians in many fertility centers will then offer the procedure to patients.

Scientific Zeal

These possibilities engender a recurring disquietude about new reproductive technologies. Scientific zeal and the profit motive combine with the desire of infertile couples for biologic offspring to create an enormous power to manipulate the earliest stages of human life in infertility centers across the country. Even before one innovation is fully assimilated, the largely unregulated billion-dollar infertility industry presents another "improvement," which separately or together threatens disturbing consequences for offspring, families, and society.

Some persons would argue that the idea of creating exact replicas of other human beings is so novel that there should be a moratorium on further research

and development until a national consultative body evaluates the ethical acceptability of the procedure and develops guidelines for research and use of the
technique. At the very least, to prevent abuses there should be strict rules about
the circumstances in which cloning by embryo splitting occurs, and about the
uses made of cloned embryos.

A closer look at the issues, however, suggests that the most likely uses of
cloning are neither so harmful nor so novel that all research and development
should now stop until the ethics of the practice are fully aired, or that governmental restrictions on cloning research or applications are needed. Indeed, there
may be no particular need for guidelines beyond the full and accurate disclosure
of risks and success rates that should always occur in assisted reproduction. . . .

Destruction of Embryos

Cloning by blastomere separation raises a number of ethical issues. Some ethical concerns derive from the stark interference with natural reproduction, or the
manipulation and destruction of embryos that cloning necessarily entails. However, those concerns are not unique to cloning, and have been voiced about embryo research, freezing, and discard, and about IVF generally. Since they are not
deemed sufficient to justify banning or restricting those accepted forms of assisted reproduction, they should not
be sufficient to ban cloning either.

"Thawing cloned embryos to provide tissue or organs for an existing child should also be ethically acceptable."

Yet persons who believe that fertilized eggs and embryos are already
persons with rights will object that
embryo splitting goes beyond the
manipulations ordinarily involved in
IVF. In this case a new unique individual will be intentionally split to serve other
ends. The very process of blastomere separation could destroy embryos that
would have developed normally, thus denigrating and undermining the value of
human life. Because human life at all stages is a preeminent value, cloning by
blastomere separation is an unethical procedure that should be banned.

There may be no way to answer the objections of persons who think that embryos are themselves persons and must be protected at all costs. The fact that
embryo cloning might yield additional human lives will not assuage their concerns, for one is ordinarily not justified in killing one person in order to save
several. One can only point to the prevailing moral and legal consensus that
views early embryos as too rudimentary in neurological development to have
interests or rights. On this view, splitting embryos can no more harm them than
freezing or discarding them can. Nor is splitting embryos to enable one or more
of them to implant and come to term inherently degrading or disrespectful of
human life. Cloning embryos thus poses no greater harm to embryos than other
IVF practices and should be permitted to the same extent that they are.

Ethical objections that are unique to cloning arise from a concern that the intentional creation of genetic replicas of an existing person denies the uniqueness of resulting offspring. This could occur from causing more than one child with the same genome to be born simultaneously. It could also occur from causing more than one child with the same genome to be born at different points in time.

Is the intentional creation of twins who are born simultaneously morally objectionable? Identical twinning occurs naturally and is not generally thought to be harmful or disadvantageous to twins. If anything, being a twin appears to create close emotional bonds that confer special advantages. If this is true, then having twins as a result of embryo splitting should be no more harmful to offspring than having twins naturally. . . .

Later Born Twins

The second ethical issue unique to cloning by embryo splitting is the possibility of genetically identical siblings being born years apart in the same or different families. Are later born children harmed because a twin or triplet already exists? The claim rests on the notion that the later born child lacks the uniqueness or individuality that we deem essential to human worth and dignity, and that human individuality is largely determined by nature or genome rather than by nurture and environmental factors. Because phenotype and genotype do diverge, and because the environment in which the child will be raised will be different from that of his older twin, the child will still have a unique individuality. Physical characteristics alone do not define individuals, and there is no reason to think that personal identity will be wholly controlled by having an older twin.

Still, there could be special problems faced by such a child. Its path through life might be difficult if the later born child is seen merely as a replica of the first and is expected to develop and show the skills and traits of the first. This might be a special danger if the later born child is used as a replacement for an earlier born child who has died. However, it will be some years before the later born child is even aware of his genetic identity relative to an older sibling and the special expectations his parents might have.

But it is also as likely that the later born child will be loved and wanted for his own sake. His status as a later born twin (or triplet) could be seen as a special status, indeed, a unique or novel status that confers attention and love. It could also lead to close ties with the older twin, if the special

> *"Cloning by embryo splitting . . . has fewer risks and more benefits than first appeared."*

bond that twins feel is genetically based. However, it could also lead to unique forms of sibling rivalry. Will the older twin feel that he is deficient because his parents wanted a newer version of him, or will he feel special and proud that his parents wanted another child like him? In any event, it is difficult to conclude that later or earlier born twins or triplets are likely to have such serious psychological problems that they should never be born at all. Even if one did so conclude, this would counsel against implanting cloned embryos only when a twin already exists, not against implanting two cloned embryos simultaneously or splitting embryos at all.

Cloning as Life or Health Insurance

Although cloning for the explicit purpose of providing parents with a replica for a lost child or as a source of organs or tissue for transplant for an earlier born child will not frequently occur, couples who have split embryos to treat infertility might occasionally be faced with thawing a cloned embryo for those purposes. Consider, for example, parents who request cloning to protect against the loss or death of a child, or who wish to thaw a cloned embryo to replace a dead child. Wanting a child to replace one who has died is not itself unethical. Nor does it become so merely because the new child will be a twin of the first. Although the parents may hope that the new child will develop and show the same traits as her deceased twin, they should very rapidly learn that the second child is different in some respects and similar in others, and would ordinarily come to treat and accept her as the individual that she is.

The use of cloned embryos as insurance against organ and tissue failure in an existing child presents a different set of issues. Here the concern is that the cloned embryo will be treated as an instrument or means to serve the needs of an older twin and will not be loved or respected for his

> *"The most unappealing applications of the technique are highly speculative and could be restricted without also stopping more valid uses."*

own sake. As the Ayala case in California showed, however, a family can be motivated to have another child to provide an existing child with bone marrow and still treat the subsequent child with the love and respect that children deserve. [Note: In the Ayala case, a family chose to have another child so that child could serve as a bone marrow donor for the family's oldest daughter who was dying of Leukemia].

If this is so, thawing cloned embryos to provide tissue or organs for an existing child should also be ethically acceptable. The key is whether the child will be loved and accepted by the family that brings her into the world, not how or why she was conceived, nor even whether she was cloned for that purpose. As long as the child's interests are protected after birth occurs, it is hard to see how being cloned or thawed to provide organs for a twin is any worse than being conceived for that purpose. Even if it were, the risk that some cloned embryos might be used to provide tissue to existing children would not justify a ban on embryo splitting to treat infertility.

Scenarios involving embryo splitting for genetic selection are extremely unlikely as long as overall demand for embryo donation is low and the buying and selling of embryos is not permitted. Since it is highly unlikely that a market in embryos will develop, there will be little incentive for couples going through IVF to clone embryos in order to sell them in the future. This is true even if recipients of donated embryos are permitted to pay some of the costs of embryo production.

It is true that the small subset of in-fertile couples who are candidates for embryo donation might wish to know the actual characteristics of existing twins or triplets of the embryos they seek to "adopt." However, neither having nor satisfying this wish is it-

> *"The case for adding [cloning] to the armamentarium of infertility treatments is a reasonable one."*

self immoral. Indeed, the right of adoptive parents to receive as full information as possible about the children whom they seek to adopt is increasingly recognized. There is no reason why the same principle should not apply to embryo "adoptions." Even though the couple seeking the embryos will be choosing them on the basis of expected characteristics, such a choice is neither invalid nor immoral. As long as the parents are realistic about what the information signifies, do not have unrealistic expectations about the child's perfection, and love the child for itself, seeking and providing such information prior to em-bryo donation should be ethically acceptable. If it were not, providing such in-formation could be banned without requiring that embryo splitting to treat in-fertility also be banned. . . .

The Permissibility of Cloning

The idea of cloning human beings initially sounds so bizarre and dangerous that one would think that such practices should be closely regulated, if permit-ted at all. Yet this survey of ethical issues in cloning by embryo splitting sug-gests that the procedure has fewer risks and more benefits than first appeared and would be ethically permissible in most cases. The most unappealing appli-cations of the technique are highly speculative and could be restricted without also stopping more valid uses.

Cloning by embryo splitting thus presents a regulatory situation that often arises with new reproductive technologies. An immediate step that seems justi-fied to meet the legitimate needs of infertile couples could open the door to fu-ture applications that are much less defensible. If we ban the immediate steps in order to prevent potentially harmful future applications, infertile couples lose the benefits of the procedure without a clear showing that future harms would necessarily have occurred.

The temptation in such situations is to defer further research and development until a national commission or ethics advisory body puts its imprimatur on the practice. While such bodies, however, have been absent from bioethical debate in the United States for some time, there now appears to be an increased will-ingness to confront such issues. For example, an advisory panel on embryo research has been created to recommend guidelines for federal funding. However, it remains uncertain when any such body will consider the complicated issues of human cloning.

As a result, we are left to elucidate and resolve on a retail basis the ethical dilemmas that each new innovation presents. Cloning by embryo splitting is another example of this policymaking process. Unless there are greater risks from its use than are now apparent, the case for adding the technique to the armamentarium of infertility treatments is a reasonable one. Its novelty will not prevent parents from loving and acting in the best interests of children born in this way.

Selling Human Organs
Can Be Ethical

by Richard A. Epstein

About the author: *Richard A. Epstein is the James Parker Hall Distinguished Service Professor of Law at the University of Chicago.*

The dominant philosophy of organ transplants today is captured in this stark opposition: to give is divine, but to sell is immoral. Since the paramount consideration is that donations be voluntary rather than coerced, donations do not go forward if there is the slightest hint of any motive other than pure altruism. Hence the reluctance of the medical establishment to encourage live donations between unrelated parties. More importantly, the sale of organs has been made a felony, and the law is rigidly enforced, no matter how many people are dying as a consequence. To save lives, altruism must be supplemented with market mechanisms that allow the sale of organs both during life and after death.

The Lengthening Queues

At present, organ donations come from two sources: cadavers—the bodies of individuals who have just died—and live humans. Cadaveric donations are the most common, but they are not easy to collect. Drug and alcohol users, those who die of illness or disease or whose organs are damaged in an accident, and those whose organs have lost efficiency due to age are not good potential donors. Neither are the poor and malnourished. The ideal donors of cadaveric organs are young individuals who have died traumatic deaths that left their internal organs fit for use. Fatal head injuries from, say, motorcycle accidents and gunshot wounds yield suitable donors, typically male, if the wounded can be kept alive long enough for their organs to be harvested in the hospital. But since fewer people are dying deaths of this sort than in the past, this supply of organs may be shrinking. Even if it should remain constant, this source does not provide enough organs to meet the expanding demand. Today there are 31,000 Americans on waiting lists for vital organs. The official and public call for altruism has not substantially increased the number of organ donors.

Take kidneys, for which the shortage is most acute. In 1992, for instance, some 7,644 kidneys were obtained from cadaveric donations. Added to these were 2,300 voluntary donations from live blood-related donors. These kidneys did not begin to cover the number of people whose lives could have been saved or bettered by a kidney transplant. The official waiting list for kidneys is up from 10,000 names in 1987 to over 23,000 names at the end of 1993. And that number does not include persons too sick to survive a transplant or those who died waiting in vain for a needed organ.

> *"To save lives, altruism must be supplemented with market mechanisms that allow the sale of organs."*

So beware of glowing reports of altruism in action, and heed the sobering voices of failure: 40 percent of possible cadaveric donations are thwarted for one reason or another. In practice, one relative opposed to the violation of the dead can block a cadaveric donation even if the rest of the family consents. Technological advances, however, now make it possible for many more individuals to become donors or recipients. Yet the number of deaths for want of an organ continues, inexorably, to rise.

Prohibitions and Markets

The legal source of our difficulties is not hard to find. The National Organ Transplant Act of 1984 makes it a felony, punishable by fines up to $50,000 or five years in prison, "for any person to knowingly acquire, receive or otherwise transfer any human organ for valuable consideration for use in human transplantation." Simply stated, this is a ban on the sale of organs. Monetary payments are allowed only for the expenses of removing, transplanting, and preserving the organ, and for lost wages from transplantation. Live donors are not compensated for the anxiety, pain, and suffering of the operation itself, or the loss of some of the amenities of life that even the successful removal of an organ entails. By design, the law prevents any gains that could flow from an organized market for organ transfers. In textbook regulatory style, the current prohibition has produced a set of complex but dubious procedures designed to expand the supply of organs: some statutes require physicians to make requests of the deceased's family for use of the organs; some proposals even presume consent to donation when no opposition has been expressed. But there is no strategy to encourage live donations other than an appeal to individual beneficence. As resistance in many cases is high, and the number of traumatic deaths is constant or declining, a complete harvest of every usable organ would still leave shortages relative to the increasing demand.

Given these shortages, organs must be rationed. This creates additional problems. The nonprice mechanisms used by the federal government to do this are inadequate. James Blumstein of Vanderbilt Law School rightly stresses the tension between private and public control over donations. Do individuals have the right to select the recipients of organs, by name or by group, or should all organs be thrown into a large public pool and allocated by the impersonal criteria (tissue matches and lotteries) usually reserved for these occasions?

Under the current policy, organs are distributed through a national allocation managed chiefly by the United Network for Organ Sharing (UNOS), a quasi-government organization in Washington. But treating all organs as "national resources" in some impersonal pool reduces the incentive for giving that comes when the donor knows, and takes an interest in the welfare of, the recipient. People tend to have greater sympathy for those who are in their local community than those who live at a distance. After all, most volunteer and charitable work is done at a local level for local citizens. The same dynamic works for organ donations, especially when controlled by family members of the recently departed. In its attempt to maximize the number of organs collected, UNOS mistakenly assumes that the rate of collection is wholly unaffected by policies of ultimate distribution.

Under the 1986 Budget Reconciliation Act, which extended its powers, UNOS has become the proverbial 900-pound gorilla: it has a de facto monopoly over every aspect of organ transplantation. Every hospital has to dance to its tune for all organ transplants or face the intolerable loss of Medicare and Medicaid reimbursement, not only for organ transplants but for all medical services. And UNOS now sets the rules for all transplant programs at every center, regardless of where or how the organs are procured. A center that does not satisfy UNOS criteria cannot in practice continue running its transplantation programs at all. The government does more than simply maintain a registry to help people arrange for good matches privately. The "benevolent dictatorship" of UNOS exerts monopoly power over organ transplantation and, worse, persists in holding to its no-sale policy in the face of enormous and predictable shortages.

> *"If ever there was a time to rethink a major portion of government policy, that time is now."*

UNOS is also unable to respond to other problems of organ distribution. With payment banned, who gets organs? Most often the experts rely on systems of antigen matchings—to see which prospective recipient is most likely to prosper with the organ. Antigen matching is the ultimate criterion of the technocrat. A perfect six-antigen match prevails over any less than perfect match. Thereafter, five may be preferred to four, four to three, and so on down the line. Lotteries may be used to break ties. But all soft criteria, such as matters of past conduct, family situation, and prospective benefit are quite simply too hot to handle, even though these would heavily influence the willingness to bid in voluntary markets or to give in charitable settings.

Even within this limited frame of reference, ambiguities abound. Unhappily, the "neutral" criterion of antigen matching carries with it an unintended but well-established racial spin. For example, kidneys from whites generally do better in white recipients and kidneys from blacks do (relatively) better in black recipients—although overall white survivorship rates are higher. Yet the suspicion or alienation of potential black donors and their families is so high that a far higher percentage of potential white donors gives than of potential black donors. A policy of local preference might increase the rate of black contributions.

Worse still, the percentage of blacks who suffer from various kidney-related diseases is far higher than the percentage of whites who suffer from the same conditions. The numbers are striking. While blacks constitute about 12 percent of the total U.S. population, they constituted about 35 percent (about 37,000) of the population with end stage renal disease (ESRD) in 1988, the last year for which data are available. ESRD confines people to dialysis unless they receive a kidney transplant. Yet there were only 1,500 black recipients of kidneys in 1992 (about 5 percent of the black population with ESRD) versus 4,900 white recipients (7 percent of those whites with the disease). Requiring an even distribution of black and white recipients would increase the overall number of deaths. But the size of any increase is subject to sharp disagreement now that immunosuppressive drugs increase the success of donations with imperfect matches.

Some ethicists have proposed that blacks be allowed to designate other blacks as their preferred organ recipients. But should similarly situated whites (or for that matter, Protestants, Catholics, or Jews) be accorded an identical privilege? Unfortunately the entire issue will be caught up in the endless debate between the color-blind and affirmative action views of the antidiscrimination principle. These weighty issues cannot be resolved here, but both sides of the current debate are wrong and for the same reason: they support different forms of state regulation on matters properly reserved to the domain of individual choice. All persons should be allowed to choose the objects of their affections, for both individual and class gifts, whether of organs or of common stock. But the current gridlock is likely to continue given that the debate over organ donations is waged in the wrong forum.

> *"A shortage in organs, like one in tomatoes or rental housing, is simply evidence of a malfunctioning market."*

Speaking of discrimination, there is another flaw in the current distribution system; it is biased against foreigners, even those who are willing to pay for the operations themselves. UNOS policy makes organs a national asset and tries to exclude patients such as the opportunistic sheiks who come to our shores in search of reliable organs. Hospitals, on the other hand, love to place these patients at the top of the queue because, although their money cannot legally be paid to existing organ donors, it can be given to the transplanting hospital free of any Medicare restrictions. UNOS, however, subjects transplant centers to special review if more than 10 percent of their organs are transplanted into foreigners, and Congress is now considering more stringent restrictions. Benevolent though it may seem, the communitarian system currently in place makes a mockery of a world without borders with its xenophobic restrictions.

Futures Market in Organs?

Current organ policy fails on two fronts. The forces of altruism work too sporadically to generate an adequate supply; and government-controlled allocations work on impersonal, technical, and arbitrary criteria that give only weak information on the expected benefit from any particular procedure. If ever there was a time to rethink a major portion of government policy, that time is now. The one policy alternative that deserves the most forceful endorsement is the one legally banned and ethically condemned: markets.

To those lacking refined ethical sensibilities, a shortage in organs, like one in tomatoes or rental housing, is simply evidence of a malfunctioning market. No surprises here, just the usual unfortunate consequences—queues and intrigue—when markets are banned. A number of able scholars have proposed limited market systems for organ transplants. Law professors Henry Hansmann and Lloyd Cohen have independently suggested the creation of a futures market in organ transplants: the organ donor would be paid for giving the government or some private firm the right to harvest a specified organ in

"Open markets could make a big dent in the area of the most acute shortage: kidneys."

the event of death. Hansmann wants the donors to receive an annual reduction in health care premiums if they agree to donate. Cohen prefers a lump sum payment at death to those persons designated by the decedent.

One problem with both proposals is that too many years and obstacles lie between today's contract and a probable death a generation later. Who will be around to see that the terms of the promise are rigorously enforced? And no matter what the contract says, the system of multiple vetoes will allow lone relatives to block desired transfers. After death, no one has absolute property rights to his or her own body, for no matter how many times we amend the Uniform Anatomical Gift Act [an act passed to encourage organ donation and promote the fair distribution of organs] to say they do, transplant surgeons and bereaved families act otherwise. The living cannot direct the use of their own bodies after death. So long as that is part of our belief system, no futures market can emerge, even if legal prohibitions on organ sales are removed. Nor do the Hansmann and Cohen proposals respond to the gridlock created on the recipient side of the market. UNOS would still do the collection and allocation.

One alternative, however, might work: allowing market sales of organs by living donors to unrelated parties. Admittedly, the proposal will not stop the shortage in needed hearts. It may help reduce the shortage of liver transplants now that partial transplants are viable, especially for children. But open markets could make a big dent in the area of the most acute shortage: kidneys.

Before yielding to any predictable howls of ethical revulsion, note some of the advantages of this proposal. First, it generates gains from trade. Again, take kidneys as an example. In general, kidneys from live donors are more beneficial for the recipient; but the transfer is inconvenient at best for the donor. A kidney removal requires a major incision, the loss of a rib, and several weeks of recuperation. An ugly scar and increased risks later in life of disorders such as high blood pressure are inevitable outcomes; in addition, there is a 1 in 20,000 chance that the donor will die during the surgery. These costs may be small compared to the gain to the recipient, who is freed from the uncertainty of waiting, the pain of being a family burden, and the suffering of endless dialysis. But they are substantial costs nonetheless. It is one thing to speak of aggregate gains. It is quite another to speak of gains shared by both parties. With live altruistic donations, all the tangible gains go in one direction and all the tangible losses go in the other. There is a classic divergence between private loss and social gain that cries out for redress. Compensation paid from the gainer to the loser is the best way to set right that private imbalance. Once the net social gain is shared by both parties, the level of transfers should increase because the gain to the person transferring increases as well. This is not the most subtle and profound account of human motivation, perhaps, but it is the most reliable.

> *"We have to fight our natural instincts in order to obtain the gains that modern medicine promises."*

A second hidden benefit of transfers from live donors is that it reduces the fear of the undue influence and coercion so likely in close family situations. The ethicists are right to worry about coercion, but they are wrong to deplore the payment system because it could help reduce the levels of pressure exerted in "voluntary" family donations.

Organ sales from live donors also overcome the bane of futures markets, the huge time gap between contract formation and contract performance. If cash were paid when the operation took place, property rights would no longer be indefinite or insecure. People who do not own their bodies after death could control the disposition of their organs during life. They could make an intelligent decision at a time of their peak competence without fear that their organs would deteriorate during any delay for reflection or contemplation. Nor would physicians need to make frantic requests to shocked and grieving family members for organ donations at the time of their great loss. So long as there was a substantial number of buyers and sellers, fraud and foul play would be effectively curbed by the amount of information available on terms and rates generated by an active market.

Above all, these changes are likely to boost supply. Don't ask whether you would sell your organs. You may be no more likely to do that than to commit murder. But just as criminal sanctions influence those most likely to commit a crime, so too our organ markets will attract those most likely to donate for a price. Millions of people have good organs and strong constitutions. If even a small fraction of 1 percent of them were to sell, organ shortages, at least for kidneys, would be over. And if something were to go wrong with the donor's remaining kidney, he or she could return to the market.

This market in organs sales from live donors obviates virtually all of the objectionable features of the current system of allocation. Foreigners would not be subject to discrimination or exclusion. No board would sit in judgment to decide on the most worthy recipient. Lotteries would be a thing of the past. And persons with inferior technical matches could pay the going price to get the needed organ.

The Objections to Markets

So with all the generative power of the market, why the opposition? It is possible here to identify three separate traditions that have opposed the development of markets for organ transplant. The first stresses inviolate natural rights; the second deals with the exploitation of the poor; and the third rests on the belief in the communitarian ideal.

Unnatural acts. The ablest modern exponent of this tradition is University of Chicago professor Leon Kass, who has raised a wide variety of objections to the sale of organs, either during life or after death. Kass is uneasy about his position and candidly admits that if the lives of his daughters were on the line, he would put aside his philosophical misgivings and participate in such a market if he thought he could save their lives. Perhaps on the general issue, Kass should follow his basic instincts and not his nuanced philosophical arguments.

At the deepest level his view is that the sale of an organ is an unnatural act because it flies in the face of the purpose of all organisms, namely, their own flourishing and survival. He regards the transfer of organs during life as a form of self-mutilation and partial murder; and transfer after death as an act defiling the integrity of the body and mocking the life of the person who has died. Taken at one level, Kass's arguments are so strong that they would preclude gifts as well as sales, but he distinguishes between the two cases on the ground that gifts are motivated by good will while sales are not. For him, organ sales are simply out of bounds, for while individuals own their bodies, in the sense of having exclusive control over them, they do not (or should not) possess the right to dispose of their body parts by contract. Even if the gain to the buyer is greater than any

> *"Today's ban on organ transplant sales is in reality no more than a misguided sense of paternalism."*

loss, subjective or objective, to the seller, making a commodity of body parts is just too repellent to tolerate, whatever its practical advantages.

It is easy to understand the natural revulsion toward the sale of body parts. Surely during our dim evolutionary past, both live and cadaveric transplantations were self-destructive acts. It was natural, therefore, that some strong revulsion grew up about them: that sentiment protected transferors (alive or dead) and recipients against the consequences of foolish acts. Technology, however, has moved faster than our biological predispositions. Now that transplants are both possible and safe, why hold to a set of instincts that no longer serve their intended function? The body has developed all sorts of natural mechanisms to ward off invasion by foreign bodies. Yet no one wants to ban surgery as an unnatural act simply because anesthesia and sterile instruments are required to overcome the body's natural defenses.

> *"We should ignore our present squeamishness. Too many lives are at stake to do anything less."*

We have to fight our natural instincts in order to obtain the gains that modern medicine promises. Over and over again systems of thought that were perfectly suited to their own time need cautious revision in the light of changed circumstances. The principles of gift, contract, and exchange are also very old, and often defended in natural rights language. They should be given their day, now that new techniques have made it possible to breach the once inviolate body in ways that better serve human interests. Today's ban on organ transplant sales is in reality no more than a misguided sense of paternalism, with harmful consequences for both parties to the transactions. Kass's categorical rejection of voluntary transplants should be rejected even by those sympathetic with the natural rights tradition.

Exploitation of the poor. It has also been claimed that an open market in organ transplants would exploit the poor. But these fears are exaggerated for at least two reasons. First, entrepreneurs are not likely to target poor people for organs because they could not be sure about the quality of what they are getting given the higher incidence of alcohol, drugs, and infectious diseases among this group. It is far better to pay increased prices and target persons whose organs are likely to prove safer and more valuable. Second, this objection is paternalist at its core. It says that persons of limited wealth may make decisions about what surgeries to receive but not what organs to give. It should be their choice whether the loss of an organ is more harmful than anticipated gains. These decisions will not be made lightly. This sort of protection of the poor only limits their opportunities to improve their position by voluntary exchange. It does not enhance their welfare. Perhaps there ought to be some rules that require disclosure, waiting periods, or counseling before the organ transfer takes place, just as there are presently with live donations. But if so, these rules would be better directed to the problems of impulsive action and incomplete information than to the problem of poverty as such. In any case, they counsel only deliberation and full disclosure, and not an inflexible ban.

Helping the Poor Buy Organs

There is a second side to the argument, namely, that the poor could not afford to buy organs that are made available through a market to rich people. The question of unequal provision of medical care based on wealth arises for all medical services, not just for organ transplants. I cannot resolve that grand question here. But for these purposes it is sufficient to note that whatever mix of charitable contributions, tax credits, and government grants is thought suitable for dealing with the poor and their medical services should be carried over to organ transplantation. The exploitation issue only raises distinctive questions with the poor as organ sellers. The issue does not arise with the poor as organ recipients, whether by purchase or gift. . . .

What is desperately needed is some new effort to end this appalling loss of life. If no one comes forward to sell organs, then we have lost little and can take some small comfort that no stone has been left unturned. If there are abuses in the market, we can try to correct them and only then consider closing down the entire market. But I suspect that this note of pessimism is misplaced, for the enormous gains from trade should lead to flourishing markets that are free of most of these problems.

The inevitable question will be: how far do we go in the sale of human flesh? What about lethal transplants that require the killing of the donor in order for the donee to live? Surely, the critic would say, I must ban these because no rational person could ever sign his own death warrant. But matters are not so clear in dealing with extreme cases, and a recent story in the *New York Times* should give everyone pause. A 48-year-old quadriplegic woman with end stage multiple sclerosis had one wish: to give, not sell, her organs after her death. After much deliberation, her physicians agreed to wean her from the respirator to die. Several hours later she died. But during this painful death, her internal organs became useless for transplant from lack of oxygen. Who among us would argue that this woman should be condemned as immoral, irrational, or self-destructive because she wanted to leave a good organ to a total stranger? And why should the result differ if she wanted to sell the organ to leave some money for a devoted friend or a needy child? There are strong counterexamples even to a categorical rule banning lethal transplants. . . .

Cutting out an organ is painful; it is self-destructive and unnatural; and it gnaws at instincts of survival that predate the emergence of human beings on this planet. So we don't let a market emerge and feed our fears. Yet the stubborn shortages are large and getting larger. Do we want a set of unpersuasive ethical objections to seal the needless deaths of thousands? Perhaps live organ sales will help. If so, then we should ignore our present squeamishness. Too many lives are at stake to do anything less.

Helping Postmenopausal Women Bear Children Is Ethical

by Alexander Morgan Capron

About the author: *Alexander Morgan Capron is Henry W. Bruce professor of law and medicine at the University of Southern California in Los Angeles.*

Not for nothing is the caduceus, with its intertwined snakes, the symbol of medicine: the snake has mystical powers for good but it can also wound. Over the last thirty years medical science has helped to liberate women by offering them greater control over reproduction. But some recent developments have provoked a reaction that could restrict rather than enhance the choices available to women about this central and highly personal issue. Indeed, in January 1994 a bill passed the French Senate that would prohibit the use of reproductive options in certain cases. . . .

Those who favor enhancing choices about reproduction have generally embraced the medical wizardry that allows them not only to avoid unwanted pregnancy and childbirth but to overcome infertility. Although they admit some distinctions between negative and positive rights, scholars like John Robertson have argued that the society should respect a constitutionally based "procreative liberty" that would protect people's choice either to avoid reproduction or to engage in it by a variety of means and with the help not only of physicians but of women who contract to undertake a pregnancy (surrogate mothers) and donors (or vendors) of eggs and sperm.

Regulating Fertility Clinics

New reproductive techniques have been producing ethical dilemmas and demands for governmental control for decades. In the United States, a number of states have adopted laws (usually restrictive) regarding contract pregnancy, but the regulation of in vitro fertilization (IVF) has aimed at ensuring the quality of the facilities that offer reproductive services. A new federal statute establishes a uniform reporting system for the clinics' success rates.

Ironically, public shock and the first signs of restriction of individual choice to reproduce have arisen not from a medical failure but from perhaps the most startling instance of "success" to date. Since 1990, several physicians both in the United States and abroad have been able to assist fifty to seventy-five women to become pregnant. The cause for alarm? The women are post-menopausal, the oldest being a sixty-two-year-old Italian who became pregnant using donated eggs, fertilized in vitro before transplantation.

While the first results were reported several years ago, the subject only received widespread attention in December 1993, when a fifty-nine-year-old British woman announced that she had given birth to twins with the help of Dr. Severino Antinori's fertility clinic in Italy. As with many biomedical developments, the first reaction (after amazement that anyone that age would want a newborn, much less two) was shock at the unnaturalness of the procedure.

Defenders responded that medicine is centrally concerned with altering the natural course of events, from preventing infections to replacing failed organs. Moreover, while menopause at forty made sense biologically when the average life span was roughly that, it makes less sense today, when most women can expect to live about twice that long.

Some people were offended at the idea that once again women were going to have more choices about becoming mothers, timing the decision to their own convenience, undeterred by the ticking of their "biological clocks." The physicians involved report, however, that most of their patients had tried to become pregnant using other methods for many years.

Other critics argued that it was cruel for children to have parents who will have difficulties dealing with the rigors of midnight feedings and the other ordeals of having young children—or worse, might not live to see the children through their teenage years or college graduation. The fact that this risk already exists regarding men—whose natural capacity to become fathers is typically present, if not undiminished, throughout life—came under the heading of "two wrongs don't make a right."

Perhaps the most far-sighted criticism was that, like any new technique, this one might become less of an option and more of an expectation. Some people attempt to overcome in-

> *"Society should respect a constitutionally based 'procreative liberty.'"*

fertility for years, at great financial and emotional expense. The hope offered by each new method may simply extend their agony and interfere with their concluding, "Enough is enough, already!"

Even the physicians offering the technology worry about the genie they've let out of the bottle, because they know they'll be faced with requests that they are now able to grant but do not want to. For example, Dr. Mark V. Sauer, a professor of obstetrics and gynecology at the University of Southern California who has pioneered the use of egg donation for pregnancies after menopause, has set a fifty-five-year cutoff age for patients. "It's simply that my comfort level gets stretched beyond that."

All of these concerns—from maternal (and paternal) health and longevity to the further commodification of children (order what you want, when you want it)—have some force. Indeed, they are among the factors that one would hope would go into the decision of any person—prospective mother or father or physician—contemplating reproduction late in life. But as such, they would remain matters of individual conscience, to be weighed according to the particular circumstances of each case. Of course, other people would be free to express their approval or disapproval, just as they do other choices one makes. And everyone involved—including the women and men from whom the gametes come—should be aware of all relevant information but protected from coercion as they make their decisions.

But the real danger would arise were society to try to ban such individual choices, as would be done by a bill on "assisted procreation" approved by the French Senate and sent to the National Assembly, where it may still be substantially amended. In its January 1994 form, it allows artificial methods only for women who are "of procreating age." Besides excluding postmenopausal women, it also rules out couples who have not been married or in a stable relationship for at least two years. Even broader legislation exists in Germany, where IVF with donated gametes is prohibited, and similar legislation was being prepared in Italy before the recent dissolution of parliament. Meanwhile, Britain's Health Secretary, Virginia Bottomley, has said she will ask the European Community to adopt uniform rules to prevent "procreative tourism."

In the United States, restrictions along the lines of the French legislation would certainly face a constitutional challenge, though perhaps not a successful one. Even while *Roe v. Wade* was under heaviest attack in recent years, a majority of the Supreme Court continued to strike down state laws that unduly burden the decision to abort. While the opposite right—to engage in childbearing rather than to avoid it—has also been described as fundamental, it has never been thought to be as strong, much less an absolute right. . . .

Procreative liberty is an attractive concept that deserves to be strongly defended. . . .

If the use of IVF and related techniques in postmenopausal women excites a French-style backlash, legislators writing the restrictions—or judges deciding on their constitutionality—could easily extend the rationales for controlling the actions of these women to other "unusual" prospective mothers—those with disabilities or less-than-normal life expectancies or eventually those with any other impediments to being ideal parents. Perhaps the only thing that would hold lawmakers back would be realizing that the same reasoning could be applied to prospective fathers, at least those who require a physician's aid to become parents!

Chapter 6

What Measures Would Promote Ethical Behavior?

CURRENT CONTROVERSIES

Overview:
Virtue and Values

by Kenneth L. Woodward

About the author: *Kenneth L. Woodward is a senior writer for* Newsweek *magazine.*

Virtue: for too many Americans, the word suggests only a bygone bluenose era, prim lectures on sexual purity—at best, something you "lose" when you finally give in or give up. But for the ancient Greeks, the great medieval theologians and a growing number of contemporary philosophers as well, virtue has little to do with sexuality. For these thinkers, the cultivation of virtue makes individuals happy, wise, courageous, competent. The result is a good person, a responsible citizen and parent, a trusted leader, possibly even a saint. Without a virtuous people, according to this tradition, society cannot function well. And without a virtuous society, individuals cannot realize either their own or the common good. That, in theory, is what the "politics of virtue" is all about.

Needing Contemporary Philosophy

But before politicians embrace virtue as their latest election-year slogan, they would do well to tune in to contemporary philosophy. Despite the call for virtue, we live in an age of moral relativism. According to the dominant school of moral philosophy, the skepticism engendered by the Enlightenment has reduced all ideas of right and wrong to matters of personal taste, emotional preference or cultural choice. Since the truth cannot be known, neither can the good. In this view, the most any government can do is carve out rules that—like a traffic cop—ensure that a rough justice prevails among its citizens. Within agreed-upon social limits, therefore, people are free to make what they will of their private lives. In the United States, this outlook has produced a strong emphasis on rights over responsibilities, and it influences much of contemporary political theory.

Against this moral relativism, advocates of the "ethics of virtue" argue that some personal choices are morally superior to others. The issue, as they see it, is not the right to choose but the right way to make choices. The disorder of contemporary American society, they insist, is proof that the "Enlightenment Project," as philosopher Alasdair MacIntyre of the University of Notre Dame puts it, has failed. What he and a variety of other influential thinkers like James Q. Wilson of UCLA, Martha Nussbaum of Brown University, Charles Taylor of McGill University in Canada and Bernard Williams of Oxford in England propose is the renewal of the idea of virtue—or character—as the basis for both personal and social ethics.

Virtue and Values

For the ordinary citizen, virtue is easily confused with "values." Since personal values differ, Americans argue over whose values ought to be taught. But "values" is a morally neutral term that merely indicates preference and can be quite banal. To choose vanilla over chocolate is not the same as deciding how to raise children, though both express values. A virtue, by contrast, is a quality of character by which individuals habitually recognize and *do* the right thing. "Instead of talking about 'family values,' says Wilson, "everybody would be better off talking about the virtues that a decent family tries to inculcate." To Wilson and thinkers like him, these are the four classical virtues, old as Aristotle and just as compelling today: prudence, justice, fortitude and temperance.

But they do need modern translation. Prudence, for example, is not cautious calculation but practical wisdom—recognizing and making the right choice in specific situations. It is the master virtue that makes all others possible. Justice, as the Greeks thought of it, includes fairness, honesty and keeping promises. Fortitude is courage—guts—not only in combat but, as President Abraham Lincoln exemplified during the U.S. Civil War, in pursuit of the right path despite great risks. And temperance involves much more than moderation in drink. It is self-discipline, the control of all the human passions and sensual pleasures—anger and frustration as well as food, drink and sex. A person of good character, then, is someone who through repeated good acts achieves an appropriate balance of these virtues in his life. Like a successful tennis professional, the virtuous person plays a consistently good game.

Traditional though they may be, the four virtues are not written on stone tablets. In *After Virtue*, the most widely read American book on moral philosophy of the 1980s, MacIntyre points out that different societies emphasize different virtues—and often add new ones. Loyalty, for example,

> *"Despite the call for virtue, we live in an age of moral relativism."*

was a highly desired virtue in the clannish world of Homeric Greece as well as feudal Europe. Obedience to God's commands was central to ancient Israel. Christianity added three theological virtues—faith, hope and charity—to Aristotle's four. To this day, Catholic candidates for sainthood are judged by those seven virtues—plus one that the Greeks never admired: humility. And in his own influential book, *The Moral Sense*, Wilson adds compassion as the virtue by which we habitually extend to strangers that concern we readily show for family and friends.

Learning Virtue by Acting Virtuous

Can virtue be taught like academic subjects? This is what a number of public-school districts are asking themselves in response to parental demands that the classroom foster the formation of good character—as it did in the 19th century. Plato, whose philosophy focused on ideas, was inclined to think it could. But Aristotle was the wiser man. Unlike science and other intellectual pursuits, he reasoned, moral virtue is acquired only through practice. "We become just by doing just acts, temperate by doing temperate acts, brave by doing brave acts," he wrote. Children, Aristotle observed, learn virtue by following rules of good behavior, hearing stories of virtuous people—like those in Bill Bennett's book [William J. Bennett, *The Book of Virtues*]—and imitating virtuous models: parents, friends and worthy public figures. A child born to bad parents or a citizen of a corrupt society, he concluded, had little chance of becoming a virtuous adult.

In short, an ethics of virtue cannot be learned alone. Nor can it be taught

> *"A virtue . . . is a quality of character by which individuals habitually recognize and do the right thing."*

from textbooks. Good character comes from living in communities—family, neighborhood, religious and civic institutions—where virtue is encouraged and rewarded. For much of American history, that responsibility fell disproportionately on women: in the home, of course, but also in Sunday schools and one-room schoolhouses. But contemporary America is as far from its small-town past as ancient Athens is from midtown Manhattan. Sociologically, all of the core institutions that once transmitted moral education are in disrepair. The family has fractured; neighborhoods have disappeared or turned surly; many schools can barely educate, and even many churches wonder what to teach. "You can't have strong virtues without strong institutions," says Jean Bethke Elshtain, professor of political science at Vanderbilt University. "And you can't have strong institutions without moral authority."

But many Americans are unprepared to recognize any moral authority outside themselves. Even so, they are not without their value systems. Believers have their God, movement feminists their liberation, intellectuals their ideas, professionals their careers. In ethics, says MacIntyre, what we have are merely shards of competing moral traditions, none of them coherent. Among them the most prevalent is "the ethics of authenticity," a phrase that Canadian philosopher Charles Taylor uses to describe those whose controlling moral purpose is personal self-fulfillment. But even this narcissistic goal, popular since the '60s, cannot do without the virtues it refuses to recognize. As Wilson puts it, "Self-fulfillment presupposes that you have a self worth fulfilling."

The ethics of virtue has its problems too. Sometimes virtues clash, as justice and compassion often do. Choices must be made, one good placed above another. Judgments must be made, too, on the behavior of others in society, even if it rubs the tarnish off their self-esteem. No ethical system is perfect, which is why religion persists, with its ethic of forgiveness. But the rising national debate over character may bring at least this much: a public rethinking of the kind of people we really want to be.

Laws Can Promote Ethical Behavior

by Robert P. George, interviewed by Jacqueline Stark

About the author: *Robert P. George is an associate professor of politics at Princeton University in New Jersey and a visiting fellow at the Ethics and Public Policy Center's Law and Society Program. He also serves on the U.S. Commission on Civil Rights. Jacqueline Stark is associate editor of* Ethics and Public Policy Center Newsletter.

Jacqueline Stark: *You called your new book* Making Men Moral. *How do you propose to accomplish that feat?*

Robert George: Not by statute certainly. The opening sentence of my book declares that "laws cannot make men moral." At most, laws can command *outward* conformity to what moral norms require, but they cannot command the *internal* acts of reason and will that are the essence of morally upright living. People make *themselves* morally good—or bad. Their free will allows them to form good characters by morally upright choosing or to form bad characters by immoral choosing.

What is the role of law, then, in "making men moral"?

Law's role is subsidiary, not merely in the sense of "secondary" but in the sense of the Latin *subsidium*, to help. Sound law and governmental policy *help* citizens to lead morally upright and valuable lives by maintaining a moral ecology that encourages virtue and is inhospitable to what used to be called "the grosser forms of vice." Of course, law and policy are not sufficient to accomplish this task. Individuals, together with the private or quasi-private associations to which they belong—families, religious communities, schools, neighborhood associations, organizations such as the Boy Scouts—play the primary role in maintaining a healthy moral ecology. Law and government should "first, do no harm" and then try to help.

What kind of help can they give?

Law can simply forbid certain powerfully corrupting vices. And where an

Robert P. George, interviewed by Jacqueline Stark, "Making Men Moral," *Ethics and Public Policy Center Newsletter*, Fall 1993. Reprinted by permission of the Ethics and Public Policy Center, Washington, D.C.

outright prohibition would be imprudent, sound policy can often use noncoercive means to discourage people from falling into vice. Moreover, government can adopt policies to strengthen families, churches, and other communities that help people live upright lives, and avoid policies that undercut and weaken these communities.

How do you answer contemporary arguments that people should be free to do as they please in private or personal matters?

First, the class of actions that is truly private and personal, in the sense of implicating no public interest, turns out to be very small indeed. Second, I question the proposition that people have a moral right to do moral wrong. In *Making Men Moral* I argue that contemporary liberal theorists who defend that proposition ultimately fail to make their case. And third, I contend that the only sort of political freedom with any real value is the liberty to choose among the vast range of morally good options. Liberty is not good in itself; it is good only when it serves as an instrument for realizing other goods.

But some people would say that the idea of legislating morality is un-American, that the Constitution is based on the libertarian idea that "your rights end only where my nose begins."

That attitude reflects a profound misunderstanding of American public philosophy and the United States Constitution. Though our constitution does withhold the power to police morality from the federal government by carefully delegating and enumerating federal powers, state governments have general jurisdiction to protect public health, safety, and *morals*. That is why morals laws—for example, laws against drugs, prostitution, obscenity, and deviant sexual practices—are, for the most part, state laws. Those responsible for framing and ratifying the Constitution believed that law and government could legitimately act to preserve the moral ecology, but they wisely decided to keep police powers like the power to uphold public morals close to the people and out of the hands of the central government.

> *"Sound law and governmental policy* help *citizens to lead morally upright and valuable lives."*

Your view of civil liberty differs quite dramatically from that of the American Civil Liberties Union.

Yes, it does. In fact, the book I plan to write during my term at the Ethics and Public Policy Center, *Honorable Liberties: A Defense of Freedom Without License,* will present a theory of civil liberties that challenges what has become the orthodoxy in organizations such as the ACLU.

Can you describe your approach in the crucial area of freedom of speech?

I disagree with civil libertarians who assume that all self-expression is intrinsically valuable and worthy of government protection. Freedom of speech is an important good and a human right, not because self-expression is good in itself, but rather because human cooperation for sound and worthy purposes depends on communication and the more or less free exchange of ideas and information. The right to free speech, as I understand it, is rooted in the human goods served by free speech—one of which, of course, is the integrity of democratic government. Thus the protection of political speech, and particularly speech that is critical of governmental policies and authority, is rightly at the core of American free-speech jurisprudence.

> *"I question the proposition that people have a moral right to do moral wrong."*

You seem to agree with some ACLU positions in practice, then, if not in theory.

That is true of some of their positions but certainly not all. Unlike the ACLU, I judge pornography, nude dancing, and a host of other forms of "expression" to be valueless or worse, and outside the scope of the right of free speech. Many well-intentioned people think that such examples of license must be condoned or at least permitted in deference to people's fundamental freedoms and constitutional rights, but I see it differently. "Liberties" of this sort are anything but honorable and may sometimes rightly be regulated.

But don't we have to permit some license in order to enjoy our honorable liberties?

Indeed we do. Overzealous attempts to combat the abuses of liberty can, in fact, jeopardize honorable liberties. So it is best to err on the side of freedom and tolerate some, perhaps many, abuses. We should dearly distinguish, however, between our toleration of wrongs as a matter of *prudence*—that is, for the sake of avoiding worse evils that might attend our efforts to prevent those wrongs—and our respect for freedom as a matter of *principle* or *right*.

A Renewed Sense of Community Would Promote Ethical Behavior

by Amitai Etzioni

About the author: *Amitai Etzioni is a professor at George Washington University in Washington, D.C., and editor of the communitarian quarterly* The Responsive Community.

A sociological prize of sorts ought to be given to the member of the television audience who, during a show about the savings-and-loan mess, exclaimed, "The taxpayers shouldn't pay for this, the government should!" He reflected quite well a major theme in American civic culture: a strong sense of entitlement that demands the community give more services and strongly uphold rights coupled with a relatively weak sense of obligation of serving the commons and without a feeling of responsibility for the country. Hence Americans called for more governmental services but showed great opposition to new taxes; they express their willingness to show the flag anywhere from Central America to the Gulf but a great reluctance to serve in the armed forces; and they even have a firm sense that one has the right to be tried before a jury of one's peers but use a variety of maneuvers to evade serving on such juries.

Rights and Responsibilities

Although the imbalance of rights and responsibilities may well have existed for a long time—some may argue it is a basic trait of the American character—in recent years leadership has exacerbated this tendency. Thus, while John F. Kennedy was still able to generate a tremendous response, including thousands of volunteers to serve in the Peace Corps, when he stated, "Ask not what your country can do for you. Ask what you can do for your country," within recent years, Ronald Reagan and George Bush preferred the less challenging course of suggesting to the citizenry that it could have its cake and eat it too, gaining ever

Amitai Etzioni, "Too Many Rights, Too Few Responsibilities." Reprinted from *National Forum: The Phi Kappa Phi Journal*, vol. 72, no. 1 (Winter 1992). Copyright ©1992 by Amitai Etzioni. By permission of the publishers.

more economic growth to pay for governmental services while paying ever less for them via tax cuts.

Avoiding Public Responsibilities

In many other areas, from public education to the war on drugs, facile nontaxing "solutions" have been offered. For example, it has been suggested that we may improve our system of education without additional expenditures by simply increasing parental choice among schools and thus, it is said, "drive the bad schools out of business." And to deal with the illicit demands for drugs, we are told to "just say no." Radical individualists, from the ACLU [American Civil Liberties Union] to libertarians, have effectively blocked most steps to increase public responsibilities, from drug-testing, even of people directly involved in public safety (such as engineers who drive trains), to dealing with those engaged in public health (e.g., requiring disclosure of sexual contacts by those who are carriers of the AIDS virus). Last but not least, in both state legislatures and in Congress the role of special-interest groups has grown so much, especially through campaign contributions, that the public interest is very often woefully neglected. Suggestions for reform have so far found only a rather small constituency.

A new communitarian movement is now taking on this set of issues, making restoration of civility and commitment to the commons its core theme. The young movement is in part social philosophy and sociology, in part a moral call, and in part a matter of adopting a different attitude toward public policies.

Communitarians point out the illogicality of demanding the right to be tried before a jury of one's peers without being willing to serve on that jury. Aside from being a selfish, indecent position (asking to be given but not willing to give), it is absurd to expect that most of us can be tried before our peers if most of us are not willing to be one of the peers. Communitarians show that in the longer run it is not possible to have ever more governmental services and at the same time pay less for them (and the longer run comes nearer every day.) They point out that a government that is trying to make do by serving numerous special interests neglects the other important matters for which there are no powerful pressure groups, from public education to public safety and health. And communitarians are showing that the Constitution, being a living document rather than a dead letter the Founding Fathers left behind, can be adapted to meeting the changing challenges of the time.

> *"What is needed most is a change in the moral climate of the country."*

A discussion of specific measures communitarians are considering follows. Before these are outlined, it is necessary to stress two points to avoid common misunderstandings. Although several of these measures involve legal matters and governmental actions, that is, matters of the state, the core of the communi-

215

tarian position is moral- and community-based rather than statist. What is needed most is a change in the moral climate of the country: a greater willingness to shoulder community responsibilities and a greater readiness to curb one's own demands. Without such change the required shifts in public service and the definition of rights will not be acceptable. Most important, the more the called-for changes are made morally acceptable and are *socially* enforced, the less need there will be for governmental actions—from policing to using courts and

> *"Societies change their moral orientation in complex, far-from-fully-predictable or controllable ways."*

jails. One example: To enhance public safety, we need fewer drunken drivers. To combat drunken driving, we need, among other things, the moral commitment of individuals to the notion of a designated driver (as in Scandinavia), that is, one person per car who will not consume alcohol during an outing, party, etc. This is best done on a moral-social base. For example, those couples who come to parties and both drink would be subject to social criticism (unless, of course, they car-pool); the people who proudly state (as if saying, "look how responsible we are!") that they are not drinking tonight because they are designated drivers would gain social approval accordingly, and so on. Similarly, we need to support sobriety check points (rather than fight them as the ACLU does) to help enforce the new social-moral dictum. The changed moral orientation ensures that drunken driving will be significantly reduced with very little state action and that whatever limited state action will be needed will merely round off new social pressures (e.g., in the form of designated drivers rather than drinking to excess being tolerated) and will be supported by the electorate.

Communitarian Writings

There is no simple recipe for building a new social-moral climate for a more communitarian orientation. Societies change their moral orientation in complex, far-from-fully-predictable or controllable ways. But just as Betty Friedan's writings helped launch the women's movement and Rachel Carson's *Silent Spring* helped the environmental movement take off, so various communitarian writings may help the social-moral climate by calling attention to the need for greater responsibility to the commons. These include Robert Bellah, R. Madsen, W. Sullivan, A. Swidler, and S. Tipton's *Habits of the Heart* and books by Michael Waltzer, Michael Sandel, Charles Taylor, and Alasdair MacIntyre. One of the newest publications, and certainly dearest to the author's heart, is the quarterly *The Responsive Community*, whose editors are James Fishkin, William Galston, Mary Ann Glendon, and yours truly, and whose editorial board includes both conservatives and liberals, ranging from Nathan Glazer and Ilene Nagel to Jane Mansbridge and Benjamin Barber. Next, a variety of public-interest groups have made communitarianism their theme, whether or not they use the term—including Common Cause and Ralph Nader's [consumer protection] groups, as well as numerous grass-roots organizations. There is also a strong communitarian element in many organizations whose explicit purpose is something other, especially the environmental movement.

Less advanced but definitely moving in the right direction are various attempts to strengthen the teaching of civics in schools by such groups as the Thomas Jefferson Center and the Ethics Resource Center. What is yet to come is a major social movement, a kind of neoprogressive movement that would shore up the commons, making its main agenda the curbing of special interests and the serving of the public interests. Unfortunately, the recent public frustration with politicians has focused on attempts to "throw out the rascals" and impose term limitations, which will only lead to a new set of politicians committed to special interests replacing the other. Until elected officials' need for private money to win elections, the main mechanism by which they become obligated to special interests, is systematically reduced by various campaign-reform laws and public financing of elections, that part of the communitarian movement will lag. Finally, suggestions for creating a year of mandatory national service are meant to further enhance education and encourage the practice of service for and to the public.

> **"We need to reset a legal thermostat to afford a climate more supportive of public concerns."**

Another misunderstanding that must be avoided is that the call for enhanced civic responsibilities and a greater measure of community service entails majoritarianism or even a measure of authoritarianism. To suggest that young Americans (or all citizens) ought to volunteer more often to serve the commons is not to say that those who refuse for reasons of conscience are to be disciplined. It is not to imply that the civic "religion" or set of values will replace the religious or secular values people uphold. Nor does the call for more sobriety check points, drug tests, and disclosure of sexual contacts by carriers of the AIDS virus legitimate the beginning of a police state. Communitarians are careful to craft suggested changes in public mores and regulation to allow for greater public safety, health, and education without falling into the opposite trap of radical communitarianism: authoritarianism.

The thrust of responsive communitarianism is illustrated by the following examples: to curb drug abuse it has been suggested that the government should conduct drug tests on all school kids, governmental employees, and corporate workers. This would entail massive violations of privacy both because a historically private function (urination) would have to be performed under controlled conditions and because the tests would often reveal private, off-the-job behavior. Persuasion not to use drugs seems more appropriate and keeps the door to a police state shut. On the other hand, drug testing of select groups of people whose drug violation directly endangers the public, e.g., pilots, seems justified on communitarian grounds. This is especially the case if they are informed when hired that their jobs will entail such tests; and that workers will be expected to give their consent to be tested when they sign their contracts.

Concerning matters of the rights of criminals versus those of their victims and public order, a wholesale removal of Miranda rights, as has been suggested by the Reagan administration, may well return us to more authoritarian days. At the same time, it seems reasonable and prudent not to throw out evidence when the Miranda rules were violated on technical grounds and clearly in good faith.

> *"The issue is not one of legal measures but a change of orientation to a stronger voice for the commons and less room for me-ism and special interests."*

Thus, for instance, one can fully support the Supreme Court's decision stipulating that when people confess before being read their rights and then again after hearing their rights that the second confession be allowed to stand.

In the same vein, sobriety check points, especially when they are announced so that those who enter public highways in effect consent to be subject to them, should be viewed more as a way to secure the right to drive freely than a curb on that right. Nor are airport screens, used to deter terrorist bombs, to be viewed as an unreasonable search and seizure, as the ACLU does. The intrusion is minimal, and the contribution to public safety, including the freedom to travel, is considerable.

Students' Rights

The debate over the rights of students provides still another example of a reasonable communitarian position between according students full-fledged Fifth Amendment rights, in effect deterring teachers and principals from suspending them, and declaring students fair game to any capricious school authority. It seems reasonable that students who are subject to expulsion and suspension should be granted due process to the extent that they are notified of the nature of their misconduct and given an opportunity to respond; both actions must occur before the expulsion takes place. Still, expulsion need not guarantee students the right of counsel or call for cross examination and the calling of witnesses because this would unduly encumber the ability of schools to maintain a satisfactory educational environment. In addition, schools need to be allowed to maintain for internal purposes further restrictions and simplified procedures for the reason that they are meant to be small communities, rather than adversarial environments. Far from a novel approach, several state courts are already modifying school policies in the directions we suggest.

Regarding the rights of people with AIDS, if to protect the public's health we choose to trace contacts, then we should also take pains to reduce deleterious offshoots of that policy. For example, AIDS testing and contact-tracing can lead to people's losing jobs and health insurance if confidentiality is not maintained. Hence, any introduction of such a program should be accompanied by a thorough review of control of access to lists of names of those tested, procedures used in contacting sexual partners, professional-education programs on the need for confidentiality, and penalties for unauthorized disclosure and especially for those who discriminate against AIDS patients or HIV carriers. All this may seem quite cumbersome, but in view of the great dangers AIDS poses for individuals and its high cost to society, these measures are clearly appropriate.

One may, and ought to, argue about the details involved in such policies. Indeed, the changes should be carefully crafted. We need to reset a legal thermostat to afford a climate more supportive of public concerns, without melting away any of the basic safeguards of individual liberties. Those who argue that the various present interpretations of the Bill of Rights are untouchable, that any modification will push us down the slippery slope toward authoritarianism, must come to realize that the greater danger to the Constitution arises out of a refusal to recognize that the Constitution is a living document that can and does adapt to the changing social situation. Without such adaptation, without some measure of increased communitarianism, the mounting frustrations of the American people over politics being governed by special interests and over unsafe cities and spreading epidemics, will lead to much more extreme adjustments. Legitimate public needs are often not attended to, in part because such reasonable adaptations as selective drug testing, sobriety check points, and other such measures are disallowed. Basically the issue is not one of legal measures but a change of orientation to a stronger voice for the commons and less room for me-ism and special interests. At this stage of American history, the danger of excessive communitarianism, theoretically always present, seems quite remote.

Teaching Individual Responsibility Would Promote Ethical Behavior

by Christina Hoff Sommers

About the author: *Christina Hoff Sommers is a philosophy professor at Clark University in Worcester, Massachusetts.*

Some time ago, I published an article called "Ethics without Virtue," in which I criticized the way ethics is being taught in American colleges. I pointed out that there is an overemphasis on social policy questions, with little or no attention being paid to private morality. I noted that students taking college ethics are debating abortion, euthanasia, capital punishment, DNA research, and the ethics of transplant surgery while they learn almost nothing about private decency, honesty, personal responsibility, or honor. Topics such as hypocrisy, self-deception, cruelty, or selfishness rarely come up. I argued that the current style of ethics teaching, which concentrates so much on social policy, is giving students the wrong ideas about ethics. Social morality is only half of the moral life; the other half is private morality. I urged that we attend to both.

Social Morality and Private Morality

A colleague of mine did not like what I said. She told me that in her classroom she would continue to focus on issues of social injustice. She taught about women's oppression, corruption in big business, multinational corporations and their transgressions in the Third World—that sort of thing. She said to me, "You are not going to have moral people until you have moral institutions. You will not have moral citizens until you have a moral government." She made it clear that I was wasting time and even doing harm by promoting bourgeois virtues instead of awakening the social conscience of my students.

At the end of the semester, she came into my office carrying a stack of exams and looking very upset.

Christina Hoff Sommers, "Teaching the Virtues." Reprinted with permission of the author and the *Public Interest*, no. 111 (Spring 1993), pp. 3-13, ©1993 by National Affairs, Inc.

"What's wrong?" I asked.

"They cheated on their social justice take-home finals. They plagiarized!" More than half of the students in her ethics class had copied long passages from the secondary literature. "What are you going to do?" I asked her. She gave me a self-mocking smile and said, "I'd like to borrow a copy of that article you wrote on ethics without virtue."

There have been major cheating scandals at many of our best universities. A survey reported in the *Boston Globe* says that 75 percent of all high school students admit to cheating; for college students the figure is 50 percent. A *U.S. News & World Report* survey asked college-age students if they would steal from an employer. Thirty-four percent said they would. Of people forty-five and over, 6 percent responded in the affirmative.

Part of the problem is that so many students come to college dogmatically committed to a moral relativism that offers them no grounds to think that cheating is just wrong. I sometimes play a macabre game with first-year students, trying to find some act they will condemn as morally wrong: Torturing a child. Starving someone to death. Humiliating an invalid in a nursing home. The reply is often: "Torture, starvation, and humiliation may be bad for you or me, but who are we to say they are bad for someone else?"

Not all students are dogmatic relativists, nor are they all cheaters and liars. Even so, it is impossible to deny that there is a great deal of

> *"Social morality is only half of the moral life; the other half is private morality."*

moral drift. Students' ability to arrive at reasonable moral judgments is severely, even bizarrely, affected. A Harvard University professor annually offers a large history class on the Second World War and the rise of the Nazis. Some years back, he was stunned to learn from his teaching assistant that the majority of students did not believe that anyone was really to blame for the Holocaust. In the students' minds the Holocaust was like a natural cataclysm: It was inevitable and unavoidable. The professor refers to his students' attitude about the past as "no-fault history."

One philosopher, Alasdair MacIntyre, has said that we may be raising a generation of "moral stutterers." Others call it moral illiteracy. Education consultant Michael Josephson says "there is a hole in the moral ozone." Well, what should the schools be doing to make children morally literate, to put fault back into no-fault history, to mend the hole in the moral ozone?

The New Ethics

First, a bit of history. Let me remind you of how ethics was once taught in American colleges. In the nineteenth century, the ethics course was a high point of college life. It was taken in the senior year, and was usually taught by the president of the college, who would uninhibitedly urge the students to become morally better and stronger. The senior ethics course was in fact the culmination of the students' college experience. But as the social sciences began to flourish in the early twentieth century, ethics courses gradually lost prominence until they became just one of several electives offered by philosophy departments. By the mid-1960s, enrollment in courses on moral philosophy reached an all-time low and, as one historian of higher education put it, "college ethics was in deep trouble."

> *"It is impossible to deny that there is a great deal of moral drift."*

At the end of the '60s, there was a rapid turnaround. To the surprise of many a department chair, applied ethics courses suddenly proved to be very popular. Philosophy departments began to attract unprecedented numbers of students to courses in medical ethics, business ethics, ethics for everyday life, ethics for lawyers, for social workers, for nurses, for journalists. More recently, the dubious behavior of some politicians and financiers has added to public concern over ethical standards, which in turn has contributed to the feeling that college ethics is needed. Today American colleges and universities are offering thousands of well-attended courses in applied ethics.

I too have been teaching applied ethics courses for several years. Yet my enthusiasm tapered off when I saw how the students reacted. I was especially disturbed by comments students made again and again on the course evaluation forms: "I learned there was no such thing as right or wrong, just good or bad arguments." Or: "I learned there is no such thing as morality." I asked myself what it was about these classes that was fostering this sort of moral agnosticism and skepticism. Perhaps the students themselves were part of the problem. Perhaps it was their high school experience that led them to become moral agnostics. Even so, I felt that my classes were doing nothing to change them.

The course I had been giving was altogether typical. At the beginning of the semester we studied a bit of moral theory, going over the strengths and weaknesses of Kantianism, utilitarianism, social contract theory, and relativism. We then took up topical moral issues such as abortion, censorship, capital punishment, world hunger, and affirmative action. Naturally, I felt it my job to present careful and well-argued positions on all sides of these popular issues. But this atmosphere of argument and counterargument was reinforcing the idea that *all* moral questions have at least two sides, i.e., that all of ethics is controversial.

Perhaps this reaction is to be expected in any ethics course primarily devoted to issues on which it is natural to have a wide range of disagreement. In a course specifically devoted to dilemmas and hard cases, it is almost impossible *not* to give the student the impression that ethics itself has no solid foundation.

Uncontroversial Truths

The relevant distinction here is between "basic" ethics and "dilemma" ethics. It is basic ethics that G.J. Warnock has in mind when he warns his fellow moral philosophers not to be bullied out of holding fast to the "plain moral facts." Because the typical course in applied ethics concentrates on problems and dilemmas, the students may easily lose sight of the fact that some things are clearly right and some are clearly wrong, that some ethical truths are not subject to serious debate.

I recently said something to this effect during a television interview in Boston, and the skeptical interviewer immediately asked me to name some uncontroversial ethical truths. After stammering for a moment I found myself rattling off several that I hold to be uncontroversial:

> It is wrong to mistreat a child, to humiliate someone, to torment an animal. To think only of yourself, to steal, to lie, to break promises. And on the positive side: It is right to be considerate and respectful of others, to be charitable and generous.

Reflecting again on that extemporaneous response, I am aware that not everyone will agree that all of these are plain moral facts. But teachers of ethics are free to give their own list or to pare down mine. In teaching ethics, one thing should be made central and prominent: Right and wrong do exist. This should be laid down as uncontroversial lest one leaves an altogether false impression that *everything* is up for grabs.

It will, I think, be granted that the average student today does not come to college steeped in a religious or ethical tradition in which he or she has uncritical confidence. In the atmosphere of a course dealing with hard and controversial cases, the contemporary student may easily find the very idea of a stable moral tradition to be an archaic illusion. I am suggesting that we may have some responsibility here for providing the student with what the philosopher Henry Sidgwick called "moral common sense." More generally, I am suggesting that we should assess some of the courses we teach for their *edificatory* effect. Our responsibility as teachers goes beyond purveying information about the leading ethical theories and developing dialectical skills. I have come to see that dilemma ethics is especially lacking in edificatory force, and indeed that it may even be a significant factor in encouraging a superficial moral relativism or agnosticism.

I shall not really argue the case for seeing the responsibility of the teacher of ethics in traditional terms. It would seem to me that the burden of argument is on those who would maintain that modern teachers of ethics should abjure the teacher's traditional concern with edification. Moreover, it seems to me that the hands-off posture is not really as neutral as it professes to be. (Author Samuel Blumenfeld is even firmer on this point. He says, "You have to be dead to be value-neutral.") One could also make a case that the new attitude of disowning responsibility probably contributes to the student's belief in the false and debilitating doctrine that there are

"There is a hole in the moral ozone."

no "plain moral facts" after all. In tacitly or explicitly promoting that doctrine, the teacher contributes to the student's lack of confidence in a moral life that could be grounded in something more than personal disposition or political fashion. I am convinced that we could be doing a far better job of moral education.

How to Teach Ethics

If one accepts the idea that moral edification is not an improper desideratum in the teaching of ethics, then the question arises: What sort of course in ethics is effective? What ethical teachings are naturally edificatory? My own experience leads me to recommend a course on the philosophy of virtue. Here, Aristotle is the best place to begin. Philosophers as diverse as Plato, Augustine, Kant, and even Mill wrote about vice and virtue. And there is an impressive contemporary literature on the subject. But the *locus classicus* is Aristotle.

Students find a great deal of plausibility in Aristotle's theory of moral education, as well as personal relevance in what he says about courage, generosity, temperance, and other virtues. I have found that an exposure to Aristotle makes an immediate inroad on dogmatic relativism; indeed the tendency to discuss morality as relative to taste or social fashion rapidly diminishes and may vanish altogether. Most students find the idea of developing virtuous character traits naturally appealing.

> *"Some things are clearly right and some are clearly wrong. . . . Some ethical truths are not subject to serious debate."*

Once the student becomes engaged with the problem of what kind of person to be, and how to *become* that kind of person, the problems of ethics become concrete and practical and, for many a student, moral development is thereafter looked on as a natural and even inescapable undertaking. I have not come across students who have taken a course in the philosophy of virtue saying that they have learned there is no such thing as morality. The writings of Aristotle and of other philosophers of virtue are full of argument and controversy, but students who read them with care are not tempted to say they learned "there is no right or wrong, only good or bad arguments."

At the elementary and secondary level students may be too young to study the philosophy of virtue, but they certainly are capable of reading stories and biographies about great men and women. Unfortunately, today's primary school teachers, many of whom are heavily influenced by what they were taught in trendy schools of education, make little use of the time-honored techniques of telling a story to young children and driving home "the moral of the story." What are they doing?

How *Not* to Teach Ethics

One favored method of moral education that has been popular for the past twenty years is called "values clarification," which maintains the principle that the teacher should never directly tell students about right and wrong; instead the students must be left to discover "values" on their own. One favored values clarification technique is to ask children about their likes and dislikes: to help them become acquainted with their personal preferences. The teacher asks the students, "How do you feel about homemade birthday presents? Do you like wall-to-wall carpeting? What is your favorite color? Which flavor of ice cream do you prefer? How do you feel about hit-and-run drivers? What are your feelings on the abortion question?" The reaction to these questions—from wall-to-wall carpeting to hit-and-run drivers—is elicited from the student in the same tone of voice, as if one's personal preferences in both instances are all that matter.

One of my favorite anecdotes concerns a teacher in Massachusetts, who had attended numerous values-clarification workshops and was assiduously applying their techniques in her class. The day came when her class of sixth graders announced that they valued cheating and wanted to be free to do it on their tests. The teacher was very uncomfortable. Her solution? She told the children that since it was *her* class, and since she was opposed to cheating, they were not free to cheat. "I personally value honesty; although you may choose to be dishonest, I shall insist that we be honest on our tests here. In other areas of your life, you may have more freedom to be dishonest. . . ."

"Good Values"

Now this fine and sincere teacher was doing her best not to indoctrinate her students. But what she was telling them is that cheating is not wrong if you can get away with it. Good values are "what one values." She valued the norm of not cheating. That made this value binding on her, and gave her the moral authority to enforce it in her classroom; others, including the students, were free to choose other values "in other areas." The teacher thought she had no right to intrude by giving the students moral direction. Of course, the price for her failure to do her job of inculcating moral principles is going to be paid by her bewildered students. They are being denied a structured way to develop values. Their teacher is not about to give it to them lest she interfere with their freedom to work out their own value systems.

This Massachusetts teacher values honesty, but her educational theory does not allow her the freedom to take a strong stand on honesty as a moral principle. Her training has led her to treat her "preference" for honesty as she treats her preference for vanilla over chocolate flavored ice cream. It is not hard to see how this doctrine is an egoistic variant of ethical relativism. For most ethical relativists, public opinion is the final court of ethical appeal; for the proponent of values clarification, the locus of moral authority is to be found in the individual's private tastes

> *"Civility, honesty, and considerate behavior must be recognized, encouraged, and rewarded."*

and preferences.

How sad that so many teachers feel intellectually and "morally" unable to justify their own belief that cheating is wrong. It is obvious that our schools must have clear behavior codes and high expectations for their students. Civility, honesty, and considerate behavior must be recognized, encouraged, and rewarded. That means that moral education must have as its *explicit* aim the moral betterment of the student. If that be indoctrination, so be it. How can we hope to equip students to face the challenge of moral responsibility in their lives if we studiously avoid telling them what is right and what is wrong?

> *"The paralyzing fear of indoctrinating children is even greater in high schools than it is in elementary schools."*

The elementary schools of Amherst, New York, provide good examples of an unabashedly directive moral education. Posters are placed around the school extolling kindness and helpfulness. Good behavior in the cafeteria is rewarded with a seat at a "high table" with tablecloth and flowers. One kindergarten student was given a special award for having taken a new Korean student under her wing. But such simple and reasonable methods as those practiced in Amherst are rare. Many school systems have given up entirely the task of character education. Children are left to fend for themselves. To my mind, leaving children alone to discover their own values is a little like putting them in a chemistry lab and saying, "Discover your own compounds, kids." If they blow themselves up, at least they have engaged in an authentic search for the self.

Ah, you may say, we do not let children fend for themselves in chemistry laboratories because we have *knowledge* about chemistry. But is there really such a thing as *moral* knowledge? The reply to that is an emphatic "Yes." Have we not learned a thing or two over the past several thousand years of civilization? To pretend we know nothing about basic decency, about human rights, about vice and virtue, is fatuous or disingenuous. Of course we know that gratuitous cruelty and political repression are wrong, that kindness and political freedom are right and good. Why should we be the first society in history that finds itself hamstrung in the vital task of passing along its moral tradition to the next generation?

Some opponents of directive moral education argue that it could be a form of brainwashing. That is a pernicious confusion. To brainwash is to diminish someone's capacity for reasoned judgment. It is perversely misleading to say that helping children to develop habits of truth telling or fair play threatens their ability to make reasoned choices. Quite the contrary: Good moral habits enhance one's capacity for rational judgments.

The paralyzing fear of indoctrinating children is even greater in high schools than it is in elementary schools. One favored teaching technique that allegedly avoids indoctrination of children—as it allegedly avoids indoctrination of college students—is dilemma ethics. Children are presented with abstract moral dilemmas: Seven people are in a lifeboat with provisions for four—what should they do? Or Lawrence Kohlberg's famous case of Heinz and the stolen drug. Should the indigent Heinz, whose dying wife needs medicine, steal it? When high school students study ethics at all, it is usually in the form of pondering such dilemmas or in the form of debates on social issues: abortion, euthanasia, capital punishment, and the like. Directive moral education is out of favor. Storytelling is out of fashion.

Telling Stories

Let's consider for a moment just how the current fashion in dilemmas differs from the older approach to moral education, which often used tales and parables to instill moral principles. Saul Bellow, for example, asserts that the survival of Jewish culture would be inconceivable without the stories that give point and meaning to the Jewish moral tradition. One such story, included in a collection of traditional Jewish tales that Bellow edited, is called "If Not Higher." I sketch it here to contrast the story approach with the dilemma approach in primary and secondary education, but the moral of the contrast applies to the teaching of ethics at the college level as well:

> There was once a rabbi in a small Jewish village in Russia who vanished every Friday for several hours. The devoted villagers boasted that during these hours their rabbi ascended to Heaven to talk with God. A skeptical newcomer arrived in town, determined to discover where the rabbi really was.

> One Friday morning the newcomer hid near the rabbi's house, watched him rise, say his prayers, and put on the clothes of a peasant. He saw him take an ax and go into the forest, chop down a tree, and gather a large bundle of wood. Next the rabbi proceeded to a shack in the poorest section of the village in which lived an old woman. He left her the wood, which was enough for the week. The rabbi then quietly returned to his own house.

> The story concludes that the newcomer stayed on in the village and became a disciple of the rabbi. And whenever he hears one of his fellow villagers say, "On Friday morning our rabbi ascends all the way to Heaven," the newcomer quietly adds, "If not higher."

In a moral dilemma such as Kohlberg's Heinz's stealing the drug, or the lifeboat case, there are no obvious heroes or villains. Not only do the characters lack moral personality, but they exist in a vacuum outside of traditions and social arrangements that shape their conduct in the problematic situations confronting them. In a

> *"An exclusive diet of dilemma ethics tends to give the student the impression that ethical thinking is a lawyer's game."*

dilemma there is no obvious right and wrong, no clear vice and virtue. The dilemma may engage the students' minds; it only marginally engages their emotions, their moral sensibilities. The issues are finely balanced, listeners are on

227

their own, and they individually decide for themselves. As one critic of dilemma ethics has observed, one cannot imagine parents passing down to their children the tale of Heinz and the stolen drug. By contrast, in the story of the rabbi and the skeptical outsider, it is not up to the listener to decide whether or not the rabbi did the right thing. The moral message is clear: "Here is a good man—merciful, compassionate, and actively helping someone weak and vulnerable. Be like that person." The message is contagious. Even the skeptic gets the point.

Stories and parables are not always appropriate for high school or college ethics courses, but the literary classics certainly are. To understand *King Lear*, *Oliver Twist*, *Huckleberry Finn*, or *Middlemarch* requires that the reader have some understanding of (and sympathy with) what the author is saying about the moral ties that bind the characters and that hold in place the social fabric in which they play their roles. Take something like filial obligation. One moral of *King Lear* is that society cannot survive when filial contempt becomes the norm. Literary figures can thus provide students with the moral paradigms that Aristotle thought were essential to moral education.

What to Do

I am not suggesting that moral puzzles and dilemmas have no place in the ethics curriculum. To teach something about the logic of moral discourse and the practice of moral reasoning in resolving conflicts of principles is clearly important. But casuistry is not the place to *start*, and, taken by itself, dilemma ethics provides little or no moral sustenance. Moreover, an exclusive diet of dilemma ethics tends to give the student the impression that ethical thinking is a lawyer's game.

If I were an educational entrepreneur I might offer you a four- or five-stage program in the manner of some of the popular educational consultants. I would have brochures, audio-visual materials. There would be workshops. But there is no need for brochures, nor for special equipment, nor for workshops. What I am recommending is not new, has worked before, and is simple:

1. Schools should have behavior codes that emphasize civility, kindness, self-discipline, and honesty.

2. Teachers should not be accused of brainwashing children when they insist on basic decency, honesty, and fairness.

3. Children should be told stories that reinforce goodness. In high school and college, students should be reading, studying, and discussing the moral classics.

I am suggesting that teachers must help children become acquainted with their moral heritage in literature, in religion, and in philosophy. I am suggesting that virtue can be taught, and that effective moral education appeals to the emotions as well as to the mind. The best moral teaching inspires students by making them keenly aware that their own character is at stake.

Deemphasizing Individualism Would Promote Ethical Behavior

by Everett C. Ladd

About the author: *Everett C. Ladd is executive director and president of the Roper Center for Public Opinion Research in Storrs, Connecticut. He has written numerous books and is a frequent contributor to periodicals such as the* Nation.

The moral state of the United States is the subject of enormous attention and concern. Although this has been a recurring theme throughout American history, there is some indication that concern has grown in our own time. Rushworth M. Kidder, President of the Institute for Global Ethics, noted in *The Public Perspective* that dozens of ethics organizations are springing up across the nation, hundreds of executive ethics seminars are conducted every year, and thousands of students are participating in character education at school. The press is now full of discussions of ethics issues. Kidder cites data showing, for example, that between 1969 and 1989 the number of stories found under "ethics" in the *New York Times* index increased four-fold.

Survey data also indicate that the proportion of the public troubled by what they perceive to be serious deficiencies in the moral state of the nation is not only large but expanding. True, throughout the span of our history for which we have survey data, large majorities have expressed dissatisfaction with such matters as the honesty and standards of behavior of their fellow citizens. Nonetheless, the proportions today are at the highest levels we have seen. For instance, in 1938, when asked if the "general morals" of young unmarried people were better or worse than they had been 10 years earlier, 42 percent of those interviewed by the Roper Organization said they were worse, compared to just 13 percent who said they were better. In 1987, 60 percent of those interviewed in a Yankelovich Clancy Shulman poll said teenagers were "less moral in their behavior at present than when [the respondents] were growing up," while only 11

From Everett C. Ladd, "The Myth of Moral Decline," *The Responsive Community*, Winter 1993/94. Reprinted by permission of *The Responsive Community*, 2020 Pennsylvania Ave. NW, Suite 282, Washington, DC 20006.

percent described young people as more moral. Every time we have located a pair of queries like this from the 1930s–50s span on the one hand, and from the 1980s–90s on the other, we have found the same pattern: Majorities always profess to see decline in moral standards, but the majority is larger in the contemporary period than earlier.

Again and again, polls show Americans expressing this kind of values nostalgia. But has there in fact been a deterioration in moral conduct in the United States, as compared to, say, the 1950s? Ethical norms and moral

> *"At every point in time, . . . ethical standards and moral conduct leave much to be desired."*

conduct are of great importance to the health of the American society and polity, and it certainly matters which way the great engines of contemporary society are pulling us with regard to them. Yet for all the importance of this question and the attention it has received, the data are not as clear as the polls might suggest.

There's Always So Much Wrong

One obstacle standing in the way of productive analysis involves the fact that at every point in time, in the view of many thoughtful people, ethical standards and moral conduct leave much to be desired. Michael Josephson and his colleagues have attempted empirical work on Americans' moral judgments and behavior which, they say, reveals that a "disturbingly high proportion of young people regularly engage in dishonest and irresponsible behavior." What an extraordinary way to put it! It is, after all, a little late in human history to present as a finding that a disturbingly high proportion of people variously err and sin. The Josephson study documents that many young people are struggling and stumbling ethically, but it tells us nothing about whether things are actually getting better or worse.

Is the contemporary U.S. beset with moral decline? If we had a "Morality Index," on which 100 was utopia and zero the modern equivalent of Sodom and Gomorrah, and found the U.S. standing at 50, that should be cause for national concern. But it would be one thing if we also found that the country's position on this mythic measure had been 80 in 1867, 70 in 1917, and 60 in 1957, quite another if we found that it had been hovering around 50 in each of those earlier years.

We don't have such an index, nor do we have the kind of imaginative and thorough data-gathering such a measure would require. We only know that moral conduct today is "deficient." I have no intention of making light of this when I note that part of the reason we think today's problems are so pressing is that they are the ones we face. Since we can do absolutely nothing about previous sins, present problems are the "worst" in the sense that they are the ones that occupy us and require our efforts at remedy.

Our contemporary ethical concerns are drawn, in part, from the recognition that a democratic polity cannot survive without a moral and virtuous citizenry.

Calvin Coolidge told a throng assembled to celebrate the 150th anniversary of the Declaration of Independence that America's founders "were a people who came under the influence of a great spiritual development and acquired a great moral power." He went on to say that "unless we cling to that, all our material property, overwhelming though it may appear, will turn to a barren sceptre in our grasp. . . . We must cultivate the reverence which they had for things that are holy. We must follow the spiritual and moral leadership which they showed." In our own day, scholars such as James Q. Wilson and Irving Kristol have written persuasively on the relationship between a nation's moral health and the successful operations of its social and political institutions.

But the contemporary ethical concerns that occupy us are also grounded in a distinctive and recurring American sense of moral anxiety. James Bryce begins his monumental study of American life, *The American Commonwealth* (1889), by observing that throughout his travels across the country he, like other European visitors before him, was constantly greeted by the query, "What do you think of our institutions?" Why was it so prevalent? he wondered, considering that Europeans did not usually care what foreigners thought of their countries. Bryce's explanation of why this question came up so often in the U.S. was that American political ideas and institutions were something "invented" rather than "grown." They represent an elaborate, highly self-conscious experiment—one whose ultimate conclusion seemed to have importance beyond America's shores.

> *"The melting pot of American citizenship requires a public with considerable virtue."*

Bryce is surely right, so far as he goes, but probably something else was also at work. Americans worried and wondered about their basic ideas and institutions in Bryce's day, and they do so today in a somewhat different but nonetheless intense fashion, because the American nation has no substantial existence apart from these ideas and institutions. The U.S. isn't, as most countries are, based on a particular ethnicity; rather, it is one erected upon and around a political philosophy. The French, Germans, English, *et al.*, have had debates aplenty about what political values and programs their nations should pursue; but no one has thought that the existence of France or Germany or England was predicated upon the validity of any one set of political or philosophical values. Yet America's national existence was, and to a considerable extent still is.

John Adams, the country's second president, wrote in 1818 that a new American nation had emerged long before the war with England. It sprang from a revolution, he argued, "in the minds and hearts of the people," one which involved a sweeping ideological transformation—of "the principles, opinions, sentiments, and affections" of the inhabitants of the 13 colonies. A new American nation, rejecting aristocratic institutions and values and replacing them with an egalitarian and individualistic order, had emerged bit by bit over the century and a half following the first settlements in Massachusetts and Virginia. The Declaration of 1776 proclaimed the formal independence of a new nationality that had already been established philosophically.

The Importance of Values to the United States

Lincoln repeatedly made a similar argument in his great speeches from 1857 on. America was a nation built on political ideals, set forth most notably in the Declaration. This explains why he saw in slavery such an enormous threat. It was more than an odious institution that wreaked great harm on those subjected to it. National acceptance of the ideas underlying slavery—of the sort Chief Justice Roger Taney urged in his 1857 majority opinion in *Scott v. Sandford* [the *Dred Scott* decision]—would entirely destroy the nation founded on the Declaration's ideals. American nationality was primarily a moral idea, not the result of a legal writ. And as Lincoln warned, quoting Scripture: "A house divided against itself cannot stand."

The English philosopher and writer G. K. Chesterton grasped the central importance of American values to American nationality itself in *What I Saw in America*. Following a visit to the U.S. in 1921, Chesterton compared the American system to the Spanish Inquisition. At first glance, that was a dubious compliment—but Chesterton in fact intended it as a compliment. "The American Constitution," he wrote, "does resemble the Spanish Inquisition in this:"

> That it is founded on a creed. America is the only nation in the world that is founded on a creed. That creed is set forth with dogmatic and even theological lucidity in the Declaration of Independence; perhaps the only piece of practical politics that is also theoretical politics and also great literature.

It is, then, the large "constitutional" role that "American values" play in defining American nationality itself, I believe, that leaves so many of us so much of the time in a state of anxiety about the capacity of these values to endure. Chesterton wrote that "the experiment of a democracy of diverse races . . . has been compared to a melting pot." That implies, he went on, that the pot must be strong and durable. It must not melt. "The original shape was traced on the lines of Jeffersonian democracy; and it will remain in that shape until it becomes shapeless. America invites all men to become citizens; but it implies the dogma that there is such a thing as citizenship." The melting pot of American citizenship requires a public with considerable virtue. A decline in the moral standards would surely leave the American experiment in grave jeopardy. Little wonder that we're constantly worried about the possibility of a decline.

> *"A decline in the moral standards would surely leave the American experiment in grave jeopardy."*

Assessing the moral state of the union is made more difficult by the fact that our standards keep changing. Moreover, the institutions through which the public gains a sense of the moral state of the nation now tend to portray social and political institutions in a negative light.

As to changing standards, consider the area of race relations. Surely we have made enormous strides along this dimension of national moral conduct since the 1850s. We have ended slavery and, all too belatedly, we must acknowledge, eradicated the system of gross exclusion of African-Americans from various facilities and entitlements, known as "Jim Crow." Survey data on racial attitudes and various behavioral data alike attest to the spread and strengthening of public support for extending to African-Americans the Declaration's lofty insistence that all people are created equal and possess inalienable rights.

> *"Americans continue . . . to describe religion as important in their own lives."*

But in assessing moral conduct, we seem largely to ignore this historical perspective. Is America now living in satisfactory accord with the norm set forth in the Declaration of Independence and in other statements of national ideals? Of course not. But today's shortcomings are the ones that now occupy us—even when we recognize marked gains from times past. *We expect more of ourselves in this area than we did 50 or 150 years ago—and we come up short.*

Media studies have for some time examined the issue of political negativism or cynicism, suggesting that press bias results not so much from political preferences as from professional outlook. The press often portrays various national institutions as seamy and even unworthy of support. Austin Ranney argues that there is not so much "a political bias in favor of liberalism or conservatism, as a structural bias . . ." which encourages a cynical and excessively manipulative view of politics. Michael Robinson's research has supported the view that the press fosters a pervasive cynicism:

> Events are frequently conveyed by television news through an inferential structure that often injects a negativistic, contentious, or anti-institutional bias. These biases, frequently dramatized by film portrayals of violence and aggression, evoke images of American politics and social life which are inordinately sinister and despairing.

In addition to America's historic sense of creedal anxiety, then, recent factors, such as changing standards of justice and press negativism, may be encouraging an even more pessimistic view. At the very least, all these factors suggest there is reason to doubt that the apparently widespread sense of moral decline is simply a reflection of the actual progression.

What the Data Actually Show

The various factors sketched above present terrible difficulties for the literature which purports to provide thoughtful guidance on the matter of which way we are headed. As a result, analysts often seem to be led to the conclusion that deterioration is occurring, even when available information is inconclusive or flat-out says otherwise.

When we look at the status of religion in America and a number of moral norms, it is not at all clear America is in moral decline. The country's religious life, for instance, is often considered a moral barometer. In the early 1980s, I was asked to prepare a conference paper reviewing what surveys had to say about the religious beliefs and practices of the American people. As the Reverend Richard John Neuhaus observed at the New York conference, the conventional wisdom had it that "America is or is rapidly becoming a secular society."

I began my paper by acknowledging that on this subject, as on so many, there are severe limits as to what polls can tell us. They are blunt instruments, unable to help us much with the searching, the ambiguity, the depth and subtlety that necessarily surround any basic set of human needs and values. Nevertheless, the story told by survey research was remarkably clear and unambiguous with regard to the general character and directions of Americans' religious life: namely, the U.S. is distinguished from most other advanced industrial democracies by the persisting strength of religious beliefs and of organized religious practice. As Seymour Martin Lipset argued in *The First New Nation*, published in 1963, "The one empirical generalization which does seem justified about American religion is that from the early nineteenth century down to the present, the United States has been among the most religious countries in the Christian world." Similarly, James Reichley concluded his examination of *Religion in American Life* with the assessment that "Americans remain, despite recent incursions of civil humanism among cultural elites and relentless promotion of egoism by advertising and entertainment media, overwhelmingly, in Justice [William O.] Douglas's words, 'a religious people.'"

> *"Norms condemning various forms of cheating, lying, and stealing seem firmly entrenched across most of the population."*

My own assessments of available survey information have supported these observations. Americans continue, for example, in virtually unchanging proportions to describe religion as important in their own lives. The proportion describing themselves as members of a church or synagogue, while down just a bit from the levels of the 1930s–50s, has, on the whole, remained both high and constant. Surveys conducted by the National Opinion Research Center have continued to find overwhelming majorities of the public describing the Bible as either "the actual word of God . . . to be taken literally, word for word" (the response of 33 percent in 1993); or as "the inspired word of God, but not everything in it should be taken literally, word for word" (49 percent stating this). Only 15 percent categorized the Bible as "an ancient book of fables, legends, history, and moral precepts recorded by men." Also, prayer remains integral to Americans, even among young adults and high-income citizens (65 percent and

69 percent of whom, respectively, agreed with the statement that "prayer is an important part of my daily life").

Perhaps most striking is the extent to which the U.S. differs religiously from other advanced industrial democracies. In 1981, Gallup conducted a series of surveys cross-nationally which found 79 percent of Americans saying they gained strength from religion, compared to 46 percent in Britain, 44 percent of West Germans, and 37 percent of the French. Similarly, 84 percent of those interviewed in the U.S. said they believed in heaven, as against 57 percent in Britain, 31 percent in West Germany, 27 percent in France, and 26 percent in Sweden.

Changes in Religion

This isn't to say that there have been no changes in the structure of American religious life. We know, for example, that over the last 30 to 40 years, while the proportion of the population which is "churched" has remained basically constant, the denominational mix has changed quite strikingly. Sociologist Benton Johnson notes that American religious groups have differed greatly in terms of membership gains and losses. He points out that evangelical churches have prospered even as main-line Protestant denominations have suffered serious membership losses during this period.

Taking a longer view of American religious experience from the eighteenth century to the present, we see many substantial shifts. Interestingly enough, though, these shifts are more often than not in the opposite direction from those assumed in most commentary. That is, *the long movement over time in the U.S. seems clearly to be toward religion*, not away from it. Pointing to the decline of organized atheism and church membership gains in the nineteenth century, sociologist Theodore Caplow suggested:

> One concedes too much when one says we're just about as religious as we used to be. We may be a good deal more religious than we used to be.

Yet, while virtually all the scholars who have reviewed the systematic data which are available to us have reached the same conclusions on American religious experience, most of the group assembled at the New York conference strongly rejected the idea that American religious commitments are notably strong and enduring. For example, George Marsden, a leading student of evangelicalism and fundamentalism, dismissed most of the

"The proportion of the populace giving of its time for charitable and social service activities has actually been increasing."

findings on religious belief as essentially meaningless because, as he saw it, they picked up only an insubstantial, superficial, essentially trivial commitment. "As you know," Marsden argued, "the common comment on fundamentalism is that it is just secularism in disguise. It is a way of endorsing a materialistic, self-centered lifestyle. And that's something that could be said about a lot of American Christianity.". . .

Individualism: Strength or Weakness?

The moral shortcomings of this society often grow out of the same elements that enhance national life. The positives and negatives are frequently but flip sides of a single structure of national values. As many analysts from Alexis de Tocqueville on down to the present have observed, the core of the sociopolitical ideology on which the U.S. was founded is a uniquely insistent and far-reaching individualism—a view of the individual person which gives unprecedented weight to his or her choices, interests, and claims. This distinctive individualism has always enriched the moral life of the country in important regards and posed serious challenges to it in yet others.

Tocqueville's *Democracy in America* has seemed so rich and fruitful an account of the nation's social dynamic precisely because Tocqueville saw individualism as a two-edged sword. He saw, on the positive side, the strength in the U.S. of voluntary associations that had grown out of a self-confident individualism. Such perspectives incline one to give money to charities, to participate in all manner of voluntary service, and to join with others of like mind. . . .

Individualism has contributed much historically to the vitality of American family life and created a distinctively American type of family. Children, nineteenth century visitors often remarked, didn't occupy a subordinate place—"to be seen and not heard"—like their European counterparts, but were exuberant, vociferous, spoiled participants. Similarly, visiting commentators often remarked on the effects of America's pervasive individualism on the status of women. Bryce, for example, saw women's rights more widely recognized in the U.S. than in Europe. This had resulted, he argued, because "the root idea of democracy cannot stop at defining men as male human beings, anymore than it could ultimately stop at defining them as white human beings. . . . Democracy is in America more respectful of the individual...than it has shown itself in Continental Europe, and this regard for the individual enured to the benefit of women."

> *"Individualism has come to emphasize the gratification of the self over the needs of various important social institutions."*

But just as the country's demanding individualism has liberated individuals to achieve productive lives for themselves and contribute to a dynamic public life, so it has also been a source of distinctive problems. Many analysts have argued that these problems with the American ideology are evident not so much in the fact that these ideals are sometimes unachieved, as that their achievement may create terrible difficulties.

In the nineteenth century, for example, visitors to the U.S. often came away arguing that individualistic America was a place of stifling conformity. Tocqueville's description of "tyranny of the majority" is the most famous instance:

> I know of no country in which there is so little independence of mind and real freedom of discussion as in America. . . . In America the majority raises formidable barriers around the liberty of opinion; within these barriers an author may write what he pleases, but woe to him if he goes beyond them. Not that he is in danger of an auto-da-fé, but he is exposed to continued obliquy and persecution. . . . Monarchs had, so to speak, materialized oppression; the democratic republics of the present day have rendered it as entirely an affair of the mind as the will which it is intended to coerce.

Cut loose from secure social status anchored in the corporate institutions of traditional society, Americans were, Tocqueville thought, especially exposed to pressures to conform to majority standards.

Present-day critics of the "dark side" of individualist America charge that individualism has come to emphasize the gratification of the self over the needs of various important social institutions including, above all, the family. In *Habits of the Heart: Individualism and Commitment in American Life*, Robert Bellah and colleagues grant that "our highest and noblest aspirations, not only for ourselves, but for those we care about, for our society in the world, are closely linked to our individualism." Moreover, America cannot abandon its individualism, for "that would mean for us to abandon our deepest identity."

Still, Bellah *et al.* insist, "some of our deepest problems both as individuals and as a society are also closely linked to our individualism." It has become far too unrestrained. Historically in the U.S., the natural tendencies within individualism toward narrow self-service were mitigated by the strength of religion and the ties of the local community. No longer. In their view, individualism has been transmogrified by a radical insistence upon individual autonomy, so profoundly corrosive of the family and other collective institutions that depend upon substantial subordination of individual claims for social goods. . . .

We have been given ample proof that extending commitment to our national idea, which centers around a profound individualism, is by no means an unmixed blessing. As the U.S. has progressed in recognizing the worth and the claims of people previously excluded from the Declaration's promise, it has also encouraged tendencies which have destructive possibilities, liable to see the individual as too radically

"Individuals can only flourish in robust communities."

autonomous and leave him too narrowly self-serving. In seeking to improve the moral conduct of the nation, earlier generations of Americans have had to build on the positive elements of the country's individualist ethic, so as to curb its dark side. Ours is surely no exception.

237

Honor Codes Can Promote Ethical Behavior on College Campuses

by Rudy Abramson

About the author: *Rudy Abramson is a journalist who writes for the* Los Angeles Times *and other publications.*

Without warning, a drum roll explodes in the darkness after midnight, echoing through the still barracks, jolting the cadets of the Virginia Military Institute out of their sleep. It is ominous and relentless, as urgent as it is foreboding.

At every door of the four-story complex, there is a heavy knock, an order to fall out and, above the drumming, a shouted, repeated announcement: "Your Honor Court has met . . . Your Honor Court has met." In every room, the lights snap on.

Within minutes, dressed in robes and pajamas, chins tucked, chests out, all 1,200 young men of the VMI Corps of Cadets stand at attention in ranks around a dim inner courtyard, assembled for the excruciatingly painful ritual of a "drumming out." One of their own has cheated. He has been banished for breaking their sacred Code of Honor.

Resplendent in dress uniforms, members of the Honor Court march through an arch into the yard. The court president announces the name of a cadet found guilty of violating the code and intones: "He has placed personal gain above personal honor. He has left the institute, never to return. His name is never to be mentioned again."

Getting Caught

It is a moment none of them will forget. After 30 years, Lt. Col. Mike Strickler, a VMI graduate now on the institute's staff, vividly remembers the spring morning when a classmate was drummed out for cheating, just 10 days before he was to graduate. During one year while Strickler was a cadet, six members

---

Rudy Abramson, "A Matter of Honor," *Los Angeles Times*, April 3, 1994. Reprinted by permission of the author.

of the regiment were drummed out. In another year, there were only two. He remembers them all.

He also remembers the 12-word code that every VMI "rat" memorizes the day he arrives: "A cadet will neither lie, cheat, steal nor tolerate those who do."

That code, said Danny Felton, one of about 225 fourth classmen due to graduate from the 155-year-old institute in the spring of 1994, "is the cadet's most cherished possession."

A Movement Toward Honor Codes

Variations on this rule of conduct are embraced by 100 or so institutions of higher learning, in addition to the Army, Navy and Air Force academies and venerable military schools such as VMI and the Citadel. They range from small private schools such as Washington and Lee and Bryn Mawr to Princeton and Rice, and to the University of Maryland with 38,000 students.

At some, they are enshrined and forgotten in student handbooks; at others, they have become the cornerstone of academic integrity.

More often than not, honor systems have been installed at the urging of students, in many cases because of concern over cheating.

Although schools with viable honor systems remain a small minority, there is, says Samuel Sadler, vice president for student affairs at the College of William and Mary, "a decided movement" toward making codes a fixture on more campuses.

Typically, the codes explicitly forbid lying, cheating and stealing, and require students to take some action when they have knowledge of violations by their peers. Punishment is usually meted out by student tribunals. In return, the school administration allows unproctored examinations, with students sometimes taking the tests at a time and place of their choosing.

Nearly every week, Washington and Lee, whose campus adjoins that of VMI, receives inquiries or visits from other schools interested in its widely regarded system. An honor system is under serious consideration at Georgetown University in Washington.

Other schools, such as Duke and Johns Hopkins, have taken steps to strengthen their codes, and others, including Stanford, are contemplating ways to enhance honor systems.

In March 1994, University of Virginia students turned out in extraordinary numbers for an honor code ref-

"More often than not, honor systems have been installed at the urging of students."

erendum, voting by a margin of 3 to 1 to retain a system that, for 152 years, had required permanent expulsion for an honor code conviction. Codes have been stiffened elsewhere, too.

So why should this 19th-century creation—expanded, codified and preserved by military academies and old schools for men of the Southern gentry—now flourish? Especially now, in a generation that hates rules? Even in mega-universities where neither race, gender, history, culture, aspiration nor personal acquaintance provide unity?

The answer is evidently a sharpened concern over academic integrity—a subject brought dramatically to mind by the cheating scandal that by April 1994 had dogged the U.S. Naval Academy for more than a year.

Many Students Cheat

Cheating, studies show, is pervasive. It involves students struggling for A's and admission to prestigious graduate schools as well as those flirting with academic failure.

A landmark survey of 6,000 students in 31 of the country's prestigious colleges and universities found that nearly 70% had cheated—if all manner of minor infractions were taken into account. The figures approached 80% for non-honor code schools and 60% for those with codes.

In non-honor code schools, 20% of the students acknowledged cheating three times or more. Only 5 in honor code schools admitted repeated infractions. "I think that difference is quite significant," said Rutgers professor Donald McCabe, who conducted the study.

A generation ago, with campuses seething over Vietnam, honor codes seemed destined to become a relic. Some schools dropped their codes outright, concluding that they were unworkable. Others eased their requirements.

> *"Cheating, studies show, is pervasive."*

"During Vietnam, there was a clear assault on anything traditional," William & Mary's Sadler said, "and the honor system was just one of the traditions that came under attack. There was a tremendous passing of honor systems. One by one colleges and universities just peeled off."

There were changes even at such honor code bastions as William & Mary and the University of Virginia. Both schools dropped their non-toleration clause, which had required a student to report any person he saw cheating or face punishment himself.

With expelled students exposed to the military draft, Virginia went four years without an honor violation being charged. Students were unwilling to bring charges because expulsion was mandatory upon conviction. In 1979, the non-toleration requirement was finally dropped from the code. For practical purposes, it had long since grown unenforceable.

Taking Back Authority

The move back to honor codes is symptomatic of a larger change on college campuses, said Gary Pavela, president of the National Center for Academic Integrity, a consortium of 60 colleges and universities collaborating on issues involving honor codes, student ethics and academic integrity.

"All across the country, college administrators are beginning to take back authority that they gave up to students in the '60s and '70s," he said. "But the area of academic integrity is the only one where authority is still moving toward the students. In part it is because faculty members are abrogating. They teach, do their research and get off campus. But there is a yearning among students and in society for more discussion of ethical issues, and honor codes provide a forum."

> *"There is a yearning among students and in society for more discussion of ethical issues, and honor codes provide a forum."*

The 1994 student vote left Virginia among a handful of schools—mostly small military academies like VMI—with expulsion as the required penalty for lying, cheating or stealing. The uncompromising attitude is unmatched even at West Point, Annapolis and Colorado Springs, the preeminent schools for Army, Navy and Air Force officers. But—ironically, perhaps—the revered national military academies have produced the country's most notorious cheating scandals.

In 1976, 152 cadets were kicked out of the U.S Military Academy for cheating on an exam. After a long investigation, 98 were reinstated the following year. In 1984, 19 Air Force Academy seniors were suspended for cheating on a physics exam, and cadet honor boards' handling of academic cheating was temporarily halted.

Cheating and Covering It Up

The most excruciating cheating affair in the history of the military service schools is still [as of April 3, 1994] being played out on the stately campus of the U.S. Naval Academy at Annapolis. There, a panel of senior officers appointed by the Secretary of the Navy is hearing the last cases of as many as 133 midshipmen involved in cheating on an electrical engineering examination in December, 1992.

What made the episode extraordinary was the ensuing cover-up and mishandling.

In the weeks after the incident, Navy investigators concluded that 28 midshipmen might have had prior knowledge of the exam's contents. Honor boards eventually found that there had been 11 cases of code violation, but 4 of them were dismissed by Capt. John B. Padgett III, the commandant of midshipmen, and a fifth was dropped by Rear Adm. Thomas C. Lynch, the superintendent of the academy. The remaining 6 were ordered expelled.

The 5 whose cases were dismissed were academy football players.

When the superintendent, himself the captain of the football team in 1963, went before the 4,200-member brigade to announce the results of the investigation and reviews, he faced a remarkable reception.

One midshipman asked point-blank about one of the exonerated football

241

players, a friend of Lynch's son, visiting the superintendent's quarters on the evening before his case was reviewed. Lynch replied that he had not engaged in any substantive conversation with the young man, but his response was greeted by the muffled jeers and chants of the football player's name.

In May 1993, nearly five months after the now-famous exam, another midshipman came forward with new allegations, and the Navy's inspector general launched another probe.

During more than 800 interviews, investigators encountered determined reluctance to cooperate by many midshipmen. They reported that some midshipmen lied to protect friends even after confessing their own guilt; 14, including 11 athletes, invoked the Fifth Amendment; 8 swore to lies, and 5 refused to be interviewed "even in the face of the Superintendent's grant of immunity and orders compelling their cooperation."

When the investigation was all over in January 1994, Vice Adm. D.M. Bennett, the naval inspector general, reported that as many as 133 students had been involved and that 81 had finally so acknowledged.

As did a separate report from the academy's Board of Visitors, the inspector general's findings called for fundamental changes. There had been no actual conflict of interest on the part of academy officials, the report concluded, but "there was a definite perception of a conflict or a lack of impartiality among the midshipmen."

"The message the investigators received from the midshipmen," the report said, "was that they viewed the honor concept as an ideal that simply could not be applied to many of the problems that arise in the daily life of a midshipman at the Academy."

Military Institutions Are Unique

Many who study academic integrity issues do not find it surprising that the most notorious cheating scandals have come at the service academies, where personal honor is the keystone of education.

"Military schools," said McCabe of Rutgers, "create a culture in which students strongly bond with each other, joining together and trying to help each other through the system.

> *"The most notorious cheating scandals have come at the service academies, where personal honor is the keystone of education."*

"If you have a rigid set of explicit rules and regulations, you can reduce cheating, but if students see an opportunity to beat the system, they will. Honor programs do best where they create an atmosphere of trust, where everyone is involved, and the honor system becomes a part of the fabric of an institution."

Because military institutions are special cases, McCabe has excluded them from his surveys on cheating. The University of Maryland also excluded them when it studied other schools' honor codes in designing a system for its campus.

The distinguishing feature of the Maryland system—aside from its being tried in a huge public institution—is its incentive for students convicted of cheating to recover.

In such a case, a student is given a grade of F-X. After a year, in which the person takes an ethics seminar, he is given the opportunity to take the course again. Otherwise the X, indicating cheating, remains a part of his permanent transcript.

At the Naval Academy, an effort is under way to restore the credibility and enhance an honor system that Midshipman Brigade Cmdr. Sean Fahey said will remain "student owned and student operated."

[It includes] a "moral remediation" program for midshipmen found guilty of honor violations deemed insufficiently serious to warrant separation from the Navy. It will involve psychological counseling, performance of service, formal instruction in ethics and work with a senior officer, who will act as the student's mentor during the remediation period.

Even as hearings continued for midshipmen implicated in the scandal, superintendent Lynch began meeting with classes and with individual midshipmen in an effort to establish the honor system more deeply in the academy's conscience.

"They are very much ashamed of what has happened," he said. "They feel they have all been tarnished by this brush. I can talk with four or five midshipmen and get four or five reasons why it happened. But we are going to keep the honor concept at the Naval Academy, and it is going to be stronger in the future than it has ever been in the past.". . .

Changes will not go so far as to adopt the single sanction that endures at VMI, several other small military and private schools, and, after 152 years, at the University of Virginia.

"There are some situations where we will say, 'You are out the door,'" Lynch said recently.

"We will do that for drugs, for sexual misconduct and for serious honor violations. But the Academy is a learning, developing, maturing experience. You can have a medical problem or you can have an academic problem. But honor violations are in all gradations. They are never black and white."

Teaching Values in Schools Would Promote Ethical Behavior

by Bill Honig

About the author: *Bill Honig is the superintendent of public instruction for the state of California. This viewpoint is excerpted from his book* Last Chance for Our Children.

Children are not automatically moral or ethical. It takes a great deal of education, social bolstering, and sustained effort at putting a culture's highest ideals, values, and inspirations before young people to help them attain their full humanity.

Schools should enshrine and celebrate the individual, but doing that tends to overshadow the requirements of the community. We should also recognize that our political life demands that we convince students to attach to the group, be it family, church, community, or country. The point is that sheer self-interest has never been a sufficient basis for any society.

Our founding fathers pledged their lives, their fortunes, and their sacred honor in defense of shared beliefs—a lofty precedent. Children need to hear about the high ideals of our collective moral order if they are to be lifted out of a self-centered existence. Our democracy and the quality of life depend on enough people making that leap. The alternative is that they will grow up feeling emotionally isolated strangers to ethics in a devil-take-the-hindmost world. They won't commit to leading moral lives. They will be relegated to a mean and unsatisfying existence. And, inevitably, we will all end up the losers. End of argument.

The reigning orthodoxy of modern intellectuals, as Daniel Bell has observed, is radical individualism and anything that asserts the interest of the community is bound to strike an uncritical adherent of this position as a threat.

There is a difference between those who want group prayer in the public

From Bill Honig, "Teaching Values Belongs in Our Public Schools," *Ethics: Easier Said Than Done*, issues 19 and 20, 1992. Adapted from the author's book *Last Chance for Our Children* (Addison-Wesley, 1985). Reprinted by permission of the author and the Josephson Institute of Ethics, Marina del Rey, California.

schools (the practice of religion) and those who want moral content in the curriculum (a fundamental purpose of the schools). Between the equally unacceptable poles of religious dogmatism and institutionalized public amorality, there is room for a rational discussion of what ideals and standards we as a society hold to be worthy of praise and emulation. The fact that many educators fail to discern this middle ground is one index of our current predicament.

Misconceptions about Public Schools

The belief that a public school is no place to teach values rests on a pair of misconceptions. The first is that morality and ethics smack of the religious and spiritual and that teaching them in a public school necessarily violates the constitutionally guaranteed separation of church and state.

The second objection is more pragmatic: it holds that, in a pluralistic society such as our own, agreement on what moral values should be conveyed can never be reached. It follows from this premise that such an attempt could only be construed as an illegitimate use of Big Brother's coercive power.

This is nonsense. The constitutional argument is plainly wrong. The First Amendment reads: "Congress shall make no law respecting an establishment of religion, or prohibiting the free exercise thereof." It does not say: "Congress shall be aggressively neutral on matters of ethics, morals, and virtue, and any discussion of shared values in the public sector is strictly prohibited." To the contrary, with their unselfconscious references to "Nature's God," "the Creator," and "divine Providence" in the Declaration of Independence (and throughout the nation's seminal documents), it is clear that the founding fathers were themselves spiritual men. They were not against the practice of religion in general and certainly not against the transmission of elevated moral sentiments in schools. What they sought to prohibit was the establishment of a single state religion in the European mold. This prohibition poses no difficulty, however, because there is no question of teaching a particular creed—Catholic, Baptist, Jewish, Mormon, Buddhist, or whatever—in the public schools.

Schools shouldn't be run by majority vote, but they are an expression of the public will, and when it comes to moral instruction, the numbers are overwhelming. In September of 1984, the Gallup Poll released its annual survey of U.S. attitudes toward education. For the survey, the public had been asked to rate the relative importance of various goals for the public schools on a scale of zero to ten. The alternatives included everything from preparing students for a high-paying job to training them to take part in our democracy, to promoting physical fitness, to showing students how to use a computer. The results? Out of twenty-five possibilities listed, the second-high-

> *"Children need to hear about the high ideals of our collective moral order if they are to be lifted out of a self-centered existence."*

est show of approval was accorded the following goal: "To develop standards of what is right and wrong." Indeed, the only educational goal that outscored moral formation (and just barely) was this classic academic mission: "To develop the ability to speak and write correctly."

Clearly, the expectation among the people in this country is that education should include some kind of moral and ethical training. But what kind?

What Doesn't Work: Values Clarification

There's something absolutely essential missing from values clarification, and that's values, as the word is generally understood. While pretending to Olympian detachment in its neutrality on moral issues, values clarification actually affirms the shallowest kind of ethical relativism. It tells students that on matters of profound moral significance, their opinion—no matter how ill-informed, far-fetched, or speciously reasoned—is all that counts. Ethics and morals are reduced to matters of personal taste. The issues of abortion and registering for the draft are weighed on the same personal, idiosyncratic scale as one's choice of spring clothing or vacation destination: it is so if you say it's so.

This blithe invitation to moral anarchy, however, is not the way the world

> *"It is clear that the founding fathers were themselves spiritual men."*

works. Our society is built on widely observed moral precepts. It isn't a matter of personal conjecture, for example, whether stealing a Walkman from a classmate's locker is right or wrong. It's wrong, and so is cheating. However, students who decide that they personally sanction using crib notes because tests are irrelevant to the real dynamic of learning, or because the teacher assigned too much material to study in so little time, or for any one of a thousand convenient reasons, are perfectly entitled to do so under the values clarification rubric. Conceding the point, a teacher put it this way: "Once you accept the idea that kids have the right to build a position with logical arguments, you have to accept what they come up with."

This is arrent nonsense, of course, but values clarification sanctions such sophisms. It uses the Socratic method of question and answer but forgets about Socrates' passionate search for a truth that is accessible to all. Worst of all, values clarification is a self-conscious abdication of the adult role in education. It says to children that we adults don't hold anything sacred, that we don't believe in anything deeply enough to stand up for it, that the cumulative wisdom of our collective culture over 3000 years of struggle and progress can be reduced to two magic words: suit yourself.

Lessons from Developmental Psychology

Everything we know from the literature of the developmental psychology of childhood and adolescence suggests that moral character is painstakingly acquired, not pulled out of a hat, but earned in predictably sequenced stages, over time. In fact, following the lead of Jean Piaget in the study of cognitive development, contemporary researchers such as Lawrence Kohlberg and Jane Loevenger have identified a pattern of development that characterizes moral growth in children and transcends cultural boundaries. Very briefly, it goes something like this: Beginning with an infantile awe in the presence of a magically potent adult world, the child first learns to behave out of a desire for reward or fear of punishment (commonly, the fear of withdrawal of parental affection). An important leap occurs when the youngster adopts the conventional mores of his or her family or school chums, out of a wish to fit in, or later, out of a sense of loyalty to the group and emotional identification with it. Eventually, the young adult breaks away, appraises the moral principles that have governed his or her life, and consciously chooses to accept some of them on rational grounds. As the individual matures, his or her ethical perspective will continue to broaden.

> *"If the goal is a refined morality in adults, the starting point is instilling a clear sense of right and wrong in children."*

This scheme can be embroidered at considerable length and there is some dispute about the details, but I think most parents will recognize the general progression from dependence to independence and from self-concern, through conformity, to conscious election of the good. The conclusion to be drawn from all these findings is plain: the adult world has a critical responsibility to discharge. It must furnish the child with a guiding morality in the form of expectations and good habits. With this foundation, the young adult can either adopt that guiding morality later on or formulate one of his or her own.

We have to keep reminding ourselves that it isn't patronizing to treat children like children—it's parental. At the heart of moral education is a paradox. Nineteenth-century sociologist Emile Durkheim expressed it best when he said, "Solely by imposing limits can a child be liberated." We want free citizens who, as an assertion of their humanity and moral identity, consciously decide to expend the enormous ethical effort it takes to be another Gandhi, Schweitzer, or Confucius. But to reach this ethical peak, we must be willing to approach the problem like a good mountaineering team. We must provision the base camps that make possible the final attempt. If the goal is a refined morality in adults, the starting point is instilling a clear sense of right and wrong in children.

The School's Role

The home is the primary locus of moral formation, of course, and religious instruction can be a key element. But the schools must participate too, along with the other social institutions. A traditional education orients the students to the high ethical expectations of the community both by what it teaches and by how it goes about it. In the traditional setting, students learn the value of self-discipline when they turn in homework assignments, of courtesy when they raise a hand before answering, of punctuality when they come to class on time. The teacher, as an exemplar of the adult world, is a closely scrutinized role model. Does he or she prepare well for class every day, and grade fairly? Is he or she good-humored, inspirational, compassionate, honest, and respectful of differences? No one could measure up to such an impossible standard of perfection, but the best teachers try.

Cultural Heritage

The other hugely important source of moral insight for the student in the traditional scheme is the course content itself, particularly in the humanities. Exposure to the cultural heritage carries with it a powerful message. Think of the great stories in our tradition: Icarus flying toward the sun on wings of wax, Oliver Twist asking for a second bowl of gruel, Nathan Hale dying for his country, Penelope remaining faithful despite the long absence of her husband. These stories speak to us with great force about the perils of pride and greed and the honor of patriotism and fidelity. In the end, the moral sensibility and social conscience of a civilization can only be learned by reading and discussing the classic works of its literature and history and the biographies of its exemplars.

We have always known this truth. Just look at the texts used to teach children in the nineteenth century, when people naturally assumed that the primary business of school was to train character. *McGuffey's Reader*, used in the first through sixth form, was the most famous of these texts, but they all resemble one another. In their pages, God was everywhere and operated according to a stern system of dire punishments and bankable rewards.

I'm not recommending a return to *McGuffey's Reader* for today's public schools. Our challenge is to identify their modern equivalent, to put before students the lives and legends and stories and speeches that adequately express the guiding morality of our modern, democratic, pluralistic society.

I say "guiding" for two reasons: first, because the distillation of adult wisdom the schools present is only a starting point, but a crucial one, in the adolescent's quest for a personal identity and value system; and second, because the best expression of this morality (as opposed to what Walter Lippmann called the "eternal verities" at the heart of it) is changing over time, which is the cause of the dated quality of the old readers.

> *"The moral sensibility and social conscience of a civilization can only be learned by reading and discussing the classic works of its literature."*

What might that guiding morality look like? No doubt the key concepts would include such broad principles as the sanctity of human life, respect for the dignity of the individual, and the importance of the family and personal moral effort. The guarantees flowing out of the principle of the individual's primacy—

the guarantees of freedom of speech, religion, association, and the press, of equality before the law, of respect for property rights and the system of free enterprise—have been encoded in the law of the land. But, to make a good man or woman, our republican and Biblical traditions tell us, more is required.

Thus, the vast majority of us would agree that a good person is generous to others, not miserly or self-absorbed; modestly self-assured, not vain or boastful; faithful, not promiscuous; prudent, not rash or prodigal; reverent to the elderly, not brusque or insolent; optimistic, not envious; forgiving, not vengeful; hospitable, discreet, loving, patient, not hostile, overbearing, cold, or slapdash. The list goes on but you get the idea. It just isn't that difficult to arrive at a consensus about what our society admires.

Bibliography

Books

Richard L. Abel	*American Lawyers*. New York: Oxford University Press, 1989.
Kenneth D. Alpern, ed.	*The Ethics of Reproductive Technology*. New York: Oxford University Press, 1992.
Myra Alperson et al.	*The Better World Investment Guide*. New York: Prentice Hall, 1991.
Robert M. Baird and Stuart E. Rosenbaum	*Morality and the Law*. Buffalo: Prometheus Books, 1988.
Alan Bear and Rita Maldonado-Bear	*Free Markets, Finance, Ethics, and Law*. Englewood Cliffs, NJ: Prentice Hall, 1994.
Linda A. Bell	*Rethinking Ethics in the Midst of Violence: A Feminist Approach to Freedom*. Lanham, MD: University Press of America, 1993.
Lynda Birke, Susan Himmelwiet, and Gail Vines	*Tomorrow's Child: Reproductive Technologies in the '90s*. London: Virago Press, 1990.
Ruth Ellen Bulger, Elizabeth Heitman, and Stanley Joel Reiser, eds.	*The Ethical Dimensions of the Biological Sciences*. New York: Cambridge University Press, 1993.
J. Douglas Butler and David F. Walbert, eds.	*Abortion, Medicine, and the Law*. New York: Facts On File, 1992.
Arthur L. Caplan	*If I Were a Rich Man Could I Buy a Pancreas? and Other Essays on the Ethics of Health*. Bloomington: Indiana University Press, 1992.
Darwin Cheney, ed.	*Ethical Issues in Research*. Frederick, MD: University Publishing Group, 1993.
Clifford E. Christians, John P. Ferre, and P. Mark Fackler	*Good News: Social Ethics and the Press*. New York: Oxford University Press, 1993.
Ralph W. Clark and Alice Darnell Lattal	*Workplace Ethics*. Lanham, MD: University Press of America, 1992.

David E. Cooper and Joy A. Palmer, eds.	*The Environment in Question: Ethics and Global Issues.* New York: Routledge, 1992.
Bette-Jane Crigger, ed.	*Cases in Bioethics: Selections from the "Hastings Center Report."* New York: St. Martin's Press, 1993.
William Damon	*The Moral Child: Nurturing Children's Natural Moral Growth.* New York: Free Press, 1990.
John Dewey	*Lectures on Ethics, 1900-1901.* Carbondale: Southern Illinois University Press, 1991.
Edwin R. DuBose, Ron P. Hamel, and Laurence J. O'Connell, eds.	*A Matter of Principles? Ferment in U.S. Bioethics.* Philadelphia: Trinity Press International, 1994.
Anthony Dyson and John Harris, eds.	*Experiments on Embryos.* New York: Routledge, 1989.
H. George Frederickson, ed.	*Ethics and Public Administration.* Armonk, NY: M.E. Sharpe, 1993.
R. Edward Freeman, ed.	*Business Ethics: The State of the Art.* New York: Oxford University Press, 1991.
Erich Fromm	*Man for Himself: An Inquiry into the Psychology of Ethics.* New York: Holt, 1990.
K. Richard Garrett	*Dialogues Concerning the Foundation of Ethics.* Savage, MD: Rowman & Littlefield, 1990.
Robert P. George	*Making Men Moral: Civil Liberties and Public Morality.* New York: Oxford University Press, Clarendon Press, 1994.
John Harris	*Wonderwoman and Superman: The Ethics of Human Biotechnology.* New York: Oxford University Press, 1992.
Richard E. Hart	*Ethics and the Environment.* Lanham, MD: University Press of America, 1992.
Milton D. Heifetz	*Easier Said Than Done: Moral Decisions in Medical Uncertainty.* Buffalo: Prometheus Books, 1992.
David Heyd	*Genetics: Moral Issues in the Creation of People.* Berkeley and Los Angeles: University of California Press, 1992.
John A. Jenkins	*The Litigators: Inside the Powerful World of America's High-Stakes Trial Lawyers.* New York: Doubleday, 1989.
Carl Junkerman and David L. Schiedermayer	*Practical Ethics for Resident Physicians.* Frederick, MD: University Publishing Group, 1994.
Daniel J. Kevles and Leroy Hood, eds.	*The Code of Codes: Scientific and Social Issues in the Human Genome Project.* Cambridge, MA: Harvard University Press, 1992.
Richard W. Kilby	*The Study of Human Values.* Lanham, MD: University Press of America, 1993.

Bibliography

James W. Kuhn and David W. Shriver	*Beyond Success: Corporations and Critics in the 1990s.* New York: Oxford University Press, 1991.
Paul Lauritzen	*Pursuing Parenthood: Ethical Issues in Assisted Reproduction.* Bloomington: Indiana University Press, 1993.
Sol M. Linowitz with Martin Mayer	*The Betrayed Profession: Lawyering at the End of the Twentieth Century.* New York: Charles Scribner's Sons, 1994.
Don MacNiven	*Creative Morality: An Introduction to Theoretical and Practical Ethics.* New York: Routledge, 1993.
Rita C. Manning	*Speaking from the Heart: A Feminist Perspective on Ethics.* Lanham, MD: University Press of America, 1992.
M.P. Miceli and J.P. Near	*Blowing the Whistle: The Organizational and Legal Implications for Companies and Employees.* New York: Lexington Books, 1992.
David Nyberg	*The Varnished Truth: Truth Telling and Deceiving in Ordinary Life.* Chicago: University of Chicago Press, 1993.
Christopher Plant and Judith Plant, eds.	*Green Business: Hope or Hoax? Toward an Authentic Strategy for Restoring the Earth.* Philadelphia: New Society Publishers, 1991.
Robyn Rowland	*Living Laboratories: Women and Reproductive Technologies.* Bloomington: Indiana University Press, 1992.
Thomas L. Shaffer	*American Lawyers and Their Communities: Ethics in the Legal Profession.* South Bend, IN: University of Notre Dame Press, 1991.
Peter Singer	*Practical Ethics.* New York: Cambridge University Press, 1993.
Peter Singer et al., eds.	*Embryo Experimentation: Ethical, Legal, and Social Issues.* New York: Cambridge University Press, 1990.
Marion Smiley	*Moral Responsibility and the Boundaries of Community.* Chicago: University of Chicago Press, 1992.
Robert Solomon	*Ethics and Excellence: Cooperation and Integrity in Business.* New York: Oxford University Press, 1992.
Allen Verhey and Stephen E. Lammers	*Theological Voices in Medical Ethics.* Grand Rapids, MI: Eerdmans Publishing Co., 1993.
Oliver F. Williams and John W. Houck	*A Virtuous Life in Business: Stories of Courage and Integrity in the Corporate World.* Lanham, MD: University Press of America, 1992.
Oliver Williams, Frank K. Reilly, and John W. Houck, eds.	*Ethics and the Investment Industry.* Lanham, MD: University Press of America, 1989.
Richard Zaner	*Troubled Voices: Stories of Ethics and Illness.* Cleveland: Pilgrim Press, 1993.

Ethics

Periodicals

Jerry Adler	"Clone Hype," *Newsweek*, November 8, 1993.
Lillian R. Bevier	"Should the Press Be Liable?" *The American Enterprise*, May/June 1994.
Amar Bhide and Howard H. Stevenson	"Why Be Honest If Honesty Doesn't Pay?" *Harvard Business Review*, September/October 1990.
Business and Society Review	Entire issue on corporate responsibility, Spring 1992.
Estelle Carota and Mario Carota	"Turning the Tables: Why We Must Find Alternatives to Interest-Based Economics," *The Other Side*, January/February 1994. Available from 300 W. Apsley St., Philadelphia, PA 19144.
CQ Researcher	"Reproductive Ethics," April 8, 1994. Available from Congressional Quarterly, Inc., 1414 22nd St. NW, Washington, DC 20037.
Ethics: Easier Said Than Done	Entire issue on business ethics, issue 22, 1993. Available from 4640 Admiralty Way, Suite 1001, Marina del Rey, CA 90292.
Ethics: Easier Said Than Done	Entire issue on ethics in the law profession, issue 23/24, 1993.
Amitai Etzioni	"American Competitiveness: The Moral Dimension," *The World & I*, October 1991. Available from 2800 New York Ave. NE, Washington, DC 20002.
Amitai Etzioni	"Good Ethics Is Good Business—Really," *The New York Times*, February 12, 1989.
First Things	"The Sanctity of Life Seduced: A Symposium on Medical Ethics," April 1994. Available from the Institute on Religion and Public Life, 156 Fifth Ave., Suite 400, New York, NY 10010.
W. Wayt Gibbs and Tim Beardsley	"Fertile Ground: IVF Researchers Pioneer the Bioethical Frontier," *Scientific American*, February 1994.
R.M. Hare	"Is Medical Ethics Lost?" *Journal of Medical Ethics*, June 1993.
Rushworth Kidder	"Ethics: A Matter of Survival," *The Futurist*, March/April 1992.
Thomas G. Labrecque	"Good Ethics Is Good Business," *USA Today*, May 1990.
Medical Ethics Advisor	"Human Embryo Cloning Causes Ethical Furor," December 1993. Available from American Health Consultants, Inc., Six Piedmont Center, Suite 400, 3525 Piedmont Rd. NE, Atlanta, GA 30305.
Zygmunt Nagorski	"Yes, Socrates, Ethics Can Be Taught," *The New York Times*, February 12, 1989.

Bibliography

Robyn Y. Nishimi	"Biomedical Ethics in U.S. Public Policy, *JAMA,* December 22/29, 1993. Available from 515 N. State St., Chicago, IL 60610.
Lyda Phillips	"Social Investing: The Wave of the Future?" *Public Citizen*, May/June 1990.
David E. Provost	"Corporate Responsibility," *The Christian Century*, April 7, 1993.
Steve Rendall, interviewed by Kevin Clarke	"Are You Getting the Whole Story?" *SALT*, March 1994. Available from 205 W. Monroe St., Chicago, IL 60606.
Frank Rose	"A New Age for Business?" *Fortune*, October 8, 1990.
Robert J. Samuelson	"R.I.P.: The Good Corporation," *Newsweek*, July 5, 1993.
Danny Schechter	"A Failure of Journalism," *The Progressive*, April 1994.
Society	Entire section on fraud in science, March/April 1994.
James Srodes	"Social Vision in the Business World?" *Ethics: Easier Said Than Done*, issue 9, 1990.
Rebecca Voelker	"A Clone by Any Other Name Is Still an Ethical Concern," *JAMA,* February 2, 1994.
Susan M. Wolf	"Health Care Reform and the Future of Physician Ethics," *Hastings Center Report*, March/April 1994.
The World & I	"Journalism on the Rocks?" Entire section on media ethics, December 1993.

Annotated List
of Periodicals

Business Ethics A bimonthly publication aimed at helping transform business by promoting ethical business practices. Available from Mavis Publications, Inc., 1107 Hazeltine Blvd., Suite 530, Chaska, MN 55318.

Common Cause Magazine A quarterly publication of Common Cause, an organization that works to improve the way government operates. Available from 2030 M St. NW, Washington, DC 20036.

Ethically Speaking Published three times a year by the Association for Practical and Professional Ethics. Available from 410 N. Park Ave., Bloomington, IN 47405.

Ethics & Behavior A quarterly publication that adresses a wide array of topics pertaining to various moral issues and conduct. Available from Journal Subscription Department, Lawrence Erlbaum Associates, Inc., 365 Broadway, Hillsdale, NJ 07642.

Ethics: Easier Said Than Done A quarterly publication of the Josephine Institute of Ethics. It addresses ethical issues in education, government, and society. Available from 4640 Admiralty Way, Suite 1001, Marina del Rey, CA 90292.

Ethics Journal A quarterly publication of the Ethics Resource Center. It seeks to present diverse perspectives and foster frank discussions concerning ethics. Available from 1120 G St. NW, Suite 200, Washington, DC 20005.

First Things A monthly journal of religion and public life published by the Institute on Religion and Public Life, 156 Fifth Ave., Suite 400, New York, NY 10010.

Hastings Center Report A bimonthly journal published by the Hastings Center, 255 Elm Rd., Briarcliff Manor, NY 10510. It explores a wide variety of ethical issues concerning medicine and medical technology.

Issues in Law & Medicine A quarterly journal published by the National Legal Center for the Medically Dependent and Disabled, Box 1586, Terre

255

Haute, IN 47808-1586. It provides technical and informational assistance to attorneys, health care professionals, educators, and administrators concerned with the health care rights of severely disabled people of all ages.

The Journal of Clinical Ethics

A quarterly publication that addresses physician-assisted suicide, the definition of death, the use of human fetal tissue, and other ethical issues in medicine. Available from 107 E. Church St., Frederick, MD 21701.

Journal of Medical Humanities

A quarterly journal published by the Institute of Medical Ethics. It is devoted to such topics as assisted suicide, termination of life-sustaining treatment, and AIDS in children. Available from PO Box 1586, Terre Haute, IN 47808-1586.

Second Opinion

A quarterly publication of the Park Ridge Center for the Study of Health, Faith, and Ethics. *Second Opinion* addresses issues that integrate health, faith, and ethics. Available from 211 E. Ontario, Suite 800, Chicago, IL 60611.

Organizations to Contact

The editors have compiled the following list of organizations concerned with the issues debated in this book. The descriptions are derived from materials provided by the organizations. All have publications or information available for interested readers. The list was compiled on the date of publication of the present volume; names, addresses, and phone numbers may change. Be aware that many organizations take several weeks or longer to respond to inquiries, so allow as much time as possible.

Accuracy in Media (AIM)
1275 K St. NW
Washington, DC 20005
(202) 371-6710
fax: (202) 371-9054

AIM is a conservative nonprofit organization dedicated to investigating complaints about media inaccuracies, informing the public about media inaccuracies, and motivating the media to adopt a high standard of ethical behavior and a responsible approach to the news. AIM publishes the *AIM Report* twice a month and distributes books such as *Trashing the Planet* and *Deconstructing the Left*.

Center for Applied Christian Ethics (CACE)
Wheaton College
Wheaton, IL 60187
(708) 752-5886

The goal of CACE is to raise moral awareness, develop conscience, and elicit moral thinking by encouraging the application of Christian ethics to public policy and personal practice. It seeks to relate theory to practice by addressing contemporary issues in the light of biblical principles, theological and philosophical ethics, and character and moral development theory. Activities and publications focus on ethics in business management, public policy, biomedical research, communications, and the arts.

Center for Applied and Professional Ethics (CAPE)
University of Tennessee
801 McClung Tower
Knoxville, TN 37996
(615) 974-7215

CAPE brings the skills and knowledge of philosophy and related humanities disciplines to bear on issues of practical ethics through research, teaching, and services to professionals, students, and the general public. CAPE is interested in how ethics relates to the issues of medicine, mental health, animal rights, the environment, war, business, law, and professional codes. The center offers courses, sponsors lectures and forums, and

257

consultation services to professionals, institutions, and policy-making bodies. It publishes curriculum materials and articles concerning ethics.

Center for Biomedical Ethics
University of Minnesota
Box 33 UMHC
420 Delaware St. SE
Minneapolis, MN 55455
(612) 625-4917
fax: (612) 626-6800

The mission of the center is to advance and disseminate knowledge concerning ethical issues in health care and the life sciences. It carries out this mission by conducting research, offering educational programs and courses, fostering public discussion and debate, and assisting in the creation of public policy. The center publishes research reports and distributes books and other materials.

Center for Ethics and Human Rights
American Nurses Association
600 Maryland Ave. SW, Suite 100 West
Washington, DC 20024-2571
(202) 554-4444, ext. 294

The American Nurses Association is the professional organization for America's two million nurses. Its Center for Ethics and Human Rights aims to promote public policies that address ethical issues in health care and to provide publications that educate the public about ethical issues in health care. The center's publications include a casebook, *Ethical Dilemmas in Contemporary Nursing Practice*; a quarterly newsletter, *Ethics and Human Rights Communiqué*; the report *Managing Genetic Information*; and guidelines on issues such as quality of life, organ and tissue donation, assisted suicide, and the reporting of incompetent, unethical, and illegal health care practices.

Center for Ethics Studies
Marquette University
Academic Support Facility 336
Milwaukee, WI 53233
(414) 288-5824

Marquette University is a Jesuit institution committed to developing citizens who appreciate the role of values and ethics in their lives. The center's primary goal is to be an ethics resource for the university and the community at large. The center sponsors speakers and programs that focus on issues such as the moral use of police power, in vitro fertilization, and the ethics of health care. The center, a clearinghouse for ethics information, publishes a volume of essays titled *Ethics Across the Curriculum*, a periodic newsletter, and pertinent lectures.

Common Cause
2030 M St. NW
Washington, DC 20036-3380
(202) 833-1200
fax: (202) 659-3716

Common Cause is a liberal lobbying organization that works to improve the ethical standards of Congress and government in general. Its priorities include campaign reform, making government officials accountable for their actions, and promoting civil rights for all citizens. Common Cause publishes the quarterly *Common Cause Magazine* in addition to position papers and reports.

Ethics Resource Center, Inc.

1120 G St. NW, Suite 200
Washington, DC 20005
(202) 434-8468

The center is a nonprofit, nonpartisan, nonsectarian organization working to restore America's ethical foundations by fostering integrity, ethical conduct, and basic values in the nation's institutions. It sponsors programs and develops materials on ethics and character education for children and adults and advises business, government, professional, and trade organizations on how to promote high standards of ethical conduct. The center produces the video series *Ethics at Work* and numerous research reports.

Hastings Center

255 Elm Rd.
Briarcliff Manor, NY 10510
(914) 762-8500

Since its founding in 1969, the Hastings Center has addressed the ethical implications of medical practices such as euthanasia and assisted suicide. The center's goals are to promote research on such issues, to stimulate universities to support the teaching of ethics, and to educate the public. It publishes the *Hastings Center Report* bimonthly.

Institute for Global Ethics

PO Box 563
Camden, ME 04843
(207) 236-6658

The Institute for Global Ethics is a nonpartisan, nonsectarian, nonprofit research and educational organization. Its goal is to discover and articulate the ethical values shared by all the peoples of the world, to analyze ethical trends, and to gather and disseminate information on global ethics. The center sponsors programs, seminars, workshops, and lectures, and publishes the monthly *Insights on Global Ethics*, the periodic *News Flash*, the book *Global Ethics: Common Values for a Shrinking World*, and the videotape "Personal Ethics and the Future of the World." The center's library has a wide variety of books and journals on ethics as well as periodicals accessible by computer networking.

The International Alliance of Holistic Lawyers (IAHL)

Holistic Justice Center
PO Box 753
Middlebury, VT 05753
(802) 388-7478

The IAHL is a group of lawyers who work to make practicing law a more humane, less aggressive profession. The alliance opposes the competitive, adversarial nature of the law profession and endeavors to help clients work out their own conflicts and to admit their guilt when necessary. Write for a list of publications.

Josephson Institute of Ethics
4640 Admiralty Way, #1001
Marina del Rey, CA 90292
(213) 306-1868
fax: (213) 827-1864

The institute is a nonprofit membership organization founded to improve the ethical quality of society by teaching and advocating principled reasoning and ethical decision making. The institute's Government Ethics Center has conducted programs and workshops for more than twenty thousand influential leaders. Publications include the periodic newsletter *Ethics in Action*; the quarterly *Ethics: Easier Said Than Done*; course materials; and reports such as *Ethics of American Youth: A Warning and a Call to Action*.

Kegley Institute of Ethics
California State University
9001 Stockdale Highway
Bakersfield, CA 93311-1099
(805) 664-3149

The Kegley Institute is a nonprofit group dedicated to enhancing society's understanding of and ability to respond to contemporary ethical dilemmas. It sponsors conferences and lectures on a wide range of topics, including ethics in journalism, the environment, health care, and business. The institute has published books on technology and ethics and ethics in journalism as well as articles on the death penalty, mental health, fetal rights, and abortion.

The Park Ridge Center for the Study of Health, Faith, and Ethics
211 E. Ontario St., Suite 800
Chicago, IL 60611-3215
(312) 266-2222
fax: (312) 266-6086

The center explores the relationships between health, faith, and ethics, focusing on the religious dimension of illness and health. It seeks to help clergy, health care professionals, ethicists, educators, and public policy makers to address ethical issues and create ethical policies. The center publishes the quarterly *Second Opinion*, the newsletter *Centerline*, and the book series *Health and Medicine in the Faith Traditions*.

Index

261

Index

266

Index

268